They Teach Without Words

The Animals of

Moose River Farm

Anne T. Phinney

Anne T. Phinney

For the Nichols Family
I hope you enjoy
reading about the
animals who inspire
me to teach. Warmly!
Anne

They Teach Without Words
The Animals of Moose River Farm

Copyright © 2019 Anne T. Phinney

First Paperback Edition, May, 2019

Cover Photograph by *Nina Betters-Tobin*
Photo edited by *Ryan McCardle*
Cover design by *Travis Kiefer*

Published by

Moose River Farm
Old Forge, NY 13420
www.mooseriverfarm.com

Printed in the United States of America through Kindle Direct Publishing

ISBN 978-1-093-29597-9

They Teach Without Words

The Animals of

Moose River Farm

Anne T. Phinney

DEDICATION

To my mother, Barbara Higley Tall Lane, from whom I inherited my love of animals and to all of my animals who have inspired me to teach.

CONTENTS

	Acknowledgments	i
1	**I am a Teacher**	Pg 3
2	**Finding My Way to Africa**	Pg 20
3	**Animals in the Classroom**	Pg 49
	Barbaro	Pg 55
	Horses Come to School	Pg 63
	Animals Return to the Classroom	Pg 69
4	**Love and Loss**	Pg 75
	Murray and Makia	Pg 79
	Goat Saga	Pg 95
	Target	Pg 121
	Rosemary	Pg 131
	Huxley's Last Breath	Pg 145
5	**Horses Make a Landscape More Beautiful**	Pg 151
	Donkeys…Who Knew?	Pg 151
	Sandeman's Port	Pg 161
	Lessons from Tango	Pg 173
	Partly Cloudy	Pg 179
	Supreme's Golden Spirit	Pg 191
	Zambezi	Pg 201
	Equi-Reflection™	Pg 216
	Gatsby	Pg 225

6   **Unusual Pets**   Pg 233

    No More Pigs   Pg 233

    Llamas; Adonis and Bravo   Pg 243

7   **I am Still a Teacher**   Pg 257

    Opposite Directions   Pg 257

    Kids Farm Day   Pg 259

    Moving Forward   Pg 265

8   **The Barn as Sanctuary**   Pg 269

ACKNOWLEDGMENTS

For over a year my editor, *Paula Roy* and I reworked this manuscript with no clear vision of what the finished product was going to look like. We were never satisfied with it being a continuation of our first book, *Finding My Way to Moose River Farm*. For a time this book appeared to be writing itself and waiting for us to notice the direction it was taking. Finally, it was Paula who declared the *eureka* moment. The stories were aligning perfectly with my professional teaching career which came to an end in June, 2018. It was Paula who recognized the connections between *teacher training* that I gleaned from animals and application of it in my day to day life and in my classroom. Thank you Paula for your endless support and wisdom throughout the long process of writing our second book.

Thank you to all of my friends and family who love *Moose River Farm* and its residents as much as I do. This includes *Jean Risley* who steps in often to care for the animals and who loves to spend time at the farm in their presence. Thank you to my sister *Sue Sutter,* with whom I share the *animal gene*. Thank you *Vicky Brazell* who shares my love of animals by caring for a miniature MRF *version* of her own. Thank you Lisa Eklund and Missy Elleman for decades of support and friendship. Special thank you to *Michele deCamp* who has captured hundreds of images of life on our farm through the lens of her camera. And finally, thank you *Rod Phinney* for keeping the infrastructure of *MRF* in top shape so that I may continue to enjoy this privileged life.

I am a Teacher

"I never teach my pupils, I only attempt to provide the conditions in which they can learn." -Albert Einstein

To the Board of Education,
Please accept this notification as my intent to retire…

Each keystroke brought the intention closer to reality. My twenty-six year career as a classroom teacher was going to end shortly. In addition to this public school experience, I had been a college instructor and teacher's aide, accumulating almost thirty years in education. Looking back on my career, I made a startling observation.

I am a teacher by accident, well, maybe by accident. As a small child, I played *school* with my friends in the basement of my family's home. An antique set of attached desks and a card table staged my classroom between an un-cozy sitting area and my brother John's makeshift hockey rink. The burgundy and beige checkered linoleum floor alternated in my imagination between slick ice and polished institutional flooring. On the pine paneled wall in front of the desks hung a two feet by three feet chalkboard. Chunks of colorful dustless chalk, treasures discovered in my Christmas stocking every year, filled the tray at its base.

I loved to play school, especially if I was the teacher. Occasionally, my friends took a turn at filling the instructor's position, but mostly I played the role. As the teacher, I read picture books, sharing the illustrations with my friends the way my teacher had modeled in the classroom where I was always the student. I liked to wear a chunky charm bracelet that jingled wildly when I wrote on the board. Mostly, I enjoyed displaying my handwriting on the blackboard the way that teachers do, neatly and correctly from A to Z.

Eventually, I grew out of the little classroom in the basement. All of the items disappeared as did the image of myself as a teacher. In fact never once did I use the word *teacher* to describe my future or the occupation I wished to pursue. My future was going to be full of animals, particularly horses. It never occurred to me then that my passion for animals would complement my teaching career.

If horses were a disease, my case was acute and chronic with a hopeless prognosis. Visions of horses ached in me. By the time I was thirteen years old, I had but one mission, to own a horse. Nothing, including school and peers, was as important to me. Frustration brought despair because my parents did not feel the same way. My father described our family as non-horse owning. To someone who loved horses more than anything in the world, my parents seemed callous about my desperation to own a horse.

The best that my parents could provide for me were weekly riding lessons at a horse stable thirty minutes from where we lived. Every Saturday morning, my mother drove me out to the barn. From our Chevy station wagon, she watched her youngest child beam while sitting astride a twelve hundred pound animal. In later years, she admitted how much she wished I could have had a horse during those years of yearning. She saw how happy horses made me.

Horse ownership had to wait because my parents were focused on accumulating the necessary capital to send their four children to college. It was my father's proudest accomplishment. My siblings George, Sue, John and I all graduated debt free from four year schools. To our father and his hard work as a sales engineer we are most grateful.

Throughout my middle school years, there were other opportunities to be with horses. My stay at home mother had saved a

2

little money of her own, mostly from birthday gifts over the years. She sent me to a riding camp in the Endless Mountain region of Pennsylvania. For four weeks, I not only rode horses but I was also involved in their care. Grooming, feeding, mucking and riding were the highlights of my day. I was assigned to care for a large bay gelding named *Never Never Land*. For a whole month, he *belonged* to me. When I returned home at the end of the summer, I was more frustrated than ever, having been given horses and then having them taken away. Like a drug, I needed horses every day.

What was it about horses that I needed? Perhaps it was the calm that I felt in their presence. Horses are herd animals who need other horses to keep the group safe. In the company of horses, I was a member of the herd. The awkwardness of adolescence completely vanished. Among horses I belonged. Decades later I can articulate what I have learned from horses, but as a young teen they simply made me happy.

Desperate for horses, I found my way to various barns that welcomed the horse starved to help out with chores. I proved that I was dependable, willing to learn and eager to perform any task that got me closer to the objects of my desire. It never felt like work. It was education. At home after a long day at the barn, I pored over my library of horse books and periodicals. Before the internet, books were the most effective means for collecting knowledge about the subjects that I loved. As a result, I accumulated a whole collection of resources that addressed everything I needed to know about horses. Some of my favorites were *A Horse of Your Own, Veterinary Notes for Horse Owners,* and George Morris' iconic riding manual, *Huntseat Equitation.* From the pages of these books, I learned how to care for horses, what maladies they suffer from and how to polish my riding style. I absorbed knowledge with the focus of a devoted scholar.

During this time, I was also given the opportunity to teach young children how to ride. While helping out at a day camp one summer, I was assigned the task of leading young riders who were mounted on horses for the first time. Sitting on a horse's back can be overwhelming, even to the most lovesick, horse crazy kid. Giving up control to a creature who has the potential to gallop off without warning is a sobering experience. Yet it is necessary on the way to learning how to control one's steed. My job was to teach the rider to hold the reins correctly and to steer by activating one rein at a time: pull the left rein to go left and the right rein to go right. Eventually, the rider was able to navigate her horse in a circle around me, a first independent effort. Little by little I began to increase my distance from the horse. Sometimes riding independently happened in the first lesson and sometimes it happened after several lessons.

The riding lesson continued when the child dismounted. After riding, the horse's needs come first. A sweaty horse must be cooled properly by hosing the entire body with water, particularly his chest and between his back legs where most of the heat from his body dissipates. An aluminum sweat-scraper drains excess water from his coat. Hand grazing a horse in the warm sun as the rider holds the lead rope is a pleasurable reward, but pay attention. Hold the lead rope taut so the horse can't step on it and scare himself. There is so much to learn about horses! By teaching, I too absorbed knowledge. It was just the beginning of an education that was molding me into my future self.

Little did I realize that I was addressing each riding student's individual needs, just as a classroom teacher is trained to recognize and teach to different learning styles. I knew instinctively that it was inappropriate to push riders beyond their levels of confidence. At the same time, I recognized that students attained mastery through a variety of learning styles. Many students improved after a visual demonstration, while others were proficient once given verbal directions. I enjoyed this role as instructor. Teaching came naturally to me although I didn't realize until much later that, in fact, I was already employing well-accepted theories of formal pedagogy. The rider's needs determined my teaching goals, something I had to remain tuned in to, as not to over face her before foundations of riding position were in place. I also paid attention to the rider's level of confidence. It was a solid indicator of how hard or soft I should push to move forward in the lesson. Watching the progress made by fellow riders was gratifying. Most of all I loved sharing my passion for horses. Apparently, there were other children just like me.

When I was sixteen years old, my father made a deal with me. I could own a horse for my last two years of high school. He would cover half of the expenses, and I would cover the other half, including the purchase of the animal. I never looked back.

Summer's Promise was a four year old chestnut American saddlebred mare. The heartwarming story of how I found her and how she became mine appears in my first book, *Finding My Way to Moose River Farm*. Needless to say, she soothed my horse craving while continuing to teach me more about horses. From the moment she was delivered to the barn where I boarded her, we were together every day during the summer and after school. Promise was the number one priority in my life. I could not have imagined the number of lessons she began teaching me, lessons that addressed my training, caring and coping skills. I was not conscious of these teachings at the time. However, now looking back, I see that she was building my confidence and paving the path toward an adult life spent caring for many horses in my own barn.

Due to the deal that my father made with me about her expenses I also needed to earn more money. Nobody was more motivated to work than I was. Since the age of twelve, I had worked for a cat breeder. Twice a week I cleaned her *Cattery* in the basement of her home. Two rooms of cages and enclosures housed up to thirty cats. Frequently, kittens were born because the breeder was trying to prolong prize winning bloodlines. My job was to clean cages and freshen litter boxes. Not all of the cats were friendly. Some of the unneutered males hissed and sprayed urine at me. I really thought they were no better than the stray tomcats that lurked about our neighborhood. The difference was that these boys were trapped in cages and had documentation that kept track of their lineage. The feral strays had a more interesting life for sure.

I worked at the *Cattery* until I went off to college, a testament to the loyalty I felt toward the breeder and she toward me. Although she was a quirky lady, I admired her female independence that enabled her to live her lifelong dream. In this respect she was a wonderful role model for a young woman who also had a big dream. She knew that the job she provided for me was a lifeline to my horse ownership. I rarely missed a day of work.

In addition to my cat cleaning job, I babysat for every family with young children in our neighborhood. One family in particular hired me to look after their three girls and toddler boy several times a week. I never turned them down. Frequently, I took all four children out to the barn to see Promise and to give them pony rides. I taught them how to brush her coat, pick her hooves and comb the tangles out of her tail. Watching over four youngsters at a barn was a huge responsibility. I was diligent about keeping them safe. Hay bales tossed out of the loft or a horse loose in the driveway provided potential for disaster. Luckily, I always returned the children home unharmed. In a way, I was already practicing what I would later learn to call classroom management.

In the meantime, Promise and I forged a bond never to be broken. At four years old, she still required training. Although she walked, trotted and cantered from my aids or cues, she needed polishing if I wished to compete with her at local horse shows. I would have benefited greatly under the watchful eye of a paid riding instructor. That expense, however, was not high on my priority list. My precious income paid for essentials such as board, blacksmith and fly spray. My father was true to his word, paying only half of Promise's upkeep. On my own, I forged ahead with her training. Sometimes I was frustrated by her stubbornness. The child in me did not understand that my communication skills did not always match her comprehension abilities. Trial and error was how we prepared for horse shows. Most of the time, she made me proud, especially when she won a blue ribbon in a hunter over fences class. When she refused a jump or engaged in some other disobedience, I could not blame her. That was a lesson I learned early on. Mistakes were *never* her fault. At the time, I could not appreciate all that she was teaching me. She reached me at a depth that few teachers had been able to touch. Like any hard working student, I always wanted to please her by practicing what she had taught me.

No matter what our competitive outcomes were, I loved Promise more than anything. She was all I wanted to be: beautiful, kind, patient, and dignified. She was the best thing that ever happened to me in those tumultuous teenage years. Promise calmed the storms that brewed within me when clouds appeared over my head. I always found my balance with my arms squeezed tightly around her neck. When I was astride her back the view from between her ears seemed more vibrant. She was the teacher who inspired me the most in my youth. Although I tumbled off her back many times, particularly if I steered her incorrectly to a jump, she never let me down.

Junior and senior year passed all too quickly. My father's deal was supposed to expire after high school graduation. Then college was to become my new priority, and Promise was to move on to a new home. So strict had my father been with our half and half deal that nobody was more surprised than I was when he relaxed the terms of the agreement. As I packed my bags for freshman year, so too did I pack my tack trunk, saddle and bridle so that Promise could come along with me. We were off to Centenary College in Hackettstown, New Jersey, to major in the Equine Studies program. At Centenary, my education was going to expand beyond what I had gleaned at the barn and in my bedroom library. My horse and I were off to college to learn together.

One learning objective at college was to become proficient at applying standing bandages to all four of a horse's legs after schooling over jumps. The leg wraps support overused tendons and ligaments while the horse stands or lies down in her stall at night. The quality of bandaging was a measurable standard that required constant practice. Over and over I applied the heavy flannel wraps around puffy cotton batting. One inch at the top and one inch at the bottom were the requirements. More or less and they had to be removed and applied again. Later as a teacher, I would make a clear connection between the joy of learning and the necessity of basic rules as foundations for exploration and discipline.

At Centenary, I rode Promise consistently under the watchful eyes of several highly qualified trainers. At first I struggled with so many changes being made to my riding style. All of the muscles in my body had to establish new memories: where to sit, where to apply my leg and how to synchronize rein aids with pressure from my calf. It was overwhelming at first. To admit that my riding wasn't as good as I believed it to be was a humbling experience. However, I wanted to be a better rider. I shut my mouth and tried harder. Eventually the training paid off. As I improved, Promise's responses became more correct. At last she understood the questions I was asking.

All of this work on the flat proved vital to our progress over fences. As my riding improved, I was able to communicate to Promise the correct number of strides between jumps. Counting strides from jump to jump enabled Promise and me to complete courses as a team. Perhaps Promise benefitted the most from my opportunities to ride other horses in the program. Horses are individuals. Upon the backs of different mounts, I filled a *toolbox* with more knowledge. I grew immeasurably as a horsewoman at every jump.

Two years of study at Centenary earned me an Associate's degree. For my junior year, I transferred to Cornell University College of Agriculture and Life Sciences. Having concentrated on horses for two years, I was now willing to broaden the scope of learning to a variety of domesticated farm animals. Statistics on dairy cattle breeding, sheep management and swine production filled an array of spiral notebooks. I spent weekly labs in the university's teaching barns that housed small herds of research animals. It was an exciting time to attend Cornell. Just as in public education, computer technology was beginning to be recognized as a means for consolidating farm data. Many of my classmates were acquiring skills that could raise the efficiency of their family farms and prepare them for the twenty-first century. At this point I wasn't certain what I was going to do with my animal science degree. There appeared to be only two choices: animal production or veterinary school.

Originally, I leaned toward the latter. However, it didn't take me long to realize that loving animals was not enough to seek acceptance into vet school. There are only thirty vet schools in the country in comparison to one hundred seventy-nine medical schools. Therefore, the vet school admissions process is much more selective. My grade point average was not high enough for consideration. I was not disappointed, but I still was not certain in what direction my degree was leading me. It appeared that the undecided group of students I attended class with were double majoring in education. They were working toward various levels of public school certification. The thought of completing a seventeen year education, Kindergarten through bachelor degree, only to continue with a career in education didn't appeal to me. I wanted something much more exciting.

Little did I know, at the same time that I was banishing the thought of a future in education, I was already on my way toward combining my love of horses with a teaching vocation. Instead of reading the signs, I focused on trying to establish a career in pharmaceutical sales. Interviews with some of the top companies in the field including *SmithKline Beckman, Schering-Plough* and *Ortho,* often resulted in follow up interviews, instilling hope that I was a potential candidate. Ultimately, jobs were awarded to middle aged men with prior sales experience. Frustration and dwindling funds forced me to accept a teaching position.

In the fall of 1984, I returned to Centenary College to teach in the Equine Studies program. I taught all but one of my assigned courses in the classroom, not out at the barn. Without any formal education credentials, I was assigned the task of teaching *Stable Management, Anatomy and Physiology* and *Theory of Equitation.* My level of knowledge for these courses came solely from my education at Centenary and Cornell. The one riding class that I taught to novice riders out at the barn was the only time I got to visit with Promise. She was also employed as a school horse, a role that lessened my financial burden while still allowing me to maintain ownership of my horse.

Back at Centenary, I thrived in my new occupation. I discovered that I loved teaching. Perhaps sharing my passion for horses with people who wanted to learn all about them was the most stimulating. More surprising was the realization that I had learned so much about my favorite subject and was fairly effective at encouraging others to do the same. After two years of teaching at Centenary, I added the experience to my resume; yet I still was not ready to pursue a career in education.

This is the point in my life where love came calling. The bond became permanent on my ring finger a year later when I married my soulmate, Rod Phinney. The story of the summer I met him while teaching horseback riding at the Raquette Lake Girls Camp in the Adirondacks is also chronicled in my first book. Before I knew it, we had settled in Inlet, New York, a town ten miles from where we met. Rod was renovating a lakeside camp that he had purchased on his own. In addition to remodeling the house, Rod also built a two stall barn for Promise and another horse named Windy, whom I had acquired shortly after we were married.

With two horses, I was looking forward to teaching riding lessons to local and summer residents. My level of youthful energy enabled me to teach riding lessons all week, then spend the weekend preparing the students and the horses to compete at horse shows. Several students had their own horses, which lightened the load for Promise and Windy. Still, the pre-daylight departures and late night arrivals home never seemed to zap my enthusiasm. I loved fueling the passion to ride in my students. Winning ribbons after all their hard work was a delight I shared with them. It brought me back to the carefree happiness of my youth when I spent my weekends showing Promise. Now, I was able to share the benefits of her training with fledgling riders.

Unfortunately, the hard work did not produce much income. To cover the cost of owning horses, liability insurance and the other expenses incurred at the beginning of marriage, I took a full time job at a local convenience store. For four years, I sweated over a donut fryer and made sure the coffee was fresh from six o'clock in the morning until noon. The schedule allowed me to teach riding later in the day when my students were out of school. The days were long, but one job made it possible for me to do the other.

In the back of my mind it often occurred to me that I possessed education that should be used in a more financially fruitful manner. But how? The answer arrived via a telephone inquiry from our local school. For years my name sat on the substitute teacher list, but I had never received a call. Now the school superintendent was desperate to find a long term substitute teacher for chemistry, earth science and environmental science. One of his teachers was going on maternity leave in a few months. At first I flat out refused. Visions of my own experience in high school chemistry prevented me from considering the offer.

"Oh no, I can't do that." The memories of my struggle were too unpleasant to revisit.

"Well, I hope you change your mind," he pleaded.

In the end, I did change my mind because the superintendent called again and assured me that my science degree would guarantee me success in the classroom. How did he know that? Perhaps it was time to step out of my comfort zone and risk this challenge. What could it hurt? After ten weeks, I would return to my life just the way I was living it, safe and under my control. I was still sure that teaching at a school was not for me.

From late January until early April, I became a science teacher. Ironically, I loved being back in the classroom, handling chalk, grading papers and designing lesson plans. Proper preparation unraveled the mysteries of chemistry so that I could teach effectively. As my own comprehension improved, I became passionate about covalent and ionic bonds. The periodic table of elements was my classroom bible because energy levels, proton numbers and nuclear configurations finally made perfect sense. I wanted the students to appreciate the world they live in on a molecular level. After all, molecules are the basic structures of our earth and of life itself. They are ingenious building blocks. Where did they come from? I realized I was learning as I was teaching! I also realized that I was experiencing the same joy in the classroom that I felt in the riding ring.

At the same time that I was delivering content, it occurred to me that teaching was an opportunity to touch lives and drive them forward into the future. If students felt my passion, then maybe a spark of interest might fuel their own ambitions to learn. Maybe teaching was an exciting career after all. The fact that I felt capable of making a difference in youngsters' lives suggested that it was at least an honorable occupation.

Ten weeks as science teacher passed too quickly. When my time was up, I reluctantly left school. For the remainder of the year, I was called several times a week to substitute. A day in second grade might be followed by a day in seventh grade social studies. Next I was asked to cover a few days of algebra. I never turned down an offer. Something had changed inside of me. My confidence to teach and to teach anything had been awakened. I began research to see what it would take for me to become certified as a New York State public school teacher.

Several years later, I was hired as a sixth grade teacher at the same school that convinced me I could teach chemistry. *The Town of Webb School* is a tiny jewel of education nestled in the resort town of Old Forge, New York. The student body fluctuates from either side of two hundred seventy-five students in grades kindergarten through twelfth grade. The school offers a private school education at a public school price. I feel fortunate to have taught my entire public school career within its welcoming walls.

The position required a Master's Degree and a stint of student teaching. I accomplished both while enrolled at *Goddard College* in Plainfield, Vermont. Goddard is a correspondence school that made it possible for me to remain at home while completing the curriculum to obtain my degree. Once a semester, I was obliged to attend a week long residency on campus. The time was used to plan my semester's work with an appointed advisor. It was an interesting education that depended on the maturity of my focus and organization. The experience opened my mind to alternative forms of education that involved what I already had learned about and from animals.

During the first year as a fully credentialed teacher, I filled my classroom with animals. The lessons that iguanas, rats and reptiles taught my students will never be found in a teacher's manual. Yet they remain among the most vivid memories for the students. From week one, the animals became co-teachers whose presence in my classroom made me a more effective new teacher.

From the cusp of retirement, I looked back over my life with animals and had an epiphany. I learned to teach long before I entered a classroom as a teacher. Horses and other animals were my most influential teachers. They taught me acceptance, patience and respect, characteristics that shape an effective educator. Working with them in the years that preceded my appointment as a classroom teacher taught me more about useful pedagogy than my methods classes in education.

Although they teach without words, the creatures in this book provide lessons in love, decision making, acceptance and loss. Strong bonds established between my animals and me empower my ability to listen closely to their messages. It is similar to how I receive verbal and nonverbal messages from my students once strong connections are established with them.

Long ago it was Promise who taught me that disobedience was the only way she could communicate confusion in what I was asking her to do. She did not wish to harm me when she reared in front of a jump and refused to leap over it. She needed support from my leg and its reassurance that yes, indeed, I was confident that she could carry me to the other side. When I fixed these components of my riding position, she rewarded me with the equivalent of an *A+,* an exhilarating trip around the jump course. Now when my students fail to master a concept, I know to ask how I could have taught better. When they fail, I have failed. When they succeed, I have done my job well as a teacher. Promise's lesson prevails in school where it is my obligation to assure that all students understand what I expect of them. No graduate course in pedagogy did as much to prepare me for the classroom.

Sandi, a sturdy bay gelding who arrived in his twilight years, delivered other lessons. He proved to be the quintessential co-teacher during beginner riding lessons at my farm. His gentle nature and confidence building ability filled in all the gaps that I couldn't articulate. When Sandi retired, a feisty paint gelding named Tango took his place. His teaching style required more participation from the rider. This trait backfired often but ultimately produced confident and gritty riding skills. A palomino gelding named Spirit robbed me of my common sense with his golden beauty. Luckily, patience and consistency polished his charm buried deep below a sunny exterior. There is also Joshua, a lost soul so completely misunderstood by the good intentions of his previous owners. His lesson involved misconceptions, perseverance and the ability to believe that a good soul lived within a strong will. Consistency and patience finally paid off when Joshua was provided with a second chance to prove that he was indeed worthy. Like my students, each horse offered unique challenges and rewards.

Many animals taught me lessons in acceptance over and over again, including a handsome bay warmblood named Murray and a faded gray thoroughbred named Target. Both forced me to open my eyes to conflicting emotions that develop when owning so many horses. In contrast, lessons in decision making are at the root of my large dark bay gelding Zambi's chapter. No matter what lessons my horses teach, they always make the landscape of life more beautiful.

In this book, I examine love and loss not only through the lives and deaths of my horses but also through the lives of other animals. Goats only live for about a decade. Like dogs, their time is up too quickly. The pain of saying goodbye to my goats Liam and Lacey was soothed when the next generation of bottle fed kids arrived. Also, a twenty-one year old iguana named Rosemary leaves behind an honorable legacy, having touched the lives of so many. Death is inevitable, but acceptance is a choice.

A trip to Africa brings full circle my understanding of the role that animals play in nature. Witnessing giraffe, lions, warthogs and antelope living by nature's rule book expands my acceptance of the difference between pets and wildlife. It also defines the necessity for zoos and an appreciation for attempts made by animal conservationists to preserve diversity until *whole* ecosystems can be restored in wild places.

From my work with horses and other animals I continue to grow as an educator. Their lessons stimulate my interest and keep me curious about traveling into a future away from the conventions of the classroom. Animal teachers have inspired me to write this book. My barn and farm have taught me more about teaching than any course in a graduate school of education. My farm is my classroom and my animals are my teachers. As the philosopher *Martin Buber* notes, *"An animal's eyes have the power to speak a great language."* Through their eyes, I learned to see myself as a teacher; from their language I learned how to teach.

Summer's Promise and me; 1978

Promise was my best friend and sturdy mount from 1977 until her death in 1990.

My siblings from top left; John, George, Sue and me with our dog Penny; 1978.

Rod and me at his family's camp, Sunny Cliff, on Raquette Lake, in the Adirondacks, 1985.

Throughout my teaching career there have been many opportunities to share animals with my students.

Finding My Way to Africa

"If I have ever seen magic, it has been in Africa." -John Hemingway

From the Adirondacks to Africa is a long way. The contrast between the two is startling. But so too, are the similarities. For Africa, like the Adirondacks, is as much lifestyle as geography. The environments of the two can be harsh, extreme and dramatic. Despite constant turmoil and unrest in many African nations, the wildlife continues to exist and adapt, relatively peacefully, through annual cycles of extreme droughts and floods. The potential to experience the bounty of beauty in both places is what enables endurance of the extremes. Although my childhood dreams did not include living in the Adirondacks, I had always dreamed about traveling to Africa someday. Until I was an adult, my curiosity about African animals had to be satisfied, however, by attending local zoos.

During frequent childhood visits to the Philadelphia Zoo I was fascinated by the various shapes and sizes of giraffe, rhinoceros, elephants, chimpanzees, lions, and every other species on display. The forty-two acre facility, nestled in Fairmount Park between Girard Avenue and 34th Street, provides an oasis of sorts. There within the graffiti tattooed asphalt decor of a city rich in American history, the zoo delivers a glimpse into the natural world.

Despite my excitement at seeing all the animals, there always appeared to be something out of context. The animals standing on concrete and behind wrought iron fences looked like pieces of a jigsaw puzzle that didn't fit together properly. I can still remember the intensity of ammonia that stung in my nostrils upon entering the large cat house where the lions and tigers lived. Pacing inside ceramic tiled cages, the large felines appeared to live without purpose.

I am proud of the city's efforts to improve the living conditions for the animals at the zoo over the past forty years. Today, many natural enclosures provide a more realistic and enriching life for zoo residents. In return the animals live a relatively stress-free life while providing education and much needed lessons in empathy for patrons. Thanks to the pioneering efforts of zoo celebrities such as *Joan Embery* (San Diego Zoo) and *Jack Hanna* (Columbus Zoo), reputable zoos have been forced to update their facilities. Chimpanzees forage for treats hidden in the grass and climb into tree like structures. Elephants, free from archaic ankle chains, move about with other elephants engaging in the social relationships on which they thrive. Zoos cannot replace a wild existence; but for the most part, zoos are stepping up to the public's demands. The trouble is it takes enormous amounts of financial support to build and maintain natural facilities. Without the fiscal commitment of wealthy donors and corporate sponsors, upgrades simply cannot happen.

In the 1970s, zoos were just beginning to address the humane needs of the animals in their collections. The animal lover inside of me was thrilled to hear the bray of a zebra, to watch the dexterous trunk of an elephant forage for treats on the ground and to inhale the manure scented musk of camels up close. However, an unsettled part of me felt compelled to observe animals in native wild habitats.

In 1985 I traveled with May, my roommate from Centenary College to California. Arriving in San Diego, we spent two days exploring the two properties of the San Diego Zoo. On day one we attended the main urban zoo, located in Balboa Park. The zoo was large, over one hundred acres developed to display animals in the most natural settings imaginable; cutting edge for the mid 1980's.

The zoo facilities were revolutionary. Careful research had gone into addressing the needs of each species on display. Dense foliage provided private areas where animals could seek refuge from patron's prying eyes. Primates romped in the sunshine, swinging from sturdy artificial branches.

The next day we drove thirty miles north to the San Diego Zoo Safari Park. Here the animals were displayed in large open spaces. Viewing them was only possible while slowly gliding along the circumference of the park on a monorail. Giraffe, zebra, rhino, antelope of all kinds, and other hoofed stock co-existed across the plains of the California countryside. The facility was impressive but offered no guarantee that every creature could be seen. Animals who chose to rest comfortably in a shady grove during the baking heat of the day were free to do so. Our attitudes were forced to change from *"I want to see..."* to *"I was lucky enough to have seen..."*

These animals, living for the most part free, appeared to be content. The rolling surroundings provided them with endless space to spend pent up energy. Still, the overgrazed vegetation and girdled tree trunks nagged at my conscience. Although fat, sleek and living stress-free within the fence line, these animals were still not totally free. With respect for the zoo's efforts, I still needed to see animals who lived by nature's rules, not restrictions thrust upon them by humans. I fully understand that truly wild means risks of predation, starvation, infant mortality, and all the stress brought on by the aforementioned. However, they do speak of a reality for what it means to be truly free.

My trip to San Diego filled me with lasting images of wildlife exhibited among striking attempts to create natural habitats. My appetite was now whetted to see exotic species in their own truly natural environments. Upon my return, my mother and I began to entertain thoughts about a day when perhaps we might travel on an authentic African safari together. At that time she and my father were beginning to plan their future retirement. Although they had dabbled in travel, the bulk of their global explorations would have to wait until my father had ended his professional career in April of 1992.

Sadly, my father passed away eleven months after he retired. He was only sixty-two. My young mother, widowed at sixty-two, looked into an uncertain future, wondering what her life amounted to now that her other half was gone. The answer came several months later when she and one of her childhood friends traveled to South America together. The experience opened a door for my grieving mother. She became a "travel bug," seeking opportunities to visit faraway places around the world.

"Annie, would you like to go to Africa with me?"

The call came during the bleakest of winter months in the

Adirondacks. Rod and I were living with our dogs, Eric, Luther and Mishka, two horses, five goats and an assortment of fowl that included our duck/chicken couple, Christopher and Louise. Lakeview Farm in Inlet was our home ten years before we moved to Moose River Farm. The snow outside the kitchen window was plowed so high I could not see Windy's and Spy's (our horses), heads hanging over their stall doors. My answer came without hesitation.

"There is a trip planned for southern Africa in August. It will tour both Botswana and Zimbabwe for a total of nineteen days. Want to go, honey?"

"Yes!"

The next six months required details of preparation. Everything from acquisition of a passport to a protocol of vaccinations against yellow fever, diphtheria, and typhoid had to be planned and scheduled. We were also prescribed a prophylactic for malaria. When the itinerary arrived, clothing suggestions accompanied it. Khaki seemed to be the new black in my wardrobe as I collected shorts, long pants, and a jacket in that neutral shade. There were also limits on luggage. Having never packed for an African adventure before, I was somewhat overwhelmed deciding what to take. Fortunately, I had two Adirondack cohorts to brainstorm with.

Shortly, after our travel plans began to take shape, Rod's mother Rachel expressed interest in going with Mom and me. She recruited Rod's sister, Karen, a fellow elementary school teacher, to accompany her. The three of us conferred, advising each other in all areas of our preparation to travel a third of the way around the world. By the middle of August, Mom and I were ready for our departure. In addition to visiting several game parks, Mom and I decided to extend our trip and visit the Okavango Delta. This excursion required that we leave a week earlier than Rachel and Karen.

On August 8th I took my nine year old gelding, Spy Hopes, for a trail ride through the Adirondack woods one more time before embarking on an adventure so far away from home. It was an exceptional ride. Blazing along under a canopy of quivering leaves soothed my anxiety, a mixture of excitement and nervousness colliding with guilt.

I was about to leave Rod for almost three weeks so that I could indulge myself in a childhood dream. Although he never objected, I could tell that he was a bit concerned about being left behind to care for my animals. At the time he was working long hours for a private family's camp on Raquette Lake. It was evident that chores in addition to his daily obligations was a lot to ask. Although we had email, access to it from Africa was not a possibility. He and I would be completely cut off from each other for nineteen days. That meant that he had the sole responsibility of our horses, dogs, and goats.

Spike the iguana was spending the summer with my friend and fellow rider. Cindy was quite enamored with him. Spike and I had spent our first year teaching in an elementary classroom together and we were looking forward to our new class to begin the school year a week after I returned from Africa. Cindy had generously volunteered to check in on Rod and the horses a few times during the weeks that I was gone.

Spy and I walked a long way home after our exuberant ride through the woods. My mood was high, anticipating yet another childhood dream coming true. After saying goodbye to Rod and my whole animal family, I officially began the trip by driving to my mother's house in Lansdale, Pennsylvania. My sister Sue and her children, Amy and John visited for the afternoon before our departure the following day. Sue was excited for us as we reviewed the trip's itinerary and surveyed the glossy photo enhanced brochures. The next day we boarded a shuttle to Newark Airport at three o'clock in the afternoon.

At seven o'clock we boarded a Virgin Atlantic jet to fly across the Atlantic Ocean to Heathrow Airport in London. An hour bus ride through the countryside delivered us to Gatwick Airport. That evening we took our seats on an Air Zimbabwe jet that delivered us ten hours later to Africa. The time changes wreak obvious havoc on the body, so lack of exercise and idle waiting in one's seat for hours had a profound effect on me. By the time we prepared to land I was fully wound up and in desperate need of a shower.

It was quarter after six in the morning when we landed at Harare National Airport. A ribbon of sunrise on the horizon lured me from my discomfort. Staring at the view below, I felt a pang of pure joy calm the butterflies that battered my stomach for most of the trip. Scrubby green and brown brush dotted the scenery. Acacia trees from every African piece of literature I had ever read stood at willowy attention to welcome us on our descent. Thus, the African adventure commenced.

Our trip began in Zimbabwe's small metropolis, capital city, Harare. Zimbabwe's political history gets in the way of its natural beauty, having cast a shadow of gloom for nearly a century (1890-1980) under a white supremacy government. During that time the nation was called Rhodesia in honor of *Cecil Rhodes,* who conquered the country for acquisition by the British Empire in 1890. The land was rich in natural resources including gold, nickel, copper, platinum and coal. Years of conflict fluctuated between periods of bureaucracy and violence after it declared independence in 1965. In 1980, Rhodesia finally broke free from Great Britain. Despite the establishment as an independent nation with a new name, Zimbabwe has yet to solve conflict among its own people. The clash between whites and blacks is still evident among its citizens. The current governing regime has been accused of corruption, violence and violation of human rights. In 1994, Zimbabwe's political issues were fairly quiet so we were advised that it was safe to travel.

For two days we explored Harare, venturing into a number of souvenir shops that sold "African" trinkets made in China. I bought dozens of postcards, one to send to each student in my sixth grade class the year before and one to send to Rod every day that I was away. For him I also bought T-shirts emblazoned with graphics of "big game" such as elephants, lions, and Cape buffalo. Soon we would be photographing them in the wild. Mom and I bought several miniature polished stone Shona sculptures, unique to the craftsmen of Zimbabwe. Each depicted a stylized human face emitting good luck and fertility.

Early the next morning we boarded a one hour flight to Victoria Falls, hailed as one of the seven natural wonders of the world. Eventually, a van drove us another hour into the remote and sparsely populated country that is Botswana. In addition to clearing customs at the border, we had to cleanse the tires of our van and our shoes in a bath of antiseptic liquid. The protocol was an effort to kill the dreaded hoof and mouth virus that can wipe out a whole herd of ruminants. Both domestic livestock and wildlife are vulnerable to the disease.

At the tiny airport in Kasane, we hopped into an eight seater plane which reduced nine hours of driving to one hour in the air. The handsome bush pilot, Keri, was a character out of a romance novel. His untamed blonde mane suggested a life full of exciting and exotic adventures. His appearance conjured up all kinds of possibilities that kept Mom and me chuckling as he chauffeured us closer to our African dream. Anticipation mounted when we flew into the Okavango Delta region of Botswana, Zimbabwe's neighbor to the southwest. After forty-five minutes in the air, my mother tapped my shoulder and pointed out the window. Below I could see a herd of elephants traversing along a path that their ancestors had forged thousands of years before. The largest land mammals on earth flowed in slow motion on a mysterious mission. Same shapes, different sizes, suggested that the group encompassed young and old, bound together by strong family ties.

Finally, as Keri announced our arrival we passengers prepared for a brisk descent that brought the plane to a halt in the middle of... nowhere. Nothing about our surroundings suggested an airfield. Keri opened the doors of the plane and immediately went about the task of emptying his cargo section of our sparse luggage. Reluctantly, we exited the plane, wondering if he planned to abandon us on the dirt airstrip. The only sign that other humans might be close by was a faded orange windsock mounted on a thirty foot pole. Presently, there was no breeze activating it which added to the anxiety we felt about being stranded now that we were all standing outside of the plane.

Shortly after our belongings were unloaded, we heard the faint sound of diesel engines in the distance. The louder the chugging noise got, the more relieved we felt. Several minutes later, two open seated Toyota Land Cruiser trucks entered the airfield. They pulled up tight to our luggage so that Keri could deposit the bags in the back cargo section.

Two native African guides stepped out of the vehicles and approached. They were meticulously dressed in pressed khaki shirts, shorts and desert boots. With smiling faces they welcomed us, extinguishing any remnants of worry about abandonment.

"Welcome, welcome everybody, to Pom Pom International Airport," exclaimed the older guide with a hearty laugh.

I liked him immediately.

"My name is Amos, and this," he gestured to the younger man who smiled at us in a more reserved manner, "is Bee. We are so happy to meet you all and to escort you into camp. Please, if you would take a seat in one of the automobiles, we can be on our way." His rich resonant accent suggested he had been educated somewhere in this southern region of Africa. Standing there listening to his melodious tone, I became aware that in these arid surroundings I was wrapped in the pungent scent of sagebrush. This was the Africa I had read about my whole life and here I was, standing right at the beginning of my own adventure.

So many questions swarmed in my head about where we were and what we were going to see. I had to resist holding up the procession so we could get underway. Meanwhile, Keri was preparing for takeoff and his next adventure. Perhaps he was off to rescue a safari damsel in distress who would surely thank him with a tryst under the Southern Cross twinkling in the night sky. Or maybe he was just headed home to share leftovers with his cat. Unthinkable!

For the next ten minutes, the eight members in our group bumped along in one of the vehicles while our luggage jostled behind us in the other. The short trip gave me a few minutes to ruminate about all that I was about to see, hear and learn in the days to come. The animals were expected to inspire me, yet the biggest surprise of all was to come from the fascinating people I was going to meet along the way.

As the trucks pulled up to Pom Pom Camp's entrance, seven staff members assembled and began singing and swinging a welcome song. Their superb alto voices and *Tswana* accents (official language of Botswana) combined with the thatched structures that dotted the camp, announced that we had truly arrived in an Africa where time stood still. No electricity, no snake venom antidote, and no roads that lead to the civilized world. Here luxury existed but required a twist in definition.

Once we were out of the vehicles, Amos gestured for us to follow him to the dining pavilion. Meanwhile, the staff was receiving orders regarding the delivery of the luggage to our assigned tents. Just outside the entrance to the dining pavilion, we passed a female warthog and her three babies foraging on the lawn.

"This is Bacon and her babies," Amos's accent accentuated *baabeez*. "They come every day hoping we will give them food. Bacon was an orphan many years ago and stayed close to camp where we fed her and looked after her. Now she returns after she has her baabeez. We have stopped feeding her but she still comes, hopeful we will change our mind." Once again his rich low laugh prompted giggles from the crowd. "She looks tame but please don't go near her, she is a wild animal and she has very sharp tusks…and there is no hospital to fix you."

He winked at us, still beaming a broad smile; however, his expression sent a message loud and clear. Keep your distance or else. I wondered how many tourists had ignored this warning.

The dining pavilion consisted of two communal areas. On one side was a gathering room complete with overstuffed couches and chairs all decorated in safari themed upholstery of fronds and wild animals. On the other side of the hut stood a table large enough to accommodate the eighteen guests who filled the camp to capacity on a daily basis. Pom Pom is only open during the dry season that lasts from March through October, winter in the southern hemisphere.

During this stretch of perfect weather, outdoor living is the rule in the Okavango Delta.

Although the region is south of the equator, its terrain is unique in that flood waters from the north flow constantly down the Okavango River and keep the land hydrated all year long. Where typical deltas empty into an ocean, the Okavango is a vast deposit of water that has established wetlands inland. Rivers and tributaries cover an area of approximately thirty-five thousand square kilometers. Eventually, the water exhausts itself and the landscape becomes the Kalahari Desert. This incredible volume of lasting water encourages a variety of mammals, reptiles and birds, not to mention plants, to thrive here year round. It is truly a jewel on a continent that struggles through two harsh seasons bone dry and oversaturated wet. Pom Pom Camp is in the heart of the Moremi Game Reserve, a mixture of marshes and savanna that hosts an intricate cohabitation of elephants, lions, giraffe, kudu, waterbuck, zebra and jackals to name a few. I couldn't wait to see them all.

We had arrived at Pom Pom at lunch time. Over a delicious gourmet buffet of lamb stew and freshly baked bread, Amos continued his orientation. He lectured about the natural history of the area, stopping to over emphasize camp rules along the way.

"Please do not go outside of the camp alone or without a trained guide. You have traveled far today and you don't realize how difficult it will be to arrange help should you be bitten by a snake or attacked by a lion. They are all a lot closer than you think, so please remain inside the walls of camp...*for your own protection.* The walls do not completely surround camp. They only mark certain boundaries to remind our guests. There is plenty of opportunity to go out in the bush and see the animals. They are waiting for you to come out and see them. They can't wait." Again Amos's belly laugh cued us to giggle. Make no mistake, his warning was no laughing matter.

After lunch, Mom and I were escorted to our tent and provided with instructions for using the toilet and the *hot water on demand* feature that made showering a luxurious event in the bush. Then we were left to settle in for an hour before our first game drive.

Once we were left alone, Mom and I stared at each other. We smiled ear to ear as we surveyed our *home* for the next three nights. The tent was comprised of a canvas ceiling and wooden platform. Between them was everything we needed to sleep bathe, and exist in the wilds of Africa. Two fully dressed twin beds, two folding chairs and a small table completed the furnishings. Screen netted walls stretched around three sides of our tent. At the rear of the tent was a more permanent structure constructed of thatched straw walls and no ceiling. It designated our bathroom space, complete with flushing toilet and propane heated shower. At the front of the tent was a small deck that looked out into the marsh where two cormorants were searching for fish in the shallow water.

After acquainting ourselves with the accommodations, we decided to venture about in camp, reminding each other of Amos's warning. Do not venture beyond the gate or walls. At the back of the tent we exited and walked about ten feet along a path that led to the swimming pool. We passed a large deposit of dry dung left by an elephant who must have passed through camp in the last day or two. We were not breaking a rule, but Amos's warning was making a lasting impression on us. Animals passed through the camp all the time because the thatched walls did not completely shut them out.

We were not sure who would need to go swimming while on safari, but Pom Pom maintained a crystal clear pool. Tucked away behind the laundry hut, the shimmering aqua blue basin seemed artificially out of place in a tented safari camp. Perhaps for those who wish to bring children, no pool would be a deal breaker.

By this time we were in the heat of the day, eighty five degrees, low humidity, around one o'clock in the afternoon; the excitement of our busy day so far had transitioned into exhaustion. Mom and I returned to our tent to stretch out on the beds and nap lightly, hoping to rejuvenate energy for our first trip into the bush.

After resting, we rendezvoused with our group and other guests to board the two Land Cruisers. Nine of us went in one direction and the other nine guests headed off in the opposite direction. Mom and I sat together, quietly taking in the details of our first ride. We had ended up in the vehicle that was driven by Amos's partner, Bee. He did not possess Amos's exuberant personality, but it didn't take us long to realize that this man was equally committed to sharing his passion for African wildlife. As we exited camp we passed Bacon and her *baabeez* just beyond the gate. Along for the meal was her *hoosban*, Sausage. The male warthog is identifiable by two extra-large warts that protrude above his snout in addition to two behind his eyes. The female only has the horny protrusions behind her eyes. From my first acquaintance with Bacon, I was smitten with warthogs. Some people think they are ugly with their warty faces and scraggly mohawk of a mane. I think they are an evolutionary marvel. The *warts* are protection from stabbing tusks during battle with other warthogs. Upon their knees they foraged the land for tidbits and sealed the deal for my endearment when the whole family trotted off with their tails straight up in the air.

Next, we encountered a tower of giraffe who were browsing in dense treetops on the side of the road. Bee's keenly trained eyes spotted their camouflaged coats. As he applied the brakes, the giraffe moved. Seeming to appear out of thin air, they glided towards us into the road. Up close one gets the true sense of how tall they are. Gazing up at eighteen feet of neck and legs makes quite an impression. A young calf, perhaps six months old sauntered out of the woods last. Even her diminutive ten foot stature dwarfed our vehicle. The whole tower floated past us in slow motion, paying no attention to our cameras clicking away to preserve their elegant images on film.

Our education with Bee continued for almost four hours. In that time he shared his enormous backyard with us. A backyard full of Africa, the way it has existed for millions of years without the effects of humans, without the devastating damage of poachers and without the rules of the civilized world.

Bee explained the intricate web that is the Okavango Delta, fiercely protected by his country's government who clearly recognizes that the tourist trade is Botswana's lifeline. Without the animals the tourists will not come; and without the tourists, the citizens will regress to un-survivable poverty. Bee made us feel appreciated for pumping our American dollars into his country's economy.

He also shared his immense knowledge of the Delta's ecosystems and animals. The elephants use the same trails over and over, cutting deeper into the terrain with every trip. This way they create deep ruts that retain water during extended dry seasons or drought. The Delta's water system is what maintains all life that lives within it. Every opportunity to conserve water is made by the animals themselves.

We learned about the iconic flat topped Acacia trees that identify African landscapes. They grow thick spiky thorns that thwart consumption by most animals. However, the giraffe has adapted and evolved with a thick tongue and lining in its mouth so it can eat Acacia blooms without wounds from pokey stickers. In fact the long neck of the giraffe is designed to gain easy access to the deeper interior branches of acacia trees, not just the ones at the top.

At one point Bee slapped the back of his neck with his hand and opened his palm to reveal a tsetse fly. This pesky insect harbors a protozoan called trypanosomatida that causes African sleeping sickness in people. Although treatable when detected early, the disease is dreaded by the African population, especially those who do not have access to routine health care. Observing a tiny menace that causes so much human suffering was truly eye opening.

For four hours we drove around the bush. We never saw the other vehicle, or any vehicles, during excursions in the Delta. What we did see were impala, waterbuck, tsessebe, red lechwe, giraffe, zebras, kudu, elephants, vultures, lions, Bateleur and fish eagles, warthogs, vervet monkeys, lilac breasted rollers, a variety of tiny colorful birds called bee-eaters, marabou storks and so many more perfectly adapted species. We came across the sun bleached skeletal remains of giraffe and elephants. The freshly killed carcass of an impala reminded us that their excessive numbers provide protein for the limited populations of carnivores living in the Delta.

Bee expertly tracked a lion who was dining on the remains of a wildebeest. The young male paid no attention to us when we pulled up within ten feet of him after our guide had spotted him from over half a mile away. Lions in the Delta have no fear of man. He is not a predator here. Since hunting is not allowed, the young male had no cause for concern about us. However, Bee did tell us that the entire mood would change if any of us stepped out of the vehicle and approached his kill.

"Instant loss of life," he assured. We believed him.

After several hours of driving, Bee pulled into a grassy picturesque vista and turned off the engine. While we admired the glowing sunset on the horizon, he opened a cooler of assorted beverages, alcoholic and nonalcoholic, and offered refreshment. After serving us, he continued with his expert commentary.

"Sunset is between 5:30 and 6:00 every night all year round. Botswana is near the Equator so hours of daylight are the same every day. The animals will be very active eating once the sun goes down. The lions become busy. When it gets dark, I look for animals who are worried, then I can track leopard and lions."

Sure enough, our ride home in the dark produced a herd of worried tsessebe. The tsessebe is a dark brown, almost black antelope with a long face and eyes that sit high on either side of its head. Although they wanted to graze on the savanna grasses, they kept moving and looking toward the trees. Bee drove toward the source of their worry to reveal a leopard with a fixed stare on the tsessebe. From her vantage point on a branch eight feet high in a tree, she watched the nervous herd with sheer determination.

"She is looking at them but the moon is too bright tonight. She will only chase them if they come close to her. They know she is there so they don't get too close. Better save her energy. She might not be able to hunt until the moon darkens in a few days."

Under full darkness, we returned to camp and our tent to prepare for dinner. A small lamp glowed through the mesh to guide Mom and me into the warm interior. Our heads were full of game sightings. It was a laborious task to organize them into retainable memory. Thankfully, our cameras did that for us.

At eight o'clock Mom and I made our way to dinner in the pavilion. Bacon and her *baabeez* had conveniently positioned themselves at the entrance, hopeful that the delicious aromas wafting from within might be shared with them. Bee and Amos played gracious hosts by delivering glasses of chardonnay. Then they invited us to sit down at the table. A generous feast of braised chicken, sautéed vegetables and roasted potatoes provided sustenance while we relived our sightings from the afternoon. Mouthwatering fresh fruits and vegetables beckoned from the buffet. Despite how delicious they looked, it is wise to avoid these in areas of the world without water purification. Digestive distress is almost a guarantee.

At the head of the table sat a woman from South Africa. Caron's ginger coloring was in contrast to the local complexion of Bee and Amos. She was the camp's hostess. By day she presided over the workers who kept the facility clean and tidy while the guests fulfilled their African dreams. At night Caron's job relaxed so that she could engage the guests in memorable conversations about Africa, the Delta and her life here. It was evident that she loved her job.

"Living out here is quite special, really," Caron offered as all eyes turned to listen to her story at the candle lit table. "I was having a difficult time finding work in Johannesburg when a friend told me about this job. There was nothing to lose so I accepted. Always wanted to see the game but never had the opportunity while living in the city. This is the best job in the world. My friends are jealous when I tell them about it. Hippos, lions, and elephants all on my daily commute! All of the employees here work for eight weeks straight and then have a week off. Most of them fly home to Gaborone, Botswana's capital city or Maun, rest for a week and return. The cycle continues through the dry season or winter, March through October. At the end of the season, we take down the tents and store them on higher ground. When the rainy season, or summer comes, we never know what will be damaged and what will be safe. Everybody must be out of camp during that time. We all go home and wait for the next season to begin."

In addition to our group and other guests, there was a mysterious stranger at the table. He was referred to as the *white hunter* and appeared to be quite familiar with Caron and the guides. Apparently, his plane needed some maintenance so he had landed at Pom Pom's airstrip to work on it the next morning. Blonde with pale complexion and uniformly dressed in safari khaki, this gentleman shared his life story. He had grown up as the son of religious missionaries stationed among the Bushmen in the Kalahari Desert, south of the Delta. Now he was a professional guide who, according to legend, was as capable of surviving for long periods of time alone in the wild just like the Bushmen who educated him throughout his childhood.

After dinner we were escorted to a small beach on the marsh just beyond the pavilion. There a campfire blazed at the center of a circle constructed by low slung fabric chairs. More wine was served as we settled in for more conversation. Caron dropped a small shovel full of hot coals under each chair so that the warmth would radiate upwards. The effect was delightful since the air temperature drops quickly after sunset. In the distance hippopotami could be heard *hmmphing* and *mmphing* as they surfaced to take a breath from under the water in the marshes. Insects chirped in the darkness and occasionally bats clicked and peeped as well. I wanted this experience to last forever, but knew full well that the memories would have to last me for the rest of my life.

When the coals under our chairs had cooled, it was time to say goodnight. Back at the tent we discovered that somebody had inserted hot water bottles between the sheets of our beds. I climbed into my flannel pajamas and crawled inside. This small luxury resulted in immense comfort. Mom and I talked quietly for a few minutes in an exchange of verbal pinches to quantify that we really were lying in a tent, in Botswana, Africa. We really were here.

I remained in a state of drowsy half sleep allowing my mind to drift wherever it pleased. I thought of Rod at home in the Adirondacks, my animals that I loved so much, and my good fortune to be sharing this experience with my mother. Suddenly, a deep throaty rumble crescendoed into a bass bellow penetrating the chirping night music around our tent. Mom and I froze.

"Is that a lion?" We asked in unison.

"Wow! They don't sound anything like that in a zoo or on TV," I whispered.

"I don't think he is very close, just sounds like he is right outside our door... that really isn't a door, just a flap of canvas," offered Mom.

After enjoying a nervous snicker over that comment, we rolled over and fell asleep.

In the morning bright sunshine poked us awake as it poured through the tent's screened windows. A humming voice approached our tent and eventually the silhouette of a woman carrying a tray on her head darkened the canvas doorway.

"Good morning," she greeted cheerily. "How did you sleep?"

"Good morning," I replied jumping out of bed to unzip the flap so she could step inside. I was not prepared for the blast of cold air that assaulted my body.

"Geez, it's so cold," I complained.

"It is three degrees, *(Celsius)*," she replied smiling. "Here, I have brought you some tea to keep you warm. Enjoy and have a good day." She placed the tray on the table.

As she turned to leave, it occurred to me that she was wearing nothing more than a light cotton dress in thirty-eight degrees Fahrenheit. In just a few hours, the temperature would soar above eighty degrees. Mom and I fixed ourselves a cup of tea and climbed back under the covers to savor it.

For three nights we remained at Pom Pom. After breakfast we loaded up in two vehicles that exited the camp in opposite directions to explore the Delta's unique terrain and thriving wildlife. One morning, Foster, a young guide, chauffeured us in a *mokoro*, a dugout canoe. The Delta marshes are quite shallow. To view the abundant bird life that lives there one needs to be pushed along by a *poler* who propels the boat through the water by thrusting a pole into the marshy weeds and giving a hearty shove. Hopefully, he never accidentally pokes at a hippopotamus. Nobody wants to encounter an angry hippo.

At water level, the Delta teems with birdlife. Against the sunshine saturated grasses, their vibrant hues and darting movements light up the environment like tiny fireworks. Malachite kingfishers, lilac breasted rollers, wattled cranes, red billed Frankolin, and a variety of bee-eaters go about the day maintaining their niche in the Delta's delicate ecosystem.

Foster brought the mokoro to rest on a small beach and offered his hand to pull Mom and me out of the boat. We stretched our stiff bodies and walked about to shake the tingling numbness from our feet while Foster prepared refreshments from a cooler he had in the canoe. He approached us with our nonalcoholic drinks while we were admiring a termite mound. These incredible feats of insect architecture are the first thing one notices about the African landscape. They are everywhere, in every height imaginable and in every state of disrepair or repair. The one we were observing was about four feet high.

"This termite mound is no longer alive," Foster exclaimed. "You can see there are large holes up and down. That means it is very old and that the termites have died long ago, few years."

Termites are social insects like bees. The whole population exists as long as the queen is alive. If she dies, the whole colony perishes with her. The mounds begin to crumble but take several years to break down completely. This four foot mound was an indication that the area that it protected underground was also four feet deep. For the entire life of the colony, the termites continue to dig deeper into the moist ground while piling the sand on the mound at the top of the ground. Simply, amazing. Mom and I stood close to the vacant mound while Foster took our picture.

In the afternoon, Mom and I separated for the afternoon game drive so that a newly arrived honeymooning couple could be together on theirs. I rode in the front seat with Bee who now seemed to recognize that I wanted to know everything about life in the Delta. He seemed intrigued by the fact that I was a school teacher who also took care of horses and goats. He had befriended an African

American science teacher from Chicago who returned to Pom Pom every northern hemisphere summer. Bee looked forward to his visit because this man also never tired of driving around in the bush. Most tourists are excited for one or two game drives and then decline to continue after a degree of boredom sets in.

Bee's keen eyes caught the rare glimpse of an Egyptian cobra sticking his head out of a hole in an old termite mound. He applied the brakes and pinpointed the location so we could all find it. Sure enough the expanded hooded head of a cobra stared directly at us from ten feet away.

"I see him. He is inside a hole of that dead termite mound," I said.

"How do you know it is dead?" Bee inquired.

"Foster taught us about them today while we were out in the mokoros. We stopped to examine one and to have our picture taken by it," I replied innocently.

Bee's face took on an expression of concern. "We do not permit the clients to get close to termite mounds unless they are alive. Dead ones are where the snakes live."

I have often wondered how my revelation turned out for poor Foster. He was a young inexperienced guide who I am certain was made aware of his error. The remote camps are fixated on the possibility of clients being bitten by snakes. It is discussed frequently. Nobody ever discloses how many tourists have met this unfortunate fate. However, it was the number one worry of our hosts and guides at camp. It even trumped being swiped by Bacon's powerful tusks, a mishap I am pretty certain would also ruin a tourist's adventure.

All too quickly the three nights we slept at Pom Pom came to an end. We were scheduled to fly out in the afternoon of our fourth day. That allowed for one more opportunity of game viewing. Our entire group, including Mom, was exhausted from the busy three days and chose to remain quietly in camp before the long afternoon of travel.

Bee invited me to see the game on foot. That meant hiking through the sagebrush and venturing beyond the camp boundaries without the protection of a vehicle. I accepted.

There were three of us on the hike that morning, Bee, me and Bee's rifle, for the rifle was as much a trusted guide in the bush as my human guide. Beyond the forbidden gate of camp, Bee led me into a vast wilderness. After the euphoria of being on foot at the level of the animals and the realization that my protection depended on Bee's gun wore off, a more sobering thought took hold. I would never be able to find my way back to camp should something happen to Bee. I was at his mercy. I swept the anxious images from my mind.

We had been told by a number of sources that guides must be able to drop an elephant with one shot from their rifle before they receive licensing credentials. They are tested out in the bush when given the order to kill. The order must be followed without question or hesitation. None of the guides wanted to admit that this was true. I have often wondered if it was.

On our hike, Bee walked in front of me with the rifle resting at attention upon his shoulder. His long lean body strode with purpose while his head rotated left and right, ever on the lookout for photographic opportunities or danger. There was something about him that suggested elegance and sophistication. I couldn't put my finger on it, but he exuded an air of humble nobility in his quiet reserve. What was his story?

I took up Bee's rhythm and tuned into my surroundings on this my last excursion in the Delta. With feet on the ground, one becomes very aware of how truly small humans are here. The land stretches for miles, emphasizing the insignificance of my presence on it. The sensation magnified my appreciation for the privilege of this experience.

Bee brought me back to the present when he pointed to a female kudu standing in the shade of an acacia tree. She startled slightly but then seemed unconcerned about our presence. We studied the copper coat and white stripes that covered her torso. Her dark face was lit up by a white beard and mustache.

A short time later we surprised a large herd of wildebeest who took off galloping. We also encountered a male waterbuck who only caught our attention when he ran off, flashing the white circle on his rump.

Along the way, Bee stopped to show me spore or footprints left on the earth by elephants, lions and cobras. He could identify scat (fecal remains) by size, shape and color. Jackals defecate large white droppings on account of the amount of bones they consume from their prey.

After more than an hour we arrived at the air strip, the first area of land that I recognized since stepping beyond the forbidden gates of camp. We stopped to rest out of the sun under the branches of a tree. Breaking the silence, I asked Bee about his life.

"Where are you from and how are you here?'

"I am from Maun. My family lives there; my wife, my children. I was raised there by my grandmother."

"What is your full name?"

"Bonetswe, Bo- net- sway," the second time he pronounced it more slowly.

"What about your family?"

"My father was the chief of our village but he was killed by the new chief," Bee's eyes remained fixed on mine as if he was waiting for a reaction.

I offered nothing.

"My grandmother did not want me to fight the chief for fear I would be killed so she sent me away to school in South Africa. It was there that I decided to become a guide. After school I went home to Maun and got married. I have been working here as a guide for eight years.

Sizing Bee up, I had guessed him to be around my age, thirty-two at the time.

"How many children do you have?"

"I have seven children. My first son was given to me by my uncle...a gift."

"That was some gift," I smiled at Bee, trying not to sound judgmental. This was not my culture so I had no opinion about this information except that it must have been a grand gesture. Bee seemed extremely proud of the fact. I was glad to learn about this man who had taught me more than I could have predicted in my African dream. He gave me an insight into a world so very different from the one that I came from so far away.

When the conversation ended, Bee hoisted the unspent rifle up over his shoulder and lead me silently back to camp. It was the perfect end to this incredible experience in the Okavango Delta.

After lunch we loaded up our belongings and boarded the small eight seater plane piloted by the handsome bush pilot, Keri. I craned my neck to watch as the Delta became smaller and smaller on our ascent. I wanted to hold onto the images as long as I could before filing them into memory. For the rest of the flight, Mom and I sat in quiet reflectivity as we headed off to our next adventure.

It was early evening when we arrived at our destination in Hwange National Park, Zimbabwe. There we met the rest of our travel group that now included Rachel and Karen at the very beginning of their African safari. It was so good to see them and to hear about home, Rod, the animals and the Adirondacks. Rod and his dad, Big Rod, were going to provide company for each other over the next two weeks. I hoped that they were managing well without us.

From here the trip took us to various national parks between Zimbabwe and Botswana. The most significant difference between a reserve and a national park was the number of tourists. We had been spoiled by the small number of guests at Pom Pom. Our Land Cruisers never crossed paths or encountered any other human life on game drives. In the parks, motor vehicles from numerous safari lodges packed the paved roads. It was common to park at a watering hole created by an electric pump to view elephants along with one hundred other tourists.

The variety of wildlife was a little different here. It included the beautiful black sable antelope and hundreds of zebra. Lions were a bit more reclusive, but our knowledgeable and well trained guides were able to find them by keeping each other informed by radio communication. There seemed to be an economic competition among the lodges to produce all the big game animals for clients. Therefore, the guides were under pressure to deliver the goods.

Our next destination was a flight and boat ride across Lake Kariba to Fothergill Island in Zimbabwe. Elephants and hippopotami shared the red clay earth with zebra and jackals. A most memorable event occurred here when I was folding some underwear I had washed earlier in the sink. It was dark so I could not see the eight inch long centipede who had taken up residence inside while they were drying. Instead I felt his stiff segmented body as he desperately tried to cling to my hand. One good frightened fling of my hand sent him unharmed to seek cover in a wall crevice. I still shudder at the memory.

Finally, we ended our African adventure at Chobe National Park in Botswana. Baboons and mongoose scampered across the lawn in front of our lodge. We had been warned not to feed the animals despite how tame they appeared and how close they came to us. One young woman in our group decided to ignore the rule when she offered a begging baboon one of her *Lorna Doone* cookies. His sweet facial expression turned into terror when he jumped up on the bench she was sitting on and exposed his three inch long canine teeth inches from her face. Luckily, having witnessed this poor decision, a guard ran screaming and yelling in his native language toward the baboon. Thankfully, the baboon abandoned his plan and ran away. Tragedy avoided. The guard continued to rage at the young woman who sat in a state of shock on the bench.

On our last morning, Mom and I were greeted by a female baboon who was foraging on the lawn three feet from our door. In her arms was a tiny baby baboon whose black eyes blinked at us from a bubblegum pink face. We watched the two of them from a respectful distance, marveling at how gentle the mother was with her newborn infant. This baby was born into a world uncontrolled by humans. His mother was the only being who could protect him long enough for him to reach independence. The odds were against his survival, a sobering fact to absorb in the company of my own mother who had succeeded with her own offspring. The laws of nature would dictate whether or not this baby lived long enough to reproduce. The unknown future of the little one, although risky, was of a design that is meant to be. Watching him cling to his mother stirred my awareness of the contrast between the protection and care I provide my own animals and the random consequences that unfold in wilderness. I realized that zoos try to meld the best of both situations into one. Presently, I accept a zoo's attempt to preserve the DNA of vanishing life forms until humans decide that wild spaces are worth maintaining. Perhaps then whole ecosystems teeming with a variety of symbiotic plant and animal species can be restored to their prehumen glory.

After our stay at Chobe, we made our way back to Victoria Falls for two more nights before it was time to embark on the return trip to New York and ultimately the Adirondacks. My mother accidentally drank water from a pitcher left in our room and spent a full twenty-four hours purging the results. Luckily, she could rest in our room until the sickness had passed. She seemed to be through the worst of it just in time to begin the long journey home.

The trip home, although exhausting, was uneventful. Endless flights provided time to process the incredible experience that all too quickly had come to an end. After nineteen days away from home, I was filled with images and knowledge that I had been longing for my whole life. I know about domestic animals, yet I have always craved the African experience. Zoos provided a stepping stone to this adventure when I was younger, but they never satisfied that itch that could only be scratched observing animals in the authentic African landscape.

In the months that followed my return from Africa, perceptions about animals swirled in my head demanding a mental sorting. At home successful animal rearing is measured by long healthy lives. A baby goat, who matures into a long-lived adult only to succumb to old age twelve years later, is deemed a success. A horse may live well into its third decade if cared for properly. My small dogs are expected to live well into their teens. Human attention is the common factor. It is this care that protects the animal. It is the "bubble wrap" applied by knowledge and good decision making during the animal's life. To date I have succeeded. The dogs are free to enter and exit the house on their own thanks to a large plastic flap by the back door. The fenced in perimeter of our backyard prevents mishaps in the driveway. My horses are neither overworked nor are they left unsupervised for long periods of time. Observation and constant monitoring of their wellbeing are essential to keep them safe. Interacting with goats forges strong bonds that keep them from roaming too far from the barn and into harm's way. In summary, my animals are safe but they are not free.

Wild animals live free. Infant mortality is high for most wild species. Only twenty-five percent of lion cubs make it to their reproductive age. Predation and failure to thrive are the most common causes of their deaths. Elephants live in constant threat of being poached by greedy humans. When a female elephant is killed, her calf is almost certain to die unless rescued by humans, a double loss for threatened populations. In Africa I was an observer. My opinions and emotions did not matter. Life cycles birth to death. If reproduction can occur between the two then so has success. The craggy skinned warthogs and elegant giraffe did not need me the way my own animals did. From the safety of an open air game vehicle, I merely spectated. Foolishly considering stepping out of the vehicle to gaze at cape buffalo at eye level is to contemplate suicide. Nobody would be able to help me, but the offending animal would be shot. This adage is verbally drilled often by game lodge employees who go out of their way to keep clients safe. By obeying the rules, safari goers assure safety for the animals.

Zoos bridge the gap between pet ownership and wildlife education. By encouraging patrons to view their collections up close, zoos encourage empathy and support. We will protect animals we know. When a child places a tiny hand on tempered glass in a high five gesture with a tiger offering a paw on the other side, a lifelong connection is made. The glass barrier keeps both of the observers safe while allowing the human to get a close-up encounter with a fellow earthling. The future of threatened wildlife all over the world is controlled by human attitudes. Education is the only way to sway these attitudes in favor of the animals. Zoos provide this opportunity.

Before my trip to Zimbabwe and Botswana, I had been issued a warning. When you visit Africa you believe you are quenching your thirst or satisfying a desire for the experience. Be prepared however, because pieces of your heart will remain scattered in the baked landscape, submerged in precious water holes or clinging to the breath of a winded antelope. Once you arrive home, a fierce desire will grow within your soul begging you to return in search of them.

When you leave Africa, as the plane lifts, you feel that more than leaving a continent you're leaving a state of mind. Whatever awaits you at the other end of your journey will be of a different order of existence." Francesca Marciano

Sharing the African experience with my mother is one of the most poignant events of my life. (Top; Standing in front of Victoria Falls, Zimbabwe), 1994.

Animals in the Classroom

"Watch any plant or animal and let it teach you acceptance of what is, surrender to the Now. Let it teach you being. Let it teach you integrity — which means to be one, to be yourself, to be real." - *Eckhart Tolle*

Animals are the most vivid features of my life. Livestock, particularly horses, were the focus of both of my undergraduate degrees. Equines were my area of professional concentration when I was hired to teach at Centenary College just after I graduated from Cornell University's School of Agriculture. Therefore, it was only natural that I would incorporate animals into my classroom shortly after I began teaching sixth grade in a public school.

At the beginning of my career, I focused on establishing a collection of unique organisms that would leave a lasting impression on young people. I cherished a vision of my students engaged with a variety of pets, including reptiles, domesticated rats and hedgehogs. From experience, I knew that most children will respond favorably to pets and form deep family like connections with them. I didn't anticipate the strong bonds that the students formed with each other for the sake of the animals. These are lessons that cannot be scribed in detailed lesson plans, read in a book or computed on a calculator. Hands-on interactions with animals encourage students to consider each other. After all, the animals belonged to everyone in the class.

"I want to hold Sunshine next," Ashley announces to Cory.

"I just got her from Cindy, so if I can have a few more minutes, then I will pass her to you," answers Cory agreeably.

Ashley has a choice now: whine and protest or accept that she will eventually be the next one to hold the hooded rat. If she chooses to squawk about it, then the rat goes back in her cage and nobody will be able to hold her. Cory also has a stake in the outcome. If he prolongs his rodent session, then he ruins the activity for everybody else in the room. These simple skills, so vital to children's social development, motivated them to choose appropriate actions.

Everybody loved the rat. Nobody wanted the privilege of holding her to be suspended. Rarely, did I need to intervene.

As for the rat? Her inquisitive intelligence and beguiling personality endeared her to the entire class. During dinner table conversations, many parents listened to lively tales that included antics of rats and other animals. When I encountered parents, while running errands at the post office or grocery store, they almost always peppered me with comments.

"I hear Sunshine has a whole collection of chalk in her cage that she stole from the blackboard."

"Is it true Spike the iguana has grown three inches this month?"

"Jimmy loves walking the iguanas up and down the hall on a leash."

"When are Sunshine's babies due to be born?"

Because the animals produced so much positive engagement in the classroom, we decided to breed Sunshine so we could experience reproduction from a rodent's eye view. A male rat named Shadow was introduced to our female rat. Three weeks later the classroom transitioned into a nursery for sixteen tiny pink erasers that Sunshine delivered. For five or six days, we viewed the rat pups from the outside of a glass tank where Sunshine tended to the babies. This gave her privacy from Shadow who would have gladly eaten the babies and bred Sunshine again. We all gleaned so many lessons from these observations. We learned acceptance of animal behavior outside of our control.

Each day the pups appeared to double in size. Rats age one *human* year every ten days. Pink wrinkly skin fuzzed into sleek fur.

"Why are they so helpless when they are born but develop so quickly? Isn't it incredible to think that Sunshine could produce a litter of babies every four to six weeks? Why is that possible?" The questions piled up in a metal *box of knowledge* located on my desk. All of the questions got answered by students, each of whom selected one to research and present to the rest of the class.

"Rodents produce lots of babies because they are easy prey for hungry predators. This way their numbers never reach dangerously low levels. Since the size of adult rat bodies are relatively small, the gestation length is short. Pups are born helpless, completely dependent on the care of their mother. That depletes a lot of her energy so babies grow quickly in order to take care of themselves sooner than later. It's all part of a plan that works in the natural world."

Many of the baby rats were adopted by students; leftovers were delivered to a local pet store. We never knew if they were sold as pets or snake food, but the students understood that either scenario was an acceptable reality. There was no way that *all* of the baby rats could grow up and live in our classroom. Certainly we were not going to turn them loose in the wild to fend for themselves. Finding an alternative solution was our responsibility. Sometimes the responsible choice isn't the ideal choice.

Then came the day when the actions of an elderly rat named Cross clearly communicated to us that she was ready to be euthanized. On average, rats live for two years. They age rapidly. Due to domestication and inbreeding, tumors, cancer and neurological disorders usually bring their lives to a swift end. Just shy of two years, Cross began to lose the use of her hind legs. For several days she dragged her useless limbs behind her. The front end of her body never seemed to notice the disability. A hearty appetite and desire to engage with her people showed no change at all. I wanted the students to still find value in her presence despite her declining physical condition.

We discussed a plan that would include euthanasia as soon as Cross showed any symptoms of pain or lethargy. Many of the children shared their family's experience of saying goodbye to an aging or injured pet. Articulating feelings and sharing events with classmates strengthened their commitment to making difficult decisions in the best interest of the animal. As our pet's humans, we take on an enormous responsibility in our capacity to decide when it is time to take away the animal's pain and make it our own.

The morning Cross showed no interest in food or being handled, I made arrangements to have her put down. During our preparation, two students had volunteered to deliver Cross to our local veterinarian. Most of the remaining students sobbed a chorus of goodbyes to the rat before she was swaddled in a towel and carried in caring hands for a brief walk down the block. The two children waited solemnly for Sunshine's heart to stop beating after Dr. Brooker had injected her with life ending medication. Then they wrapped her body in the towel and brought her back to school. Eager ears awaited the students' return, anxious for full details of what transpired in the vet's office. Student curiosity persuaded me to unwrap the towel so that they could see Cross's lifeless shell.

"It wasn't scary. Cross went to sleep and then became completely still. Dr. Brooker was so kind to us. She explained every step of the procedure. Next thing we knew, it was over," summarized the witnesses, thus bringing the whole episode and lesson to its conclusion. The class could now process and accept death. I took the dead rat home to Rod for a burial in our woods.

For over six years, animals resided in my classroom, combining endless lessons in life science, math, writing, reading, empathy and love. They encouraged the students not only to care about animals but also to care about each other; to step out of the center of their own universe and notice that helping others, whether human or creature, had a profound effect on how good they felt about themselves. Because of the animals, sixth grade could not have had a happier classroom. Therefore, nobody was more surprised than I was when I was ordered to remove them from my classroom.

Although teachers tend to remain in one school for the duration of their careers, administrators are different. Several years after I began teaching, our school hired a new superintendent, the second of five in my career. Shortly after her arrival, she made it clear to me that she was not enamored of the animals in the classroom. They made her terribly uncomfortable, especially the rats' tails and the iguana's elimination of waste on a designated tray.

At first I expressed no concern for her personal opinions. Surely they could have no bearing on all of the positives that animals brought to the classroom. But they did. By mid-October of the following year, the classroom was empty of my co-teacher creatures who had contributed so much to my instructional style. How could I ever teach without them? Stripped of their endearing engagements, teachable moments and class bonding strategies, I faced my students alone and moved on. The sequence of events left me professionally battered. The students were confused and heartbroken. Sadly, I was ordered by the superintendent not to share details of the animal removal with them so they never received a definitive explanation for this major shift in their classroom environment. In fact I was never convinced that I had received an acceptable explanation. That was a low point of my career.

Although I gave the rats to a student who took care of them for the remainder of their short lives, my house had to absorb several enclosures that contained hedgehogs, iguanas and a veiled chameleon. Their lives changed drastically without daily handling from their children. As hard as I tried to interact with them, it wasn't the same. A purpose was missing.

Yet life moved on, new classes arrived in September and dispersed in June. With each passing year, the animals faded into the past, their six year residency a legend in my creature-less classroom.

Meanwhile, in my personal life, Moose River Farm blossomed. After eighteen years of managing horses on a tiny parcel of lakefront property in Inlet, my husband Rod and I made the decision to build a farm on larger acreage. It took almost five years between the time that we selected seventy-seven acres of Adirondack woods and the day Rod finished transforming it into an eighty-four feet long barn, several fenced paddocks, and a few miles of meandering trails. The most sublime feature is the two story home that we currently live in. Every window gazes out upon animals who delight our eyes and lift our spirits. Moose River Farm is a perfect place.

The new farm's barn needed furry residents to occupy ten stalls assembled on either side of its central aisle. A steady stream of carefully considered horses arrived and have stayed for good. At the end of long lives, we have euthanized a total of seven horses so far at Moose River Farm. Losing them to death is the price one pays for providing them a forever home. Each additional horse filled a niche for my growing riding lesson business, providing a platform for me to continue to teach children about animals. In addition to horses we added more goats, donkeys, chickens and geese. My barn filled up with different species and took the place of my classroom that was once alive with animals.

Although I missed my classroom animals, I continued to grow as an educator without my scaled and furry colleagues. Along the way there were several opportunities to incorporate animals into lesson plans. Although books, videos, photographs and other visual examples never fully replaced the experience of engaging with real animals, they provided suitable, if bland, alternatives. Then came a unique opportunity to bring an animal back into my classroom, back into the curriculum and back into the hearts of my students.

Barbaro

For two college summers I had the great fortune of working for Olympic show jumper rider and consummate horseman, Michael Matz. At the time I was attending Cornell University but returned home to Philadelphia so that I could spend my vacation immersed in all aspects of his world class show jumper sport horses. My experience at the iconic Erdenheim Farm working for this top athlete is chronicled in my first book and remains at the apex of my career with horses. Caring for finely trained and conditioned equines provided me with tried and true skills that I still employ today while caring for my own horses.

Over the years since those two memorable summers, I have followed Michael's achievements and news making events. Among the most memorable are several Olympic Games and a horrific plane crash. From the latter he emerged a hero, having comforted three children while delivering them to safety. As a school teacher, I have often shared my previous work experience with my students who were fascinated to learn about Michael Matz's Olympic endeavors. The Olympic dream dances in the heads of many youngsters.

Early in the spring of 2006, I learned that Michael, who had retired from show jumping to train racehorses fulltime, was training a horse who had qualified for the Kentucky Derby. Barbaro became the six to one favorite to win during the week that led up to the first Saturday in May, otherwise known as *Derby Day*. During that week, the media was abuzz with snippets about Michael's horse. Everywhere, from the *Nightly News* to the Internet, Barbaro was expected to win the Derby and possibly achieve winning the *Triple Crown*. Doing so would be the first time after a twenty-eight year drought. As a result of his public presence, Barbaro became an effective teacher in my classroom. Lessons in anatomy, physiology and the math behind racing probability filled our week in anticipation for the big event.

After Barbaro's incredible win in the *Kentucky Derby*, my sixth grade students felt even more connected with this special bay horse. They kept daily tabs on him, learning about all the people involved in the horse's life. Owners, trainers, exercise riders, and jockeys, collectively referred to as connections, go to intricate measures to keep racehorse athletes in prime condition, but content at the same time. Videos that documented the stallion frolicking in his grassy paddock, kicking up his heels and rolling on the ground bore evidence of a pampered life.

Two weeks after the Derby, Barbaro, the odds on favorite to win, was headed to the *Preakness*, the second jewel of the *Triple Crown,* that is run at Maryland's Pimlico Race Course. Of course Barbaro never finished that race. His career came to a snapping halt shortly after the gate released the field of horses. Before the official beginning of the race, Barbaro lurched out of the gate unexpectedly. The false start elevated concern in the millions of fans watching that day, but mostly in his connections: trainer Michael Matz, jockey Edgar Prado and the horse's owners Gretchen and Roy Jackson. After a quick veterinary inspection, Barbaro was deemed fit to reenter the starting gate. Shortly after the official start, it became apparent that jockey Edgar Prado realized that something was wrong with Barbaro's gait. In response, he desperately *pulled* the horse up to stop him, a next to impossible feat considering that the rest of the horses were surging away at top thoroughbred speed. Although Barbaro was still galloping, his right hind leg swung grotesquely behind him. He soldiered on, however, because instinct reminds horses to stay with the herd. Yet, Prado's one-hundred-fifteen pound body somehow restrained Barbaro from galloping down the track on three legs. Gradually the great horse slowed, then stopped. Until a veterinary ambulance arrived on the scene, spectators and television viewers didn't realize what was happening and could only stare in horror at Barbaro's right hind limb swinging behind him.

Devastating diagnosis, blame and speculation about whether or not the horse should be saved filled newscasts while the public waited anxiously for updates. On Monday morning after the Preakness, many of my sixth grade students greeted me at the classroom door with expressions of despair. They needed to know what happened to a horse with whom they felt such a connection.

What had gone wrong? How bad was his injury? Would Barbaro ever race again? Many of these questions had no definitive answers; and frankly, I was at a loss to explain any part of it except for the scientific facts.

"Barbaro's leg was shattered in several places. Surgery was performed and he is still alive, but no, he will never race again. He has a long recovery ahead of him," was all I could offer.

As the students expressed their feelings in class, an idea began to take shape in my head. As a group we decided to create a student illustrated picture book of Barbaro's first three years of life. The class brainstormed a storyboard, selecting the events that led him to his big win at the Kentucky Derby and on to the Preakness. Each student then selected an episode that he/she wished to illustrate and contribute to the overall story. By the afternoon most of the class was engaged in the project. We were feeling much better as the sequence of the pages sprang forth into the incredible story of Barbaro's short life so far.

While the book was taking shape, the class and I decided to send it to Michael Matz as an expression of our *get well* wishes for Barbaro and his trainer during that uncertain and difficult time. The students took comfort in their efforts as we packaged the book and sent it on its way. They were quite aware that Barbaro and his connections were receiving thousands of well wishes in all forms of communication, including emails, pictures, carrots, apples and cards. We didn't expect a response. The students were content with the fact that they had expressed themselves in their book. The news was out of their control, and watching it only promoted feelings of helplessness. Reaching out to Barbaro offered the students hope. Lessons in empathy, compassion and consideration for others returned to my classroom via the teaching efforts of a broken horse.

About two weeks after we sent the Barbaro book, I received a phone call from Gretchen Jackson, Barbaro's owner. This gracious woman called to express her deepest appreciation for the book and the students' illustrations. She was deeply touched by all of the pictures and the research that went into such an accurate account of the horse's first three years. Mrs. Jackson wanted the students to know that Barbaro was pain free and that as long as he remained that way, she would continue to provide all that was possible to bring him through the injury. He was a model patient who seemed to understand that humans were helping him and therefore, did not protest their care. Barbaro's owner and her family were overwhelmed by the outpouring from so many people who wished the very best for the horse's full recovery.

The sixth grade students were delighted to receive Mrs. Jackson's message. They were uplifted, knowing that their book had offered comfort during a difficult challenge. At that time neither my students nor I could predict that our involvement in Barbaro's tragedy was not yet over.

Over the summer months, Barbaro continued to recover, despite solvable setbacks along the way. Media reports kept the world updated on his progress and over the periods of no news is good news, it appeared that the courageous horse was winning the battle.

In August, several friends and I attended a luncheon for the *Barbaro Fund.* The fundraiser was a benefit for the University of Pennsylvania Veterinary School's Large Animal Facility at New Bolton where Barbaro was recovering. The event was held at Saratoga Race Course, a two hour drive from my home. The Fund was set up to promote research on laminitis, a crippling condition that plagues horses who can't distribute weight evenly on all four hooves. Although Barbaro's fractures were healing well, he had continued to suffer from the debilitating condition in his *good* feet, now compromised by disproportionately supporting his weight.

Aside from this fundraiser being a lovely trackside event, it enabled me to meet Gretchen and Roy Jackson along with Dr. Dean Richardson, the surgeon responsible for Barbaro's remarkable recovery. I was also able to visit with Michael Matz, the genius horseman I had worked with so many years ago. My friend Michele took over one hundred pictures that day, documenting a truly incredible day in my life.

Barbaro's recovery stretched into the fall. Eventually his fans were treated to video footage of the horse taking his first steps outside to feel the sunshine on his back and to nibble grass. The images inspired us to hope that the Kentucky Derby winner was going to make it after all.

Then in late January, word was broadcast that Barbaro had been euthanized. The efforts to relieve his pain from *laminitis* were losing their effectiveness. As promised by Mrs. Jackson in her phone call eight month earlier, they would not extend Barbaro's suffering once he indicated that he was in pain. I applaud their decision although I am certain it was difficult to make.

Prior to the euthanasia, I had submitted an article to *Practical Horseman Magazine* about the involvement of my sixth grade students at the time of Barbaro's injury. Immediately after the horse was put down, they decided to run the story in the April issue. The next two weeks demanded frenzied editing to get the article shaped for publication. On top of my fulltime job, there were horses to care for on either side of my professional day. I pulled it off and completed the article on time. It included quotes from many of my students. At that point I thought I had breathed my last breath into the Barbaro episode. However, more was on the way.

In the spring of 2007, my school was actively in search of a new principal, a long process. An interim was hired to carry out vital administrative duties. Mrs. Rivett, a retired administrator, had not been in charge for long when she received a confusing phone call. Since she did not know me or anything about my association with animals, least of all horses, it took her a day or two to find me. Through persistence and guidance from my colleagues, she finally delivered a prophetic message.

"A woman from HBO called me last week, looking for the teacher who knows a horse," read Mrs. Rivett from a small note in her hand. As she delivered the message, her eyes darted above her glasses, hopeful for a sign of comprehension on my face.

I stared blankly waiting for more.

"Ok...the woman who called said she was looking for the school that had students who wrote about a horse." Again her eyes pleaded with me to understand. "Is this the school? They were sixth graders who wrote about some horse."

My mind sprang into recognition. "Yes, my sixth graders wrote about the Kentucky Derby winner who broke his leg. Is that what you mean?"

The relief on Mrs. Rivett's face was evident as she handed me the telephone number that ultimately cast my students in an HBO Sports documentary about Barbaro.

Immediately, life got interesting. Once again Barbaro returned to my classroom. The school administration went out of its way to make this happen for our students. They arranged for and paid to ship my photo copy of the book overnight to the production office for review. The class was now in seventh grade. They had to return to my classroom and *act* like sixth graders working on their book. Meanwhile, my present sixth graders had to move out and be kept on task by a substitute teacher. The plans were mind boggling. Lighting, sound and camera equipment crowded the classroom and spilled out into the hallway. The young cast members sat at desks recreating their pictures for over three hours. Several students were selected to recite the text that accompanied the illustrations. Newspapers from Utica arrived to report on the event. I was interviewed on a local radio station the next morning to share our filming experience on the air. If this wasn't enough of a thrill, the administration granted me a day off to travel with Rod to New York City for the documentary premiere.

After arriving by train in Manhattan, we spent the evening rubbing elbows with elite players of the racing and sports writer industries over cocktails and dinner. Actor *Tony Serico* from the television show *The Sopranos* attended as an avid racehorse enthusiast. When we took our seats in the movie screening room, I was not prepared for emotions I felt. As Barbaro's story unfolded larger than life and in living color, my heart swelled with pride. Halfway through the film, my students appeared on the screen.

Listening to their voices and watching their illustrations sprout on paper brought tears to my eyes.

The HBO Sports CEO sent me home with a copy of the documentary on CD. A week later the program aired on HBO and the day after, we celebrated at school with a private screening to which students and their parents were invited. Considering the general impression that the film industry is cold and calculating, I was most impressed to notice that this production team made certain that *every* child appeared in the scene. With the documentary completed, our magical moment in the history of Barbaro's life came to a close. Today, those students are beyond college age, living in various areas around the country. I hope that the memories of this special horse who joined our class over a decade ago include inspiring lessons that stuck with them. They certainly have for me.

Barbaro's remains are buried under his statue at Churchill Downs in Louisville, KY, 2014.

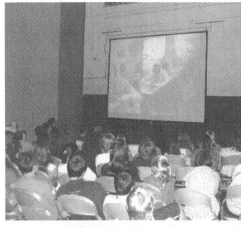

Student Lizzy Getty's illustration of Barbaro.
Filming the HBO Sports Documentary, 2007 .photo by M. deCamp
Meeting actor Tony Serico at the HBO Sports Barbaro Doc. premiere in NYC; 2007.
The students attended their own premiere at school, 2007.
Catching up with Michael Matz at a Thoroughbred Makeover event in Saratoga, 2015. photo by M. deCamp

Horses Come to School

Just before the end of June each year, I invite my class to spend a day at Moose River Farm. It is a highly anticipated field trip. Recalling the countless animal stories I have shared over the school year, students exit the bus with elevated excitement. One by one, I introduce them to my animal family and, of course, to Rod. It's interesting to watch each student gravitate toward a particular horse.

"Spirit is my favorite because I can tell he likes me," Jason declares.

"I like Joshua because he is big," Ryan announces.

"Can I brush Skippy?" Amy inquires. "I like him because he is small."

And so the proclamations ring as students set out to claim one of the animals as their special friend. The scenario rarely varies. When it is time to ride the horses, each student desperately tries to secure a mount by letting me know how much the horse likes him or her.

"I have to ride Target or he will be disappointed."

"Gatsby keeps looking for me, so I really need to ride him."

"I want to ride Easau because he massaged my hair."

This long awaited visit to the farm by my students is my favorite school day of the year. After our many discussions about how to act at the farm, they are on their best behavior.

"The first thing you will notice about our farm is how quiet it is. Occasionally, a horse whinnies or a donkey brays but mostly the animals exist here in a state of calm," I pause so the class can listen. "It's important that we keep this level of calm so that everybody, animals and people, remain safe. If the horses get excited because kids are running and screaming around the barn, everybody's safety will be jeopardized."

Their actions indicate that they understand. For the remainder of the day, they choose behaviors that keep animals calm. So successful are these visits to the farm that I did not hesitate to say yes when asked if I could bring a horse to school for a special event.

Civil War Day is an interactive affair for middle school students. Various stations set up on the school ball field offer opportunities to step into this devastating era of American history. Samples of tasteless hardtack and visits to tightly quartered canvas tents sober student's thoughts as they consider the misery of fighting an endless war. The school nurse, dressed as Clara Barton, toils over her display of bloodied severed limbs. Her crude saws and implements were used to amputate in a struggle to save lives.

To lift the dire mood, students keep tempo with a snare drum during marching practice, then gaze at magic created when a miniature simulation of the *Union Army Balloon Corps* rises toward the heavens. It is quite an educational day.

My goal was to explain the role of horses. While in the company of my own equids, I often contemplate the reality of war for horses. Like my own eclectic assortment, there must have been a variety of different personalities that charged onto the battlefield with ground troops. Clearly, some of these horses were braver than others. But there must have been many who, along with their riders, felt tremendous fear when the call to attack was issued. I can only imagine the intensity of this fear when their senses caught a whiff of death surrounding them.

I brought my Friesian mare, Lowtchee, to represent a war horse. Although her stout breed does not resemble those enlisted at the time, her training does. A horse's obedience was essential for improving the rider's chances of survival during a bloody attack. Mounted high on my zaftig black horse, I rode among a small group of students assembled in a makeshift riding ring adjacent to the baseball field. Although the mare offered her most gentle demeanor, I wanted the students to imagine the intimidation that a mounted officer could convey to lowly grounds troops. Then I steered Lowtchee away from the students to demonstrate her level of training and obedience. We trotted and cantered in a small circle, a difficult effort for a large horse. As a mounted officer, I had a stake in her training that could cost me my life if she didn't understand exactly what I needed her to do. Add to this the frenzied chaos of a battle, and her compliance was imperative. Next, I walked her back to the group and offered them a chance to pat her face and neck, to feel the living flesh that was my vehicle for war. I reminded them that it was in a soldier's best interest to establish trust with his horse. After all, the horse was as mortal as he was. Did the soldiers find comfort in quiet moments, grooming their horses, feeding them and caring for them? Did the connection provide them with comforting reminders of home and family? I wasn't sure, but I suspected, that for some, the horse touched a soft spot buried deep within a traumatized psyche.

By participating in the activities on *Civil War Day,* the students were able to catch an empathetic glimpse of the fear and anxiety that fought that devastating war. I have no doubt that the students were impressed with Lowtchee's gentleness. They all wanted to stroke her long mane and damp neck. With eyes half closed, she stood relaxed, absorbing the tactile praise, evidence of her ability to teach.

Lowtchee is not the only horse who visited school. When I taught fifth grade, my friend Vicky, who owns miniature horses, brought one directly into my classroom. *Little River Man* arrived in the backseat of Vicky's pickup truck. A throng of adoring fans greeted him with the enthusiasm directed at rock stars as he pulled into the bus circle at the front of the building. After delivering an official welcome speech our principal, Mr. Swick, secured a visitor's pass around his neck and led the tiny horse through the door and down the hallway. River visited each elementary classroom where he allowed students to fuss all over him.

"What does he eat?"

"Does he live in your house?"

"Why do you put him in your truck? Does he like to go for a ride?"

"Can I take him home with me?"

Vicky answered the barrage of questions good naturedly, no matter how many times she responded to the same inquiries. Meanwhile, River absorbed the adoration willingly, never once displaying signs of irritability. He remained alert and attentive when several fifth grade students read to him from a children's book about a miniature service horse who assisted a blind woman with her daily routine. For River, all of this commotion was an introductory test to determine if he was a suitable therapy horse. No doubt he passed. Today, River visits schools and public events.

Nursing homes invite Vicky and her minis to promote smiles among people who have little left in life to inspire them. I have witnessed nonverbal Alzheimer's patients babble incoherently while petting River. His posture suggests complete relaxation despite unpredictable vocal outbursts from elderly residents. Some geriatric brains labor with effort to rewire blocked pathways. Perhaps River is stimulating distorted memories of a beloved pet or animal from the past. Oh, the power of animals to awaken our deepest emotions and escort them to the surface of our thoughts! Every one of these encounters enables me to witness powerful dynamics activated when humans interact with animals. I never tire of bearing witness to the magic of the human-animal connection.

Lowtchee attends Civil War Day for middle school students. photo by M. deCamp

Miniature horse, Little River Man visits the elementary school during PARP, (Parents as Reading Partners), 2015.

Animals Return to the Classroom

Administrators come and go. I am happy to admit that the last superintendent and principal for whom I worked were both proponents of children interacting with animals. With their encouragement, I ended my career as a teacher much the way I started, with two special animal co-teachers in my classroom.

After Rosemary, our twenty-one year old green iguana, was euthanized a few years ago, I was certain that my life with reptiles had come to an end. Fond memories of Rosemary spiked every time I perused the produce section at the grocery store or pinched off wilted petunia blossoms, a treat she savored from flower boxes around the farm. How I missed her. Not all reptiles are emotionless, cold blooded organisms that spend daytime absorbing solar rays and conserving energy. Rosemary had learned to exit and enter our dog door on summer days and anticipated food when she heard my voice at dinnertime. We owe reptiles more credit. They are unique relics of creatures who successfully existed and evolved long before mammals arrived to populate the earth with more mobile metabolic furnaces.

My menagerie consists mostly of mammals and birds. When life is prickly, palpating their warm bodies, soft fur and dense feathers soothes me. However, I missed the presence of my scaly green pal navigating the radiant heated wood floor between the kitchen and living room of our house.

Meanwhile, I was struggling to make a connection with my sixth graders newly thrust into the fast lane routine of changing classes in middle school. I wanted something in the room that made them feel at home when attending science and math class. Our current administration, almost twenty years after the administration that banished the animals from my classroom, hinted often that they would gladly support animals in my classroom. With a great deal of thought, I contemplated what kind of animal was best for the students. Unlike twenty years ago, I now had a huge commitment to the animals at Moose River Farm. Taking time out on the weekends to care for the animals at school was out of the question. Low maintenance and portability were mandatory.

While visiting the *Fort Rickey Game Farm* in Rome, New York, I became enamored of two Russian tortoises on display. Active and alert, they explored the interior of their outdoor enclosure with purpose. They even stretched their heads up to be patted when I reached my hand in to touch them. For days after my visit, I could not stop thinking about them. From Google research I determined that they remain small, topping out at a mere eight or nine inches. Most tortoise species grow into very large specimens, some reaching fifty pounds or more. The Russian tortoise's vegetarian diet affirmed that they would be relatively easy to provide for year round. By November I successfully located and purchased a one year old male and a two year old female Russian tortoise for my classroom.

Oliver and Pandora were a huge hit with my students. The way they stretched their necks up and out to gaze through a plexiglas window of their enclosure made an endearing first impression. Over the years I have had many adorable pets who lack something when it comes to human interactions. Hedgehogs spend their days sleeping in a spiky ball, while chameleons remain motionless except for the constantly rotating eyeballs that scan the environment for crickets, not caressing fingertips. But Russians get excited when you approach them with food and stretch their necks up, cat like, to encourage a good scratch on the top of their heads. In fact, it would not surprise me if a hind leg began scratching the air in ecstatic pleasure like a dog's.

Russian tortoises are active and love to dig. The students had to become accustomed to the rhythmic scraping that Pandora and Oliver enjoyed at various intervals during the school day. When the tortoises are at home, my husband Rod reacts to Oliver's digging by setting him free on the floor. The tortoise responds with a brisk exploration of our first floor. From his turtle eye view, he *thunks* his way under the sofa before emerging at the other end and making his way out into the front hall. At the dining room door, he pauses to make a decision. When urgency sparks in his brain, he is underway again. Eventually, he appears to have arrived at his sought out destination, a corner of the dining room under a chair.

Oliver has been so busy on these forays around the house that it has become necessary to track him with a GPS monitor. After countless episodes of searching under every piece of furniture on the first floor to find him, Rod invested in a small plastic monitoring device that attaches with Velcro to the rear of Oliver's carapace or shell. The tap of an app on my phone activates a staccato of strong beeps pinpointing his exact location. Now we release Oliver confident that we can't lose him.

"Ah ha...there you are," we chant effortlessly before returning him to his enclosure where kale leaves and rest under a heat lamp await.

Pandora, unlike Oliver, is not adventuresome. When we set her free she prefers to snuggle under the dog beds by the fireplace. Rarely does she travel too far and shows no interest in exploring beyond the shadows of table leg forests or beneath the canopy of an ottoman. When the time comes for her to return to her enclosure, she is easily located and returned without stress. No GPS tracker for her.

During the warm weather months, the tortoises spend sunny days outside in a large enclosure built just for them. Natural sunlight penetrates their skin, activating vitamin D and calcium to strengthen their bones. They graze on grass, dandelion greens and Rosemary the iguana's favorite petunia flowers. At their choosing, they can seek refuge from the sun in the *Flintstone* house nestled in a corner of their enclosure. Two bricks support a stone roof providing shade and a cool place to dig in damp sand.

With ease the tortoises travel back and forth to a large enclosure in my classroom. Since Pandora is not enamored of Oliver's intense interest in her, it has become necessary to separate them. Every Monday I return to school after the weekend with a tortoise secured for travel in a vintage *Igloo* lunchbox. The tortoises take turns; a week at home followed by a week at school. Otherwise Pandora would be unable to escape Oliver's unwelcome advances.

The timeless magic performed by children and animals happens once again where it has always belonged, in my classroom as students interact with the calm tortoises.

"Hold her like a hamburger," students remind each other how to hold a tortoise with one hand clutching each side of the saucer shaped bodies. Oliver's back feet flip back and forth searching for security against the palm of a hand. Pandora is more content to relax unmoving in a student's grasp, a sign of the contrast in personalities. Students smile at the tortoises' individual mannerisms. They discuss the position of items in the enclosure, a rock on which to serve kale and collard greens, a half log to hide under and potting soil substrate for absorbing waste.

"He's pooping," somebody shares, referring to the two shiny fecal droppings that have appeared on a towel where Oliver rests.

"I will clean it up," says a volunteer as she reaches for a diaper wipe.

These actions and matter of fact statements speak volumes about the education our resident tortoises provide. For the length of my career, my opinion of animals in the classroom has never varied. They deliver messages that teachers can't always convey through words and lesson plans. I chalk it up to animal alchemy. As *John Muir* notes, *"Any glimpse into the life of an animal quickens our own and makes it so much the larger and better in every way."*

Oliver is an attentive listener when students practice reading out loud.

Pandora poses for her back to school picture.2018.

Love and Loss

"Grief is the price we all pay for love." -Gretchen Jackson

Perhaps the most important decision I make in an animal's lifetime is when to end it. Euthanasia is not only the kindest gesture I offer ailing or aging pets, it is also my obligation. Although the decision is personal, I must decide only in the best interest of the animal. Avoiding my own grief is not an excuse to prolong an animal's suffering. Of course this is my head talking. I have to keep my heart quiet as I impose a fate that has no compassionate alternative. Every one of us is going to die. Every time new animals arrive at the farm, a rehomed horse, a gaggle of goslings, an eight week old puppy, my excitement is shadowed by the sober realization of inevitable loss. I think, "Although you are here for your forever, you will not live forever. The day will come when…"

Happy moments pummel the dark thought away…for now. I think to myself, "How lucky I am to spend what I hope will be a long and meaningful quality of time with you. How I will embrace every moment we are together."

Over years of love and loss, I have learned to find peace when an old horse dies after having lived a healthy life under my care… When a dog dies having known nothing but human closeness and daily walks in the woods… When an iguana dies after thriving for twenty-one cycles of the seasons…These facts translate into no regrets and the ability to let go when the time comes. When I hold an animal as it slips into unconsciousness, I believe I offer death with dignity. If only we allowed humans such grace. To the animal's last breath, my hands touch and my lips whisper the final farewell. I want this good death for all of my creatures who spend their lives teaching wisdom and giving me joy.

When the vet extinguishes an animal's pain, anxiety, or illness, I feel a sense of relief. Strangely, I feel even more connected with the rest of my animal family immediately following the euthanasia of one. It's as if the loss itself creates a new force that strengthens bonds between death and life, tightening us up a notch. During this time, my senses are more attuned to the sanctuary that is my barn. The sweet, pungent mixture of hay and ammonia tingles in my nostrils. The distant rumbling motor of the backhoe makes me grateful to Rod who stoically digs the hole and finalizes the aftermath of death on the farm. Meanwhile, horses nicker and donkeys bray for my attention. Goats rub against me, offering condolences by demanding I scratch their backs. All of them need me. This fact catches me like a safety net. Minus one life, our routines stay the same. Life goes on.

The next day, I remain busy in the barn, filling a void left by a creature now nestled in the earth. It is a day of quiet reflection and acceptance. I also take care to focus attention on the living creatures still with me. It is not an unhappy day.

The moments leading up to death are not as predictable. The best case scenario occurs at the end of a long life, lived well. However, the death of an animal is not always in my control. From the day a horse, donkey, goat or puppy arrives at Moose River Farm, I am aware that a last day is just as certain as a first. Not only do I have to accept this fact, but I also must shoulder the responsibility of making decisions about infirmed or aging pets. It is my duty. Still, I learn more about myself every time I decide that an animal must be euthanized.

Years ago, I avoided thinking about the inevitable end of an animal's life. There was nothing to compare it to because I had yet to experience the loss of my own pets. The deaths of two dogs and several cats were shared experiences with my parents, brothers and sister. Although my father wept uncontrollably when our collie Bonnie died, sadness faded because life moved forward with focus on school, horses, college and beyond. My parents were in charge of decisions that affected our pets so I didn't have to consider the ends of our animals' lives. All that changed when I began to acquire animals that were my own responsibility.

I remember vividly the moment I realized that my dachshund, Eric might be doomed to live a much shorter life than expected. He had been diagnosed with a cancerous skin growth. Our vet at the time told me that the tumor would either metastasize quickly and spread to other parts of his body or it would remain slow growing for years to come. The ramifications of the diagnosis punched me in the gut. Eric was only seven years old at the time. He was the first dog in my independent life. Both of us were too young to die. For days I remained in a funk as the thought of life without my dog broke my heart.

Thankfully, Eric lived to be fifteen years old. Assessing his quality of life as a blind, deaf and incontinent elderly hound finally persuaded me to make the painful decision to let him go. His euthanasia was the first I arranged for a dog I loved. In the days that followed Eric's death, I was surprised at how smoothly my grief settled into relief and finally peace. I was certain that the loss would bring me down to the lowest level of despair. Perhaps that is why it took me so long to decide to euthanize Eric. The experience proved that although death is inevitable, it is only final for the dying. Left behind in death's wake, I was capable of moving forward into a happy and productive future. Now I expect this emotional transformation to occur each time that one of my animals dies. I must admit that it is easier to accept death at the end of a long life, which most of my animals live. However, acceptance takes much longer when an animal dies unexpectedly or at a young age. In those instances my mind has to process whether or not I missed symptoms that should have been treated and, therefore, might have prevented the animal from dying. I am grateful that this scenario has occurred very few times in my life with so many animals.

The decision to euthanize is a process in itself. I am always shocked when it enters my thoughts. Usually the animal begins exhibiting peculiar behaviors. Old dogs begin to wander anxiously around the house searching for me. Bending down to stroke a panting head, I seek to soothe. "I am right here," I assure while gazing into milky eyes. Unconvinced, the animal continues on his trek to seek comfort elsewhere. I cannot deny that this is a sign that *the time* is drawing near. At first I resist the thought, but eventually the reality of age, anxiety and the inevitability of death forces me to admit the option. Only when my own foreboding ebbs, enabling me to see truth in the situation, am I ready to make final arrangements.

Isaac Asimov says it best: *"Life is pleasant. Death is peaceful. It's the transition that is troublesome."* That transition falls on me. Knowing when to make the arrangements with a veterinarian to end an animal's life is the most complex aspect of the transition. Wait too long, the animal suffers. Decide hastily, I suffer with guilt. Despite the challenge of the decision making phase, my burden is lifted in the days that follow death when I am able to feel that the animal and I are at peace.

Over a four year period, I remained suspended in drama that featured animals young and old. My emotions stretched the gamut between calm acceptance and brokenhearted devastation. When the melancholy debris had settled, I was left in a haze of emotional conflict that forced me to examine my philosophy of loss on a deeper level.

Murray and Makia

"Of all creatures God made at the Creation, there is none more excellent, or so much to be respected as a horse." -Bedouin Legend

"You know, Anne, I have been working this little thoroughbred mare that belongs to Deb, my neighbor. She is the sweetest girl. Are you looking for more horses?"

Those dreaded words slipped through my friend Meg's lips. She was visiting my barn, assisting her daughters as they prepared to ride my horses.

Reflexively I gave her my canned answer. "No thank you, the barn is full and I really don't want a mare."

Luckily, Meg kept the horse in our conversation over the next eighteen months.

"Remember the mare, I was telling you about? She is going so nicely. I wish you could just come down, [to Connecticut], and have a look."

"No room, no mares, no thank you," I replied.

"I know, I know, but Deb, really wants to find a home for Makia. I was riding her this week and she was such a great horse. Very comfortable and well mannered. Sure you don't want to...?"

"No room, no mares, no thank you."

And so the conversation continued back and forth between Meg and me. Then in late August, tragedy struck our farm.

One week before the new school year was about to begin, Murray, an aged bay gelding, began to exhibit signs of extreme abdominal distress. The symptoms are enough to send shocks of fear through every horse owner. While the horse nips and kicks at his sides, attempts to lie down to roll, and refuses to eat, the owner must decide whether or not the case is severe enough to summon the vet. Our vet clinic is an hour away, but it may take the vet as long as two or three hours to arrive, depending on where she is when the message gets to her.

Before calling the vet, I followed my standard protocol of walking the horse in hopes that his intestines might dislodge the gas or source of discomfort. Murray and I walked round and round the island in our driveway, stopping every once in a while so that I could assess his condition. When there appeared to be no improvement, I decided to inject him with a strong painkiller I keep on hand that would, at least, relieve his discomfort until the gas dissipated.

By early evening, Murray's symptoms appeared to be subsiding, but his appetite had yet to return. Eventually, the heat of the summer day released its grip and darkness began to fall. By then, Murray had chosen to lie quietly, resting in his stall. Due to my elevated concern, I dragged a portable hammock from our patio out to the indoor arena where Murray was living. By the time I wrapped myself in a blanket and curled up in the hammock, Murray seemed at ease. All that separated the two of us were the metal fence panels that had been fabricated into a temporary stall. At the moment, all of the stalls in the barn were occupied. Due to Murray's good natured, confident personality and lack of anxiety about being alone in the indoor ring, I had chosen him to live out there. In truth he was less than thirty feet from the rest of the herd.

A check of the time revealed that it was close to 11:00. I reached my hand through the rails of the panel and lightly stroked Murray's ear and jowl. His eyes closed and his breathing became the normal wheezy effort that horses, lying heavily on their lungs, produce.

In that moment, I was acutely aware of the clear summer sky, its sparkling lights and waning illumination from the crescent moon twinkling through the large door. With my hand on Murray's face, I began to wonder if his condition was more serious than the gas colic I had treated him for earlier that afternoon. The weight of this worry turned my attention to Michele, Murray's financial sponsor through the summer months. Although I was Murray's owner and caregiver, providing him with all of his equine needs, Michele was Murray's kindred spirit. This role she played with every carrot that they shared, every grooming session they spent engaged in conversation and every ride on which they traversed the Adirondacks basking in each other's company.

At this point, Michele was not even aware that Murray had taken ill. I resisted the temptation to call her because she was scheduled to take pictures at a wedding the following day. Fearing the news would prevent her from focusing on her job, I had chosen to wait until after Saturday to tell her, when surely Murray would have recovered. As crickets and frogs serenaded Murray and me under that brilliant night sky, I fell asleep.

Two or three hours later, I woke up shivering under my lightweight blanket. Murray was still resting comfortably so I decided, reluctantly, to seek out my warm bed in the house. After a restless night in which I returned to the indoor arena to check on Murray twice, I got out of bed early and dressed quickly.

The air was warming up with no clouds in the sky. I found Murray dozing on his feet. His appetite had not returned, but he was not displaying any signs of colic either. After feeding the rest of the hungry herd, I called the vet clinic. It was only seven o'clock. Luckily a voice answered the phone, setting into motion the events of the coming day. Since it was a weekend they were going to send the veterinarian who was on call for emergencies. The clinic had just hired several vet school graduates who were not familiar to me yet.

All I could do was wait. Back to the house I trudged to make breakfast for Rod. Our surveillance system allowed me to watch Murray from the kitchen on the computer monitor. For the entire time, he appeared to be standing quietly. I puttered a bit around the house, trying to keep busy while waiting for the vet to arrive. Shortly after breakfast, Rod headed out to the barn to tend to a maintenance matter. He stopped to see how the big gelding was doing. In less than five minutes, he was back at the house looking concerned.

"He's not looking good. He is covered with sweat all over his body. You need to do something," he pleaded, unable to bear the sight of any animal in pain.

From the grainy image projected by the camera, the sweat was impossible to see. Murray was still standing quietly, but when I arrived back at his stall, his expression and overall condition alarmed me. Immediately, I moved him into the wash stall and began to sponge him down with *Vetrolin*, a cooling body wash or brace that I added to a bucket of warm water. Next, I covered Murray with a special fleece blanket called a cooler to prevent him from getting a chill. Finally, I walked him out into the driveway where the sun could help warm him up. By this time he wanted nothing more than to drop into the sand and roll. Fearful that his abdominal pain had returned, I prevented him from reclining and kept him moving.

At nine o'clock, my friend Jean drove up the driveway just as Murray planted his feet and refused to move any further. Now my mind wondered if he was perhaps *tying up,* a condition medically referred to as Azoturia. If this was so, the large muscles of his hindquarters were beginning to cook from a metabolic failure to eliminate lactic acid, a byproduct of anaerobic respiration. In addition, Murray was now sweating so profusely that a puddle of water was collecting in the sand from below his belly. Even his ears were wet.

My level of anxiety rose. I searched in my head to make sense of his symptoms. No, I am not a veterinarian, but I have witnessed many cases of colic, one or two cases of *tying up,* and an assortment of other conditions that torment horses. As a knowledgeable horsewoman, I believed I was prepared to identify just about any common ailment that afflicts the horse from time to time. This time I was stumped.

Just before ten o'clock, a large pickup truck appeared in the driveway. Professional help was finally here. The responsibility of trying to determine what was wrong with Murray was no longer mine. Before I had completely let go of my anxiety, a tiny woman with a long dark braid down her back, wearing a pair of large Wellington boots emerged from the truck. She was so petite that her coveralls had been hoisted up and tied in position by a string behind her neck. I was immediately reminded of how we kept our bathing suit straps up on our shoulders when we were shapeless children. I have to admit that I was skeptical about the abilities of such a young person. Was she capable of saving my horse?

Dr. Jennifer Nightingale had just graduated in May, 2011, from Cornell University's prestigious veterinary school. She would need years to develop her skills through hard knocks and experience. By the end of the day, however, she proved to me what a great vet she was on her way to becoming. Now my respect for her is immense. But that morning, there was a long day of problem solving ahead before I would have a chance to sum up my regard for Dr. Nightingale.

The vet's first impression of Murray's condition ruled out colic. She was certain that he was experiencing something more metabolic in nature. She mentioned *tying up* and wondered if he had in fact ingested something that was toxic. By this time, my friend Vicky had arrived to spend some quality time with her horse Tango. Vicky was a veterinary assistant for the same clinic that Dr. Nightingale represented. Fortunately, the office that Vicky worked for was fairly close by. Without hesitation, Vicky abandoned her plans with Tango and headed back to the vet clinic to run tests on vials of Murray's blood.

While we waited for the results, Dr. Nightingale began to treat Murray's symptoms. First she inserted a catheter into his jugular vein so that she could replace the precious fluids seeping out through his skin. My other friend and boarder, Irene, was also present by this time, offering her support for Murray. Suddenly, we all became aware of a loud thumping sound pounding from the inside of Murray. Dr. Nightingale issued a warning for us to stand clear for she worried that he might drop at any second. Apparently Murray's extreme dehydration caused a spasm of his diaphragm resulting in a serious case of equine hiccups or *thumps* as it is referred to in horses. In that instant it hit me that there was a very good chance that we might be fighting a losing battle for Murray. The race was on to try to save him.

While fluids dripped into Murray's body, he appeared briefly to recover. The thumping slowed and dissipated while the horse's skin began to cool and dry. He even stretched to urinate, a sign that the fluids were doing their job. However, the urine was dark, the volume limited.

For several hours, Dr. Nightingale worked on Murray. The blood tests indicated that his kidneys were in trouble, yet another finger pointing at toxic ingestion. What in the world could he have eaten?

Eventually, Murray appeared to be holding his own; the vet, having done all that she could for the time being, prepared to leave. Before she disappeared, she set me up with vials, syringes and liters of lifesaving chemicals along with several handwritten pages of instructions. Many of the medications were substances that I had never heard of before. They had to be carefully recorded for they were also controlled substances. My stomach felt sick looking at all these measures that might or might not save Murray. I believe at this time I knew that we were going to lose him in the end. But my heart wanted to keep going, because perhaps there was a chance. I wasn't yet able to accept that Murray had eaten something toxic on our carefully maintained horse property. It was all too much to accept...yet.

As Dr. Nightingale drove away from our farm, the feeling of helplessness returned with a vengeance. And shortly thereafter so did Murray's symptoms. By midafternoon the powerful sweats had returned and Murray was clearly uncomfortable, indicated by his bulging eyes and grinding teeth. Among Jean, Irene, Vicky and me, Murray was never alone. Luckily, when I called Dr. Nightingale to report the latest observations, she had not yet left the Adirondacks. Shortly, she was on her way back to Moose River Farm.

One of the first observations about Dr. Nightingale that I made was her willingness to confer with colleagues by phone when she had questions about how to treat Murray. This humility impressed me. It showed that she lacked ego, wanted the best outcome for *my* horse, and recognized her limited time in the field. It ultimately made me feel that Murray was under the best care, with many professionals putting their heads together to see to it.

Upon Dr. Nightingale's return, there was only one treatment left to try: the diuretic *Lasix*. It was clear that Murray's extreme discomfort was stemming from an inability to urinate. As hard as he strained, pushed and willed himself to pee, he could not. What little did squeeze through was thick and brown, clearly a bad sign. With one more valid treatment possible and an agreement that if this didn't work, the kindest thing to do would be to put him down, the vet injected yet another chemical into Murray's body. In the end, it wasn't meant to be. After we waited and hoped for twenty minutes, Dr. Nightingale headed out to her truck to prepare the one injection that would relieve Murray's pain forever.

I led the big gelding out slowly along the same path that only two other horses, Windy and Spy, so far had trekked to their final resting places. My body, now numb, resisted feeling the enormity of the decision to end an animal's life. Dr. Nightingale and Vicky followed. At the spot where Rod chose to dig the hole to receive Murray's body, we stopped. I kissed the bridge of his nose and hugged his thick neck. Tears burned in my tired eyes.

After asking if I was ready, the vet acted swiftly. Acknowledging the nod of my head, she plunged the first syringe full of sodium pentobarbital or *blue juice* into Murray's catheter. Murray's large body immediately dropped to the ground, so quickly that it almost rolled completely over from the force.

Through my tears, I looked up at the vet and said, "Wow, you're good!"

Through her own tears, she half smiled in reply.

Dr. Nightingale then quickly plunged another syringe full of the heart stopping drug through the catheter to make absolutely certain that her mission had been accomplished. Moments later her stethoscope confirmed that Murray was gone. She left me with my prone horse to pack up her truck for the long road home. Only then was I aware of Vicky making her way back to me. She had gone to the barn to get scissors so that I could cut a lock of my own hair and braid it into Murray's mane, a piece of me to be with him forever in the ground. My short hair made the task difficult but I managed. Vicky had also returned with several hairs that she had plucked from Michele's riding helmet. Her thoughtfulness was most touching. We tucked the hairs inside Murray's ear as a token of Michele's love and devotion to him.

It was late afternoon when the drama of the past twenty-four hours came to an end. All that was left to do was tend to the other horses still alive and well on the farm and in need of our undivided attention. Back at the barn, I was feeling overwhelmingly sad. Vicky sent me to walk the dogs and goats while she tended to the horses. I took her up on the offer, immediately collected my charges and headed into the woods.

For the entire walk, my mind was a blur as the events of the previous hours replayed over and over. What could I have done differently? Should I have called the vet sooner? Should I have not left Murray out on the lawn to graze yesterday? This was the first horse that I had been responsible for putting down because of an acute condition that could not be treated. The feeling was so unfamiliar to me. Windy and Spy had required planning and Promise had taken care of the matter herself when an accidental fall in the paddock broke her neck and claimed her life. But Murray had been ridden in a lesson in perfect health only thirty-six hours prior to his demise. What had gone wrong?

As the dogs, goats and I turned for home, a new thought popped into my mind. I had two tickets for that evening to attend a concert by melancholy 70's artist Janis Ian. She was giving an intimate performance at Great Camp Sagamore in Raquette Lake. Although Vicky and I had planned to attend, we had decided not to go when the events of the day became so dire. There was still time for us to change our minds. By the time I returned to the barn, I was prepared to talk Vicky into going to the concert.

"Let's go anyway. What's done is done and there is no reason that we shouldn't go," I reasoned.

Vicky hesitated. The day had been long for her too, but in the end she saw my point. We weren't leaving the patient to attend the concert. We were escaping the sad scene. Perhaps we might find comfort in Ian's somber lyrics from songs such as *At Seventeen, In the Winter* and *Tea and Sympathy.* We were right! Our seats were less than twenty feet from Janis Ian's acoustic stage setting. Her soothing vocals and sad verses allowed me to wallow in heartache. For the first time that day, I did not fight the sadness; instead I let it penetrate deep into my core.

For two hours, Janis Ian sang to us about the trials and tribulations of her musical career. From such a diminutive and unassuming person, her vocals still packed a soulful punch. She ended the concert early in order to get ahead of Hurricane Irene, which was menacingly stalking the east coast.

Thoroughly exhausted, I arrived home from the concert, cared for the horses and poured myself into bed. The events of last night, the morning and the afternoon seemed as if they had taken place months ago. I fell asleep quickly, but woke up frequently as the reality of losing Murray began to take hold.

The next day dawned dreary with rain and wind, a perfect setting for grief. My first task, after caring for the horses, was to call Michele.

"Hi," she said in a low voice, recognizing my number from caller I.D.

For a split second, I thought perhaps she already knew. "What do you know?" I asked hastily.

"I don't know anything. Why, what don't I know?"

"I am so sorry to have to tell you this, but we put Murray down yesterday afternoon," I sobbed into the phone.

Silence.

I blurted out the whole story as quickly as I could so that her emotions could catch up with mine. I'm sure my words drilled a hole through Michele's heart. But typical of Michele, she tried to comfort me through her tears while assuring me that she had no doubt Murray was in a better place.

For most of the day, I remained in the house, having tended only to the necessary care of my animals in the barn. They spent the day in clean stalls, munching hay while waiting for gale force winds and driving rain to subside. In the kitchen I worked at the computer while Rod pickled an overabundance of cucumbers from the garden.

Meanwhile, Vicky, having started out for the barn from her house in Otter Lake, was forced by her emotions and gusts of wind to turn around and go home.

Murray's loss hit the rest of our barn family hard. A young girl named Haley had been the last one to ride him on the morning of the day he became ill. She was concerned that she had been the cause of his illness. I wanted her to know how grateful I was that she was the last one to ride him so that he had left us on a high note, as the fabulous teacher we knew him to be. Another child named Alex was going to have to forge a relationship with a new mount for her lessons. Of course Michele had lost her best friend, making us all wonder who could ever fill that void.

And me? I couldn't wait to get back to school, away from the barn air that was thick with sadness. Instead, I needed the view from the windows in my classroom, where I could look out and put this event into perspective before allowing myself to move on. Unlike the closure that I felt for Windy and Spy, Murray's death left me dealing with guilt. He had been the *Giving Tree* in Shel Silverstein's beautiful children's story with its blunt message about selflessness and selfishness. I felt that I had somehow failed the big horse. It was not surprising that Murray's obituary on *Facebook* collected over 30 comments. They provided great comfort by reminding me just how many lives the handsome bay gelding had touched.

When Meg and her girls arrived, on Labor Day weekend they never mentioned the mare Meg had been praising, to me. Out of respect for Murray's death, Meg left the idea of a new horse completely out of our conversation. As September and the new school year provided a much needed distraction from Murray's death, however, I began to contemplate acquiring the mare to fill the vacant stall.

By Columbus Day weekend, Meg and the girls were on their way back to the Adirondacks for some much needed therapy with the horses at the barn. This time when I initiated the conversation, Meg couldn't talk fast enough. Whatever she said changed everything for a thoroughbred mare named Makia.

A lengthy phone discussion between Deb (the mare's owner) and me ensued shortly after Meg's visit. In that chat, Deb was reassured that I was a knowledgeable horsewoman whose animals were an important part of her life. I, in turn, was able to garner that Deb cared deeply about Makia, (Hawaiian for "where attention goes, energy flows"), but together they were not cohesive riding partners. She wanted the horse to have a good home where a new owner might provide the attention that could unlock Makia's potential and allow her exuberant energy to be useful in a riding lesson program.

On the last Saturday of October, after a fairly comfortable and dry fall, the north winds drove icy temperatures from Canada into the Adirondacks. Bundled in fleece and a wool cap, I spent the day waiting for the newest member of our herd to arrive. Late in the afternoon, the shiny silver horse van from the well-respected fleet of *Judge Manning's* transportation company pulled up in front of the barn. Makia was here at last!

Over the long winter, in which I made Makia's training and conditioning my priority among the horses, I began to wonder if she could ever make a good lesson horse. Although she was gentle by nature, the mare's initial reaction to being ridden was to pull against the rider with the strength of a freight train. She ground her teeth and stewed in frustration while bracing against the reins. The rider had no choice but to pull back and hold the mare's head up. No wonder Deb didn't enjoy riding her, especially if it was not possible to devote daily training sessions to address Makia's issues. At this point, I didn't want to give up on my *gift* horse, but I began to wonder if anybody else would ever be able to ride her. She left me exhausted. Was I headed in the right direction with her training?

The other piece of the equation required that Makia be given ample opportunity to spend her racehorse energy. Therefore, she was *chased* before each ride. That means she was turned out with another horse, usually a gelding, and encouraged to run freely at top speed around the ring. If she felt the need to buck, roll or gallop, she was allowed to do so. When her rib cage heaved and her nostrils flared with every breath, I knew that she had spent most of the energy that distracted her under saddle.

Once tacked up and mounted, Makia was able to focus on schooling sessions because of the incredible work ethic she had inherited in her thoroughbred genes. It didn't take me long to realize how serious Makia was about the world around her. This is a mare characteristic that I had not experienced since I owned Promise. Mares are wired to be moms, and mothering is a survival skill. Makia had one foal in her lifetime and that exposure had flipped the *on* switch of her maternal instincts. Mares apply these behaviors to all aspects of their existence; training was no exception.

Because Makia was in need of conditioning, she was not able to work for extended sessions. I constantly had to monitor her attention span. It took me a long time to comprehend the signals and decide which ones I should heed and which ones I needed to challenge. For a break in the monotony of training, I rode her through the woods on the mile of snow covered trail that encircles the farm. The groomed footing and crisp air worked wonders on her attitude. She pushed her ears forward and snorted at the glistening snow, both expressions of a horse in high spirits.

Many evenings, I was able to work Makia in the outdoor ring. She always performed at her best under the floodlights, accompanied by music. These rides left me smiling all evening long, hardly able to wait until the next day when, conditions permitting, we might be able to work outside again. The indoor ring made Makia feel claustrophobic, causing her to careen about in the smaller space. Despite this problem, I was beginning to sense that she was making real progress with her balance, patience and stamina. After dismounting, I always threw my arms around her neck and hugged her tight.

"You are such a good girl," I beamed. A carrot or an apple provided more tangible praise. Riding a mare with a gentle disposition and desire to take care of her human is a delightful experience. I felt serendipitously blessed that she had been given to me.

By February, Makia was able to teach a few riding lessons; two of her frequent riders became Meg's girls, Danielle and Emily. They were able to use their training skills to prevent the mare from pulling them out of the saddle. This was progress. It was such a pleasure to witness how far Makia had come in her training and conditioning since her arrival last fall.

Around the first of May, Michele was on her way back to the Adirondacks after waiting out the winter months in Florida. She was eager to ride, but resigned to the fact that this summer she would not come to the barn to spend time with Murray. Instead, she would simply ride any horse that was available. Still stuck thinking inside the box, I pictured her enjoying leisurely rides with Joshua, a hefty paint gelding, or Spirit, a sinewy palomino American saddlebred gelding or Lowtchee, my plucky Friesian mare or Welby, my niece, Amy's aged ex-racehorse. What I didn't picture was Michele making that special connection with any one of them. She had loved them for years, but she wasn't bonded specifically to one of them.

Michele wasn't home twenty-four hours before she was on her way to the barn. It was good to have her back after a six month absence, and she was eager to spend time with horses...any horses. She didn't care who I assigned her to ride that day, but first I had to introduce her to the new addition, Makia. Michele was instantly taken by Makia's gentle, social nature.

"Can I ride her?" she asked casually.

"Of course," I replied, unable to think of a single reason why Michele couldn't handle Makia.

Michele and Makia hit it off from the first ride. Theirs is a different relationship from the one Michele shared with Murray. Where Murray was Michele's baby, Makia is Michele's peer, a sister of sorts who, like Michele, had one child and views the world from a mother's watchful perspective. I am humbled by my doubts that Michele could ever find a horse with whom to form a special bond after the loss of Murray. A wise horsey friend once commented, "We never stop loving them and somehow our heart can keep growing as the next horse is loved just as much, although she will never replace the one before."

The loss of Murray and the arrival of Makia mark a significant shift in my understanding about love and loss. Murray's death forced me to accept that, although I try to control every factor of the environment where I tend to animals, there may be situations that are simply out of my control. If I believe that these sorrowful episodes define my skills, than I am missing the point. Instead, I now know that the privilege of caring for all these horses, dogs, goats and all of my other animals is of itself the reward. They will not be with me forever. Whether or not they stay a few years or live into old age I owe them the best of my skills on a daily basis. Murray's death was out of my control but it opened an opportunity for Makia to find her way to Moose River Farm where she has been able to succeed as a rideable horse, companion and teacher.

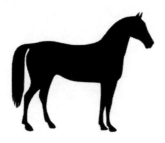

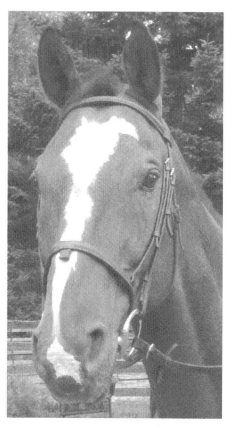

Murray was a handsome gelding of unknown Warmblood breeding. He was kind, bold and all other attributes of a safe horse. photo by M. deCamp

Makia became Michele's new partner after Murray's untimely death.

Murray, Michele, Joshua and I rode in the Old Forge Memorial Day Parade; 2007. Lesson horse Murray. Makia's previous owner delivered her to MRF; 2010. Makia became a favorite of many MRF riders. photo by M. deCamp

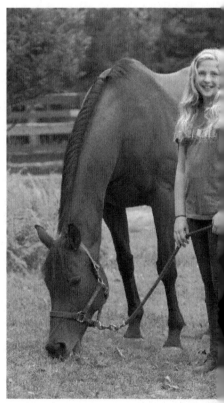

Goat Saga

By early spring one year, we had lost four animals at Moose River Farm. Beginning with our nine year old goat Lilly, in October, after a uterine/vaginal tumor made it necessary to euthanize her, the trend continued with Rosemary the iguana in December and Huxley the dachshund in mid-January. At the end of March our thirty-one year old gelding Sandi was put down as well. We had also survived the most brutal winter that I can ever remember in thirty years of living in the Adirondacks.

Just about every night that February, the temperature dropped into double digits below zero. The horses spent weeks bundled up in blankets, more for protection against biting wind than bulk against the cold. Our chickens live in a heated coop that rarely drops below ten degrees above zero, relieving any worry about fowl freezing to death. Liam, our enormous Boer goat, sprouted a layer of thick cashmere that rivaled the highest quality down parka, suitable for climbing Mt. Everest. I did not worry about him at all; he could take the cold, perhaps even luxuriated in it. But at age thirteen, Lacey, our Nubian cross doe, was not as robust. Compared to the winters of her youth, she was no longer producing a significant quality or quantity of cashmere. Although she was in relatively good health, her top coat was long and sparse. In the extreme cold, she was a source of considerable worry. The only additional defense I could provide for her was a layering system of fitted blankets. One blanket when the temperature remained above ten degrees, two blankets when the temperature dipped below zero, and three blankets when the temperature dropped below negative fifteen.

Many a night, Lacey wore the third layer, but even that was not enough to insulate my concern for her wellbeing. At night I tossed and turned, agonizing about Lacey as the trees crackled and groaned in the plummeting temperature. I wondered how low it had to drop before Lacey's body suffered the consequences of extended chills. How much could she endure? Yet every morning when I stuck my head over her stall door, anticipating the worst, she was there gazing up at me, her head extending out from puffy layers of thermal protection. Despite the frost that clung to her muzzle, she always bleated a strong greeting. Then she sucked down her grain and filled up on hay.

I left her stall door open all day so she could choose where she wanted to be. Later in the morning, Lacey was usually standing in front of the barn, particularly after the coldest nights, soaking up sunshine that flooded the driveway. Her half-closed eyes and permanent smiley expression seemed to suggest that she held no grudge against Mother Nature. I did not share her sentiment. Every morning, however, I was grateful that Lacey had survived.

In March, Lacey went lame as a result of a condition that causes symptoms in goats that are similar to rheumatoid arthritis in people. Caprine Arthritic Encephalitis or CAE is a viral infection that causes crippling lameness in adult goats who carry the virus. At nine years old, Lacey began to develop bony enlargements on the carpal joints in her forelegs that caused her to become bow legged. Despite the disfigurements, she didn't really begin to show stiffness until a year or two later. Eventually, pain prevented her from joining us on our daily walks through the woods. Occasionally, she would go along but paid dearly for it with intense stiffness over the next several days. Through it all, her demeanor never wavered from anything other than her pleasant, loving self.

After the bitter cold subsided, I discussed medicating Lacey for pain with our veterinarian, Dr. Jennifer Nightingale. She agreed that medications were available that would prolong a quality life for our elderly goat. Within a week of administering Lacey's new medication, we began to witness significant improvement. She ambled about the barn with little stiffness and began to venture out on walks with us. It was so uplifting to watch the return of such enthusiasm in our old girl. But after two weeks, her condition slid into a swift decline.

At first, Lacey simply stopped eating. Nothing could tempt her appetite; not her favorite puff peppermints, not her coveted horse treats, not even her distinctive beloved banana peels could motivate her to eat. Conferring with Dr. Jen on the phone, we decided that the medication had probably soured, maybe even ulcerated, her delicate ruminant digestive system.

Ruminants are a category of cloven hoofed animals that include cattle, sheep, llamas, deer, moose and kangaroos, to name a few. The rumen is a large vat-like organ that uses bacteria to break down leafy vegetation and stalky browse that goats can eat. This initial phase of digestion is followed by a period of rumination and eructation. During this time, the animal rests quietly and regurgitates the contents of the rumen for re-chewing. Rumen bacteria also produce a large quantity of gas that requires release in the process of burping. Once the re-chewed food has been reduced to smaller pieces, thus increasing the overall surface area, it is swallowed and enters the abomasum or true stomach of the goat. Just like the human stomach, the abomasum secretes acids that further reduce the cud or chyme and prepare it for absorption in the intestines. It is no wonder that so much is understood about ruminant digestion since cattle sheep and goats have been the focus of agriculture for centuries. Since the rumen relies on fermentation to break down cellulose in plant material, proper *pH* is of the utmost importance. It doesn't take much to offset the chemical balance within. So we took Lacey off her medication.

Lacey refused to eat for four days before I packed her in the car and took her to visit Dr. Nightingale. Extensive blood work revealed that she was indeed in distress. Goats are stoic creatures who rarely display suffering. Through the whole ordeal, Lacey remained her pleasant self, sniffing about my pockets and hands, hoping that I would produce something that piqued her appetite. Nothing did.

After all the tests were run, Dr. Jen sutured a catheter into Lacey's jugular vein and pumped hydrating solution into the goat's body. She sent me home with bags of solution and four or five medications that had to be administered at specific times of the day. I had to be careful not to give adversarial medications at the same time. I posted a chart on the tackroom counter to keep track of the process.

For the next five days, my life revolved around Lacey's medication and IV schedule. My school day went along uninterrupted, but early mornings and late into the evening she was my priority. My friend Irene's veterinary technician skills served Lacey well during the day when I was at school. Our collaboration brought Lacey around. Two weeks after her visit to the vet, Lacey began to eat on her own. Elation filled the barn now that the elderly goat appeared to push her health issues and the bitter cold winter behind her.

In the euphoria of Lacey's miraculous recovery, I forgot that no creature lives forever. Lacey had a fairly comfortable summer. We decided not to medicate her for the arthritic pain. Another bout of ulcers would surely mark the end of her. Instead, we allowed her to decide what was good for her. Every day she hobbled around the barn searching for tidbits of grain guaranteed by horses who dropped food from their mouths or flung grain out of their feed bins. Occasionally, Lacey could be encouraged to accompany us on our daily walk with the dogs. It was difficult not to worry about next winter. Would it be kind to us after three harsh winters in a row? Could Lacey survive another difficult winter? As luck would have it, *El Nino* kept the Pacific Ocean in check so that glorious fall weather extended right through Christmas. Sunny skies and balmy temperatures dominated in the early weeks following the winter solstice. Lake effect snow and plummeting conditions did not attack until well into January. Lacey's health thrived during the unseasonal bonus. But, just as I began to think she would live longer, Lacey deteriorated under an acute attack of CAE.

At first she became severely lame. However, she willed herself to get up and to hobble about the barn. Her pain appeared to ease after she had loosened up. Lacey sought the sunny areas of the barn and lay there languishing in the solar warmth for hours on end. Eventually, she refused to get up at all. I served her grain while she lay upright on her breast bone and kept hay close at all times. We syringed water into her mouth frequently during the day. In the meantime, I conferred with Dr. Jen who immediately placed Lacey back on the medication that had offended her rumen ten months earlier. This time the vet reduced the dose and added a protocol of antacids and acid reducers along with the pain killer. Then we watched and waited for another miracle.

Dr. Jen and I agreed that the medication had to make a profound improvement over the long President's weekend. Otherwise, we also agreed, Lacey had to be euthanized. With fingers crossed, I waited for improvement to postpone the inevitable. Briefly it appeared that she might be getting better. Her improvement was short lived.

Unfortunately, Mother Nature turned the February holiday weekend into a nightmare of record breaking cold for three consecutive days. At night an average temperature of negative thirty degrees held firm, rising only to a negative seventeen degrees as the daily high. For three days, we kept Lacey snug inside the lean-to that Rod had constructed to provide a cozy place away from open barn doors. We tucked two heavy wool horse blankets around Lacey, already snug in her layers.

By Monday morning, it was evident that Lacey wasn't getting better. I had no choice but to surrender the fight. I called Dr. Jen to make final arrangements. Later in the afternoon, friends Irene and

Vicky accompanied me to the vet's office. I asked Vicky to drive so I could sit in the backseat with my goat for the forty minute drive to Boonville. In our final hour together, Lacey disclosed no signs of pain. Her head rested in my arms as I silently communicated my feelings for her. The trip reminded me of the car ride made thirteen years earlier when Rod and I drove to Saratoga Springs to purchase Lacey as a young doe. She was brought home to keep our ancient goat, Hannah, company in her final days. We plucked Lacey away from her herd, shoved her in our car and headed back to the Adirondacks. Although she had been removed from all that she knew, she seemed pleased to make my acquaintance in the backseat. I held her then as I did now, having kept the promise of a long happy life as a member of our family. On this trip she lay content in my arms, perhaps hopeful that I would end her suffering. I did just that. I asked the vet to take her pain away...and made it my own.

After Rod buried Lacey on that blustery bitter cold February day, our goat herd dwindled to one. Liam, now age eleven, had been in relatively good health until he began to experience bouts of frothy bloat. During an episode, he regurgitated large volumes of white or green foamy liquid while he was *ruminating* or chewing his cud. Alarmed by the symptoms, I feared that he had eaten something poisonous growing on our property. A call to our vet on a Sunday afternoon put me at ease. She recommended that I squirt a few syringes full of cooking oil into his mouth. The oil decreased the bubbly reaction and put him right within an hour. I didn't give much thought to the episode for several weeks until it happened again. Why it was happening didn't seem to be as important as my ability to dilute the bubbles. After another treatment of cooking oil, Liam was back to normal. Well, almost normal.

In addition to the bloat, I noticed an enlargement at the base of his neck, just above his chest. A sloshy accumulation of some unknown liquid increased and decreased over time, depending on how much hay and grass he had eaten. Liam appeared unimpressed by the mass and continued to go about his day performing his bodily functions with ease. At this point I was more worried about his morale as our only remaining goat. Liam appeared to be looking for Lacey or for another goat with whom to associate himself as a herd member.

The instinct to establish and belong to a herd is necessary in all ungulates or hoofed species. In a group, these prey animals are more capable of avoiding attacks from predators. Herd membership reduces stress, allowing them to feel less vulnerable than they would existing as a singleton. *Safety in numbers* is a creed shared by goats.

Ironically, for his whole life Liam had either ignored Lacey or had searched for ways to torment her. For the last three years, I had kept the two goats separated at night for fear he might hurt her with his brutish head butting attacks. When not confined to stalls, the goats were able to roam freely around the barn and lawn. However, Lacey, always leery of Liam kept an eye out at all times. Now without her, he seemed lost. If I was working in the barn, he hovered close by. Sometimes through a window, I could see him standing in the middle of the driveway, gazing back as if willing me to come out to keep him company. It was rather sad to think of him all alone. Once the horses had been turned outside for the day, Liam was the only living creature in the barn.

We considered adding more goats to our menagerie but not until the weather was more hospitable, perhaps late spring. Until that time I had to keep Liam's spirits up by spending quality time with him in the barn. For the next several months, I made an attempt every day to be with him, touch him and assure him that he was not alone. During this time, he began to accompany us on our daily dog walks again, something he had stopped doing when Lacey's advanced arthritis prevented her from coming along. Despite his bullying behavior, she had been the other member of his herd; his loyalty to that bond was stronger than our beckoning gestures and proffers of treats.

Spring evolved at a snail's pace. March through May teased with hints of spring, a sunny day here, a sprig of vegetation there. Mostly, however, conditions remained damp and cold, preventing the explosion of delicate green so anticipated after an Adirondack winter. Liam's bouts of frothy bloat increased. It was difficult to identify a trigger. Was it something specific he was eating? Was it related to the mass that accumulated at the base of his neck? Was it a symptom of something more serious going on deep within, a tumor, an infection or an anatomical malfunction in his body?

Dr. Jen examined him several times. Her ultrasound machine produced inconclusive images. Without the sophisticated, expensive imaging equipment available at Cornell University Hospital for Animals, it was impossible to diagnose Liam's condition. I was not willing to subject Liam to a long drive and an expensive battery of tests. Dr. Jen and I agreed that even with a diagnosis, we probably could not heal this aging goat.

Advancements in veterinary medicine are simply amazing. Chemotherapy adds months of life to ailing canines, and protocols for colic surgery in horses are increasing the odds of full recovery. But research and development of such procedures comes at a huge expense that is passed along to owners who often pay more than they can afford because they can't bear the thought of losing their beloved pets. I couldn't take care of all of these animals if I didn't adopt a practical and realistic approach to their care. Making a decision to let an animal die does not mean I am callous. While they are alive, healthy and comfortable, I commit myself fully to my animals. When it is time to let them go, I avoid sentimentality in favor of the compassionate imperative to help them to an easy death. I am thankful that Dr. Nightingale professionally agrees with my decisions.

My acceptance of Liam's inevitable demise pushed me to a nearby dairy goat farm that produces artisan goat cheese from the one hundred fifty head that they raise. After searching all spring for suitable baby goats, I returned home with twin doelings of Nubian and Boer lineage.* They were only two days old.

I had enlisted friends, Vicky and Michele, to help pick out my next generation of goats. Michele volunteered to drive my car so that I could sit in the backseat and hold my new acquisitions on the way home. Vicky sat in the back with me to hold the other tiny goat. Frequently, we switched the babies back and forth. By the time we arrived home, we had christened them Audrey and Hazel.

Audrey had a tan base coat saddled with patches of black. Tan markings randomly crisscrossed her black face, an atypical pattern for goats. Hazel's coat was the opposite. It fluctuated between light and dark caramel colored patches distributed evenly from her head to her hooves. Her exquisite brown and tan striped facial markings assured that she would be a caprine beauty.

Both doelings possessed amber eyes that promised mischief and all the fun that was about to begin in our lives. Their tiny nursing muzzles reminded me that four times every day for the next twelve weeks, I would be responsible for bottle feeding them. Nothing measures up to the advantages of bottle feeding goats on formula for ten weeks. A tight parent-child bond forms between human and kid. The goats see their people as members of the herd and crave human companionship constantly.

Bottle feeding baby goats is a pleasure I love to share, especially with children. Every bottle that I prepare for babies delivers the building blocks for our future together. There is no possibility of forgetting to feed them. I can't put it off until tomorrow or only feed them at my convenience. The clock dictates when the babies get fed. Sticking to a schedule means the goats won't be stressed. By keeping the temperature and the proportions of the formula consistent, I eliminate factors that could harm my babies. I had forgotten how stressful it is when one baby doesn't finish a whole bottle or the other bolts down the liquid so quickly it causes her to cough. It is a serious game, this raising of baby goats.

Once we arrived home, I was eager to introduce the doelings to Rod. Unlike many of our animal acquisitions, Rod approved of adding these goats! He smiled at the tiny ones standing in our driveway. Their high pitched bleats sent me scurrying to the kitchen to prepare formula for our first bottle feeding. Rod kept an eye on the babies while I carefully measured and mixed.

Maa, maa meaaaa!" they screamed making it clear that they were long overdue for a feeding.

Vicky and I each secured a kid under an arm and inserted the nipples of the bottles into their infant mouths. Michele continued documenting this special day through the lens of her camera. Baby goats had arrived; and from this moment forward, they would be the focal point of life on the farm for the rest of the summer. The other animals' routines were not interrupted. Their needs were never compromised, but the extra attention they usually received took a backseat to the constant demands of the nursling goats until they were finally weaned.

The next day was predicted to be twenty-five degrees and snowy, a far cry from what is expected in mid-May. Rod and I agreed that the doelings should be kept in our laundry room for a few days until mild temperatures returned. We placed a large plastic tote on the tile floor and filled it with clean sweet hay. That first night I slept without worry, knowing that the babies were snug in our home as Mother Nature tumbled springtime progress back into winter conditions. The next day Audrey and Hazel shivered under polar fleece dog coats in which I wrapped them to go outside. They tended to business quickly and bleated at me to take them back inside, out of the blowing snow that dusted the landscape. We kept our house warm with blazing logs in our fireplace, the heat having been turned off for the season. Sitting on the floor by the hearth, I tucked each kid under an elbow and held them close to me while they drained their bottles. To be responsible for the upbringing of infants is a humbling experience. These two tiny life forms depended on me to prepare and deliver nourishment in a timely manner so that they could thrive and grow. I loved the dependency and was determined to make all the right decisions that would deliver them safely to adulthood.

The next day was Monday, a school day, and luckily I did not have to leave the babies at home. In preparation for their arrival, I had made arrangements with my school administrators to bring the kids to school every day during that first week.

"John, do you have a moment?" I asked our young principal, getting right to the point. "I am about to acquire two baby goats for my farm. They will only be a few days old and will need to be fed several times a day for a while. I suppose a maternity leave is out of the question."

"Yes, I think that is out of the question," he chuckled.

"I thought so, but not to worry, I have a great idea!"

I proceeded to tell him about the plan I had hatched with my elementary school colleagues. Each teacher had agreed to have the baby goats spend at least one day in her classroom during that first week. The babies would be integrated into lessons that allowed the students to handle, feed, and care for them. The teachers were excited to offer the children this opportunity. Not only was our principal in favor of this idea, but our superintendent became excited about it as well.

The next morning I woke up earlier than usual. The outdoor temperature was still in the twenties, but the forecast was for sun by midday. After feeding the dogs and the pig and making Rod's and my lunches, I prepared formula for the doelings. When I entered the laundry room, they stirred in their tote. I wrapped them in the dog coats and escorted them to the backyard. Snow still clung to the tender grass and the air was saturated with a damp chill. They peed and pooped quickly in anticipation of returning to the warm house. Back inside, I sat on the floor with my back against the door that shielded us from the cruel cold. The warmth of the babies' bodies on each side of my ribs penetrated my sweatshirt as if I was wearing a goat vest. The pleasure of sitting with nothing to do but hold the bottles that nourished my babies was emotionally satisfying. I leaned back and closed my eyes in gratitude for this privilege. I embraced peace.

The clock ticked away the minutes, but I sat motionless, tuned into the slurping sounds on either side of me. "Swerzzz, swerzzz, swerzzz." They sucked so vigorously the formula rushed with every draw.

After they finished their bottles, we returned to the backyard for a few more minutes to frolic and bounce off their pent up energy. Then I secured them in the tote so that I could go out to the barn and perform chores. An hour later the little goats and I were on our way to school.

I will always remember that magical week. The babies charmed the entire school community. Young students took great pride in caring for their every need, especially feeding them with a bottle. Teacher cell phones recorded adorable moments of child/goat interactions. Many images wound up on the cover of our local newspaper, *The Weekly Adirondack.* As educators, we were witnessing the effect that the babies had on students, particularly those who struggle to focus. With arms wrapped around a sleeping doeling, one young person with *ADD* (attention deficit disorder) was not only able to track a conversation with the teacher, but was also able to process information and reply in complex sentences that exercised vocabulary and comprehension. It was as if the tiny goat sleeping in the child's arms quieted the chatter in the child's head, preventing the cacophony of distractions from competing with the ability to pay attention. There is promising research in the field of animal therapy that supports the theory that animals can have a positive effect on learning.

Empathy often surfaced during goat week at school. Children shared the goats, recognizing those who waited patiently for their turn to hold or feed the babies. Others, particularly middle school and high school students, were surprised by the emotions that the babies evoked. A senior girl holding tiny Hazel shared a revelation.

"Wow, I feel like I am going to cry,"

"Imagine how you will feel when it is your own child," I replied. We both giggled.

By the end of *goat week*, Audrey and Hazel were seven days old and thriving. The constant attention from the staff and students ensured that they bonded with people. They had been held, fed and played with constantly. In return they had delighted all who came in contact with them. The timing worked out perfectly because the baby goats were becoming more active. In the second week of their lives, they were not content to sit in laps for long stretches of time. They had discovered their dancing legs and were eager to practice their moves.

One of the pleasures of goat ownership is watching kids perform their jaunty goatie dance. They are like creatures possessed by joy. Although necessary for them to strengthen their agility skills, their routines are also a comical source of entertainment. Spastic twists, twirls, leaps and hops enable them to jump up high. Their hooves can cling to the narrowest surfaces. Audrey and Hazel viewed their world as one big obstacle course to be ascended and conquered. Initially, the mounting block in our driveway was their favorite. At first glance, this mandatory piece of equestrian equipment appears to be nothing more than three steps up to nowhere. However, when a horse is led to it, the mounting block provides proper elevation for a rider to mount comfortably. But for infant goats, the top of the mounting block is the ultimate mountain. The babies practiced leaping to the ground from the summit. Eventually, they graduated to the two story hay pile neatly stacked in our indoor arena. I had to hold my breath once they discovered the joy of flying through the air from eight bales high only to turn around and bounce up to the top of the hay for a repeat. My affection for these two tiny sprites swelled into parental pride. Every minute spent with them was pure joy.

Each week they grew, their legs sprouting like bamboo shoots. Bottle feeding was so popular among friends that I could have sold tickets four times a day. It was not uncommon to find adults and children sitting on my cushioned patio furniture with one arm wrapped around a goat and the other holding tight to a bottle of formula. I never minded sharing the duty but was thankful that the task was all mine early in the morning and late in the evening. It was the best way to begin and end my days.

For four weeks I existed in goatie bliss. The babies were the focal point of my farm life. Although provided with essential daily needs, my other animals did not receive the extra attention they were used to on account of the baby goats. I promised them the situation was temporary and that in time life would return to normal. The one exception was Liam.

The euphoria of caring for baby goats was frequently challenged with the knowledge that Liam was beginning to fade. I so wanted him to know the goatlings, hopeful that their presence would lift his mood. In a way it did. I began to notice that he appeared wherever the babies were playing. He seemed to understand that they were his kind and that he belonged to their herd. His deterioration and age kept him from engaging in their antics, but he clearly enjoyed their company. I made a point to engage with him often by brushing him, sitting with him and wrapping my arms around him for extended stretches of time. In return he stood quietly, allowing me to indulge myself in his presence. He was the last from our second generation of goats. Despite the exuberant energy generated by my baby girls in the background, I allowed myself to feel profoundly sad in these moments of reflection.

Audrey and Hazel turned one month old just two weeks before the end of the school year. With summer vacation on the horizon, I was ecstatic at the prospect of spending long lazy summer days with my little girls. Therefore, nothing could have prepared me for the devastating loss that swiftly and painfully erased that vision.

The mild winter did not transform into early spring. In fact spring was continually postponed by long bouts of bone chilling dampness. May was rainy, even snowy, with frosty nights that dipped into the teens. During the day there was hope from time to time with sunny moments that penetrated the bleakness, but they never established themselves as a trend. At ten days old, the baby goats were acclimated enough to the swing in temperatures to take up residency day and night in the barn. They snuggled together in a nest of hay protected from wind and blowing snow inside a vacant horse stall. Across the aisle, Liam rested in the designated goat stall, also protected from the elements.

On one particularly numbing damp day, Hazel began to exhibit symptoms of abdominal discomfort and chill. Late on a Sunday afternoon, she wanted nothing more than to curl up in a round rubber feed tub and be left alone. At first I was only mildly concerned, having convinced myself that she was just cold and crampy. An hour later when I offered her formula, she flat out refused to suckle. Meanwhile, Audrey attacked her bottle with gusto. On closer inspection, I noticed that the left side of Hazel's abdomen, the rumen side, was slightly enlarged. The skin was tight like a balloon. Although the possibility of bloat, a deadly condition in young ruminants, surfaced in the recesses of my brain, I wasn't too terribly concerned. Hazel acted fairly normal except for the fact that she would not eat.

I remembered a similar event when Lilly as a baby displayed similar symptoms. By the next morning Lilly's gas had dissipated and she was back to her normal formula guzzling self. Surely Hazel needed nothing more than a good night's rest to dissipate the gas. For the entire evening, however, I felt uneasy. After Rod and I ate dinner, he suggested that I bring the babies into the house for the night where we could keep a watchful eye on them. Within minutes of his suggestion, I had the tote in the laundry room filled with fresh hay, just as it was when they first arrived four weeks ago. The little goats spent the evening snuggled together, Hazel taking comfort from the warmth of her sister.

I remained with them for hours, escorting them frequently to the backyard where Hazel proved to me that she could still pass manure and urine without straining. I wanted to believe that these were positive signs of a temporary condition. I administered Pepto Bismol to help neutralize the gas. By midnight Hazel's enlarged abdomen appeared to be shrinking. She seemed more comfortable. After completing chores in the barn, I secured the girls in their tote and went to bed.

At three o'clock in the morning, I was startled awake by loud baby goat bleats. With my heart racing, I couldn't hit the light switch fast enough. Both girls had leapt out of the tote and were standing on the tile floor blinking at me in the bright light. I held my breath and searched Hazel for signs of her gastric distress. Her belly was still distended, but her eyes sparkled with alertness. A good sign I hoped. I took both babies outdoors to relieve themselves before we returned to the laundry room for more observation. Hazel was still not interested in eating. When I picked her up, she cried pitifully as if pressure on her gassy stomach hurt. A blade of fear slashed my own gut. Bloat in baby goats can be deadly. I had been confident that Hazel's outcome would mirror Lilly's. I was wrong.

Within fifteen minutes, I had run through the protocols that put one in touch with a veterinarian in the wee hours of the morning. A young vet named Erin delivered the hard news.

"This sounds like bloat, so listen carefully. I will help you over the phone but you haven't much time. First you need to get that gas out of her rumen. To do this you need to puncture the rumen with a hypodermic needle. Do you have one?"

The words were firing at my sleep deprived brain like darts.

"Yes, I do," I stammered. "Are you really going to make me do this?"

"If you don't, your goat is going to die. It's not that difficult. Just place the tip of the needle…"

I willed my brain to review the directions as I ran to the barn for a needle. By now I was trying hard to keep my emotions in check in the best interest of Hazel. The vet remained on the phone as my shaky hands plunged the needle into Hazel's side. The little goat screamed at the top of her lungs, adding a whole extra level of drama to the bleak situation. Having never used a needle like this before, I wasn't sure what I was supposed to witness as a result. It appeared that nothing was happening. The vet assured me that I should hear the hiss of air rush out of the needle if I had inserted it correctly. I tried again and again, but nothing escaped the needle. Of course pitiful Hazel screamed with each jab. By now Rod had arrived in the laundry room to help by holding Hazel. He witnessed the entire episode, absorbing the trauma.

"I think she is beyond help," said the vet solemnly. "Her rumen must be full of froth which will not escape through the needle. I am so sorry. This is not going to have a good outcome."

"Is she going to die?" I asked in disbelief, so unprepared to begin the day, let alone the week, with such tragic loss.

"I am afraid so." She hesitated before continuing on. "This sounds like classic clostridium bloat. I am so sorry."

"Well, do I need to bring her to you to be put down? It will take me about an hour to get there." My voice had degraded to a thin choke.

"I don't think you have time," the vet replied.

She was right. I hung up the phone and gathered Hazel in my arms. Rod had been holding her, not speaking as he struggled to comprehend the reality of the situation. Hazel was not silent. She bleated loudly and pathetically, no doubt from intense pain. I sat in the chair and held her as she panted and screamed. My body felt numb, my brain helpless. All I could do was hold her and wait for the end.

After twenty minutes, I had one final thought. "Lacey, come take Hazel, please come get her…."

One minute later, the little goat bellowed her last proclamation and sagged in my arms.

It was shortly before five o'clock in the morning. The silent laundry room now blared a deafening realization. Hazel was dead, and Audrey was all alone. Liam would offer no comfort to her as she was too young to be penned in with him. The sadness on Rod's face and the limp little body in my arms humbled me. I had failed this little creature. Something in my management had gone terribly wrong. Worse than the responsibility was my not knowing what had gone wrong. In the days to come, there would be time to reflect and reform, but right now I had a barn full of animals who needed me and a four week old living baby goat who needed consolation. I also had to get ready for the last day of classes at school, a day that I could not miss.

Although the sun had risen, the day was bleak and drizzly. Rod dressed quickly, then lifted Hazel's still form and carried her out of the house. When the door shut and her sister disappeared, Audrey began bleating in protest. As a herd animal, Audrey was alone and afraid. I held her for the duration of Rod's absence. I could hear the diesel engine of the backhoe come to life. It would dig a small hole for a tiny body. When horses are euthanized, Rod can plan and dig ahead. Today, Hazel's shell would lie motionless on the ground waiting for her grave to be dug.

I tried to comfort Audrey in my arms. Her bleats were not responses to physical pain, but her emotional distress was unnerving. I tried to console her. Then I got an idea. With one hand, I pecked out an email to our superintendent, Rex Germer. Rex and I share a love of animals that dates back to when he was a freshman in high school. I was not surprised when he immediately replied,

"Yes, you may bring her to school."

When Rod returned from burial duty, he held Audrey while I did chores and got ready for the school day. At school we were met by so many concerned faces who eagerly offered to comfort Audrey while I taught my classes. The little goat's feet never hit the floor. Every time I saw her, she was quietly lounging in loving arms. The school nurse tended to the baby goat in her office so that I could work on my report cards and other end of year tasks that could not be postponed. Audrey and I got through the long day with the support of the entire school.

In a haze of exhaustion, my baby goat and I returned home later that afternoon. Only hours ago, we had left the farm in despair. Without changing into my barn clothes, I hurried to the barn. Old Liam was standing in the doorway transfixed by the scene. I was not surprised to see Rod sitting on a milk crate with a bottle in both hands. Each nipple was embedded in the mouth of a tiny goat. Their minute sizes were a reminder of just how far Audrey and Hazel had developed before the tragedy of the last twenty-four hours.

Before I left for school Rod was already planning to drive to Nettle Meadow Farm where Audrey and Hazel had come from. His mission was to acquire more doelings. He had been traumatized by the pathetic cries of our dying goat. Getting these new goats was his way of dealing with the sad situation. As I studied the two new babies pumping formula from the bottles, I was ashamed of my lack of emotion. The goats were beautiful and their presence was necessary for Audrey's wellbeing. However, I felt nothing toward them. I reached down to pick the smaller one up so that I could inspect her from head to hoof. She was mostly white with a few smudges of gray randomly distributed around her head. Light tan patches blotted her white torso. The skin around her eyes and flat nose was rose petal pink. Her long ears hung at forty-five degree angles from her head like mini wings catching a cool breeze. The little doeling had ice blue eyes, a color I had never seen before in goats.

"How old is she?" I asked Rod, eager to hear the whole tale of his adventure. In the waning afternoon sun, he regaled me with his visit to the nursery barn at the dairy goat farm. The farmers presented him with a doe that they had suggested we take after hearing my sad tale on the phone earlier in the day. I had then asked Rod to consider bringing two doelings home so that if we were faced with a similar tragedy, the remaining goat would not suddenly find herself abandoned. Sometimes grief must give way to practical planning.

"The little white one is only eight days old." I could tell he was already attached to her.

I picked up the other little doe. She had a very different body, stockier and sturdier than Audrey's spindly triangular build. Her coat was completely white, but her head and neck were a rich mahogany color accentuated by a dark cap between her ears that tapered to a point between her eyes. This little one possessed the same light blue eyes, a stunning contrast to her dark complexion. She had machete shaped ears that stood erect, clearly a sign of Alpine goat breeding rather than Nubian blood.

"That one is two weeks old," Rod told me.

Audrey and I spent the rest of the afternoon getting to know our two newcomers. It surprised me that they were not shy or fearful of their new surroundings. I escorted them out to the driveway so they could play on Audrey's pile of lumber and the mounting block. Liam watched the new babies' antics from the barn door. I could only imagine what he wondered about more additions to his herd.

Bonding with the doelings was difficult for me so soon after Hazel's death. However, I made myself hold them with the same warmth and affection that I had lavished on Audrey. Initially, they just didn't feel like they belonged to me. They didn't smell like sweet formula and hay, the way Audrey did. They showed no attachment to me either. Their lives up to this point had been spent in small groups of newborns with little human contact. They suckled bottles that were mounted in a frame so lots of babies could eat at one time. The doelings had lived in clean stalls, but had never ventured outside to play and practice the spastic goatie dance. They were terrible jumpers. Try as they might to leap up on Audrey's lumber pile, they missed and landed spatchcock on the ground. The same humiliation occurred at the mounting block. Their failures never deterred them, however. And my failure to feel for them did not deter me.

Bonding is a delicate force. In time my affection for the two doelings equaled my connection with Audrey. I put Hazel's loss in perspective, vowing to keep my three kids safe with the lessons I had learned. Unlike the instant christening of the first two, naming these two additions took several days. The younger one's fair coloring earned her the name Pearl. Rod, so taken by her tiny size, referred to her often as his Pearl drop. We named the older baby with the standup ears Ivy for no particular reason at all.

Ten days after the arrival of the two doelings, I knew Liam had to be euthanized. His condition fluctuated between normal and dramatic episodes of frothy bloat. Several late nights I found him in gassy distress as his rumen swelled so large that he couldn't even lie down. By morning the gas had dissipated, but the mysterious mass in his neck had not. Lying in bed I made the hard decision while Liam spent one more miserable night in his stall. I tossed and turned, wondering if he would even be alive in the morning. Shame on me if he wasn't. Rarely does an animal on our farm die alone. Liam deserved the dignity afforded his herd mates, Lacey and Lilly. In the morning I made the phone call that I am obligated to make as an animal owner.

Dr. Jen arrived that afternoon to put Liam down. Afterwards we both agreed that we needed to know what was going on inside of the goat's neck. When she performed a post mortem inspection of his esophagus, she found that he had an anatomical defect called megaesophagus, a condition found more often in dogs than ruminants. Over time the esophagus had lost tone and was unable to perform peristalsis vigorously. Vegetation consumed by the goat was not being pushed efficiently into the rumen. Food remained stagnant at the base of the tube, building up and making it impossible for Liam to belch or chew his cud. This explained the gas build up in the rumen and the discomfort that prevailed for long stretches of time. Dr. Jen found no sign of cancer or other obstructions that we had suspected over the past ten months. It was an answer I could live with. Liam may have survived for several more months through the ups and downs of frothy bloat. There was, however, no cure for the condition. I was at peace with my decision to end his life.

In the days that followed his euthanasia, we missed Liam's large presence. I expected to see his ginger colored face at the tackroom door every time I slammed it behind me to prevent his sneaky entry in search of grain. I missed his big goatie body soaking up sun at the front of the barn on early summer days. I simply missed him as the final member of a herd that had included Lacey and Lilly. A new herd was now establishing itself on the farm and in my heart. In time we all move on and open ourselves to the possibility of happiness in a future that does not include those who have died. For me it is a way to validate what was, tucking it neatly away in a file of memories while I prepare to live my life into the future with those who have just arrived.

By the end of the summer, the baby goats had established themselves with three distinct personalities. Audrey, no doubt because she is the oldest, is bossy. She leads the trio around our property, deciding where they will browse and for how long. When she is feeling disconnected from me, she sounds the alarm of *"maaa"* that ignites a bleating chorus from all three as they dash back to the barn in search of me. I often tell people that I own Ivy and Pearl but Audrey owns me.

Ivy is the sweet middle child. She wants nothing more than to please me and often joins me for a nap on days when I spread a blanket out on the lawn. There she will snuggle up next to me and quietly chew her cud while I snooze. It is one of the most blissful moments of my day. Little Pearl, the apple of Rod's eye, follows Audrey's orders without complaint or challenge. Her disposition is loving and demure.

I am prepared for the lightning speed with which these goats' lives will be lived. I am prepared for them to grow old and succumb to whatever malady or event takes their lives. If it should happen at the end of a long and happy one, I will consider it a blessing. And if I can plan it so that I can hold each one in my arms while the vet performs euthanasia, I will consider myself to be the luckiest person in the world.

For thirty years I have lived with goats. Although I don't manage them for milking or breeding, they do offer me companionship. They escort me on hikes in the woods or huddle close to me when I seek moments of calm. The goats and I spend so much time together that I recognize them as individual personalities. Because I have raised most of my goats from infancy, I am privileged to live among them for their entire lifespan. When they die, grief cuts me deeply, but never in vain. Each loss forces me to reexamine my philosophy of life and death. Questions arise about our shared mortal journey. I yearn for simple answers in the daily life of the farm, in Hazel's too early death and in the new life of Pearl and Ivy. Given time, answers surface, often with quiet clarity. As I watch my goats dance and frolic, I begin to find a spiritual wholeness, a center of acceptance and understanding.

Brad Kessler, author of the critically acclaimed memoir, *Goat Song,* reflects on his decision to make a life with his goats, managing the cycle of goat rearing, breeding, kidding, milking and cheese making. *"A goat has led me here. I am the Yiddish boy in the tale who's followed her all along- she always knew the way back home."* As I lie on my blanket in the late summer sun, three goats snuggled against my body, I come back home to a peaceful acceptance of both love and loss. Risking love of another creature who will quite likely predecease me means I have to embrace life's joyful dance and also its inevitable loss and grief. I come home over and over again to a deeper understanding that allows me to celebrate when a goat is dancing her goatie dance, even as I know that I will one day mourn her passing.

Although the breed was developed in England, Nubian lineage originated in the desert region of the Middle East. Their two outstanding characteristics are the Roman nose that develops in adulthood and the long pendulous ears that hang down on either side of their head. Nubian ancestors are among the oldest domesticated animals in the world. Alpine goats originated in Europe. In contrast to Nubian ears, Alpine ears stand erect and point forward. Both Nubian and Alpines are strong milk producers desired in the dairy goat industry.

Our current goat herd, Pearl, Ivy and Audrey, (under the table) with Rod and our West Highland terrier, Nina, 2017.

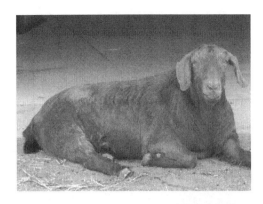

Lacey and Liam were farm fixtures for over a decade. The next generation of goats began with Hazel and Audrey who spent their first week of life at school. After losing Hazel, Pearl and Ivy were acquired to complete a herd for Audrey. 2016.

Lacey's photo by M. deCamp.

Target

"It's time," I confirmed calmly.

I finally conceded to the euthanasia of my twenty-one year old thoroughbred gelding *Final Target*. Unlike *Rosemary* the iguana, *Sandi*, the dependable lesson mount and *Huxley*, the dachshund, Target's obituary never appeared on Facebook or Twitter. Subsequently, there was no outpouring of condolences assuring me that he had lived a wonderful life thanks to my love and devotion. I couldn't bear to hear these things because I wasn't convinced they were true. Over the ten years that I had owned Target, I had contemplated putting him down several times. When the moment of truth arrived each time, I dashed the thought from my brain.

Target was originally purchased as a lesson horse shortly before we moved from tiny Lakeview Farm to the sprawling landscape that is Moose River Farm. I found him on a specialty website dedicated to connecting thoroughbred enthusiasts from around the country so they could sell members of one of my favorite breeds.

After driving for over two hours one late afternoon through a dreary March landscape, my friend Michele and I arrived at a sagging barn with fifteen empty stalls and only two horses. The owners were clearing out and closing a long chapter of their lives: years spent retraining thoroughbreds off the race track. They were heading into retirement without horses. Target, whose name was Peewee at the time, stood tall, well over sixteen hands. He was the offspring of one of their own thoroughbred mares who died two weeks after he was foaled. Orphan foals typically struggle in life as they grow up under the care of a human nanny. Good intentions can turn sour because these horses never learn the rules of being a horse from their dam. I believe this lack of maternal education had an effect on Target throughout his whole life. He remained rather aloof to other horses. At times he also lacked respect for humans, often plowing into his handler when walking in from his paddock or refusing to accept the bridle by raising his head just out of reach. His dingy white coat revealed only a few remaining faded dapples from younger days. In just another year or two, he would turn completely white. The big horse had not been ridden in over two years; however, the owner assured me that there would be no behavioral issue if I got on him.

From the moment I mounted him, I could tell that he was not going to buck or rear, a deal breaker for me in the purchase of any horse. Target complied willingly with my leg and rein aids. If anything he seemed a bit dull, a characteristic that to me is a better feature of a lesson horse than a flighty demeanor that reacts too quickly to the rider's leg. This first and only ride was enough to convince me to purchase the horse on the spot.

Two weeks later, Target was on his way to a life in the Adirondacks. He settled into our routine easily. Shortly after his arrival, I began the task of conditioning him for my lesson program. Initially, I walked and trotted him in short intervals around the ring. Keeping in mind that he hadn't had a saddle or bridle on for years, I didn't want his back to be sore while his limbs and large muscles developed strength. As I got to know him better and to feel more comfortable with his reactions to external forces such as wind, cars, and deer, I began to walk him around my neighborhood.

By late spring I had been conditioning the horse for six weeks when it became apparent that he was becoming physically irritated when ridden. I had made a conscious effort to ease him slowly into a routine that would eventually build the muscles that had not worked in two years. Training sessions began with stretchy walks where the horse is encouraged to extend his neck and back muscles while taking long slow strides. I loved to feel the swing of his haunches while his belly swayed between my soft calves. Next I used pressure from my legs to signal my desire for him to trot. Between my contact on the reins and my quiet leg, Target maintained a slow but forward gait. The goal was for the horse to engage his powerful hind end muscles and to maintain what is called impulsion without translating the effort into speed. I wanted balance not velocity. I kept the work intervals short and the walk breaks long, but built his stamina by increasing the work gradually during each ride.

As the days passed I realized that my bargain horse had some strange quirks. Out of the blue he began to stop and refuse to move forward. Applying my leg aids only resulted in his drifting left and right, absolutely refusing any advancement forward. The only way I could interrupt the behavior was to circle him a few times. Only then could I break his trance and make him proceed forward. He did so as if nothing had interrupted our training. Target pulled the same stunt out on the trail. The trigger appeared when I asked him to pass the horse who was in front of him. Not only did he stop and plant his feet in refusal, but he paid no concern to the lead horse who continued on, increasing the distance between them. Horses believe in safety in numbers. They do not wish to be left behind, especially if one becomes a lone horse as a result. Target did not seem to care about being left alone. By asking him to circle two or three times, I was able to get him moving once again. Was this a sign of pain? Stubbornness? Was it related to his orphan status? Attributing this change in behavior to physical pain as a result of conditioning, I backed off and rode him ever so lightly.

Conditioning a horse is like conditioning any athlete. After all, horses are built out of bone, muscle and other soft tissue such as tendons and ligaments too. All of these structures need to be considered when riding horses who lack tone. Target had not been ridden for two years. Just tightening a saddle around his torso was enough to cause pain and discomfort to soft or underdeveloped muscles. I assumed that any soreness or irritability I observed was probably due to the stress of conditioning. All athletes experience these periods of discomfort. Trainers back off or choose alternative exercise to avoid causing long term injury. With Target, I was trying my best.

Then the tripping began. At first the bobbles were subtle, a loss of rhythm here, a balance issue there. I paid little attention to it until one day I counted the number of trips. On average the great white horse lost rhythm in his stride fifteen times in a forty-five minute session. Imagination on my part or a physical issue on his? Did he need more conditioning? Did he need protective pads applied under the shoes on his front feet? As his conditioning progressed, he developed balance and elasticity in his back but required a knowledgeable rider to help him hold himself together. His large size made this a difficult task for beginner riders. At the time most of my students were beginner children.

Eventually, I used him more and more for adult riders with experience. They loved him. His trot and canter were just challenging enough to teach the rider's leg and hand how to respond. The bobbles appeared often, but they never seemed to result in anything more than a hiccup in rhythm. In the meantime, I rode Target as often as I could. The behavioral quirks reduced measurably once he became acquainted with the trails at our new farm. Away from the schooling ring, he picked up his feet with enthusiasm, minimizing the imbalance episodes. I used to joke with barn family and friends about developing a sport called "road dressage." As long as Target was moving forward in a straight line, he seemed to be able to round his back and float laterally from one of my leg aids to the other. He also kept his ears on alert, waiting for the faintest distraction in the woods to give cause for enormous spooks. More than once he unseated the most experienced riders on excursions in the woods.

Then one day while I was giving a lesson to an experienced college student in the ring, the inevitable happened. Betty was cantering Target on a longer rein than I am comfortable with. He was more under control when the rider supported him with both reins and leg. However, Betty's confidence and Target's balance appeared to be synchronized. Although his frame was long, he was in no way careening around the ring. Suddenly, without warning, he crashed to the ground. The momentum of his fall caused Betty's body to project forward along his neck and over his head.

Thankfully, Betty, although a bit stunned, was not hurt. After all there had been no warning, no bad footing, no explanation for the sudden loss of balance. Betty had done nothing wrong. I had no words of advice. "You should have done this....You should have done that...." I had nothing to offer her.

Target's fall resulted in a melon sized hematoma on his chest and a rattling of confidence in both him and me. What did this mean? What malfunctioned? Was there really something wrong with him? Should I put him down? This event forced me to pull him out of my lesson program. So far he hadn't hurt anybody seriously, but I was not willing to run that risk.

I continued to ride him after he healed from his bruise. In fact I spent the next winter in the indoor arena focusing on his balance through exercises and conditioning. Some days, instead of riding Target, I chased him around the ring, encouraging him to gallop as fast as he could. I wanted to observe his abilities without the weight of a rider on his back. During our ten years together, I had seldom seen him bobble without a rider.

Over the winter Target improved. I rode him six or seven times without stumbles. Some of my best rides took place on the great white horse. These sessions occasionally occurred in my lighted outdoor ring under falling snow. Accompanied by the festive notes of *Manheim Steamroller's* popular Christmas music, Target glided across the powdery surface, effortlessly responding to my leg requests. The powerful experiences kept me smiling all evening after a long professional day at school. I owe Target a debt of gratitude for those unforgettable rides.

Although the years went by, the bobbles became something I accepted; although unbeknownst to me, they were having a detrimental effect on my riding in general. I began to ride all horses defensively, afraid of tripping and falling. I needed to feel that I could control and thwart a possible fall. To do this I stared at the ground so I could steer around suspicious soft or uneven spots that might cause a fall. This wariness became the new normal.

Meanwhile, Target was beginning to exhibit abnormal behavior around the barn. He acted terrified when his halter was placed behind his ears. Bridling him in the wash stall was impossible as he hoisted his head as high as he could, shaking with fear, eyes bulging. In his stall, however, there was no bridling issue. Sometimes after I removed his bridle, he twisted his neck and held it stiffly in this position for several minutes. I wondered if he was having mini seizures, but our vet could diagnose nothing wrong with him. Was it time to put him down? His issues began to accumulate. He suffered intermittent lameness that required long stretches of rest. The lameness returned after a few weeks of light work.

Then one day while riding him on a glorious June morning, it happened. The great white horse was cantering effortlessly around the ring. My legs and reins were communicating with him effortlessly when suddenly he dropped to his knees. The event occurred so quickly, I didn't have time to react as I had convinced myself I could. However, he did not fall. Miraculously, he caught himself and took two more strides on his knees. Next thing I knew he was standing. Not only was I still on his back but my feet were still in the stirrups. Target's entire body was shaking. Fear? Pain? I too was suffering the effects of being startled into the realization that I had been lucky this time. Immediately, I steered him toward the gate and exited the ring for the last time astride this great white horse. While walking him in the woods to cool him down and calm his nerves, I had to face some difficult questions. By the time I pulled him up at the front of the barn to dismount, I had decided that he would not be ridden again.

It would have cost me thousands of dollars to run diagnostic tests on Target. I also knew that whatever ailed him was probably not fixable enough to deem him safe to ride. Was it time to put him down? All summer I pondered this question. What was his life now that he could not be ridden? Yes, he could live in a state of permanent retirement, lounging in the luxury of care without giving anything back. Had he earned that? Could I justify the expense of nearly three thousand dollars a year? Every other horse who had retired at Moose River Farm did so after a long and productive life. Horses are expensive. Target could live another fifteen years in retirement. The questions were difficult for me to answer. Perhaps I didn't want to admit some of the answers. Four years later, Target was still living in full retirement.

By the time gray horses have completely faded to white, they have most likely developed melanomas at various locations all over their bodies. Target was no exception. The tumors tend to grow slowly and rarely end the animal's life unless they interfere with the mechanics of breathing or digestion. For years, melanomas had been growing rapidly under Target's tail and all around his rectum. The unsightly large black tumors stretched out to nearly a ten inch diameter mass when he lifted his tail to defecate.

In the spring of 2015, I declined to give Target his routine annual vaccines. I was pretty certain this was the year I was going to put him down. Summer passed. As the horse sprouted his winter coat in preparation for his twenty-second winter, our vet provided the courage I needed to make the decision final. We agreed that the mass of tumors under his tail was probably going to become problematic in the future. Finally, it was okay for me to let him go.

Target's death brought closure to horse ownership at its most complicated. Although I loved this horse, ending his life was a relief allowing me to move forward, so he and I could be at peace. There is no question that I made decisions for Target differently than decisions for other horses. For instance, Zambi is still living a carefree life in retirement at age twenty-eight. Although I monitor his health and physical abilities constantly, I am in no hurry to end his life. He is an aging shadow of his robust youthful condition. Hip bones protrude under his shaggy pelt. Withers at the base of his neck protrude high above his spine due to a sinking topline where his back muscles have atrophied. Flecks of gray hair on his dark brown coat emphasize the hollow depressions above his eyes and along his cheekbones. He looks old, like a well-loved teddy bear, yet none of these features prompt me to consider his euthanasia. As long as Zambi maintains enthusiasm for hay and grain, as long as he gallops with exuberance around his field and as long as he can eventually get back on his feet after a hardy roll on the ground or nap in the sun, I will keep him alive. Sometimes I catch him struggling to rise. My heart appears to stop beating while I wait for the grand effort that thrusts him up on all fours. For Zambi I seem to be willing to break my own rule so we can continue to share the pleasures of retirement as soulmates who have lived through a long and productive human/horse relationship together.

I didn't afford Target the same luxury. Instead, I kept track of his assets and liabilities like figures in an expense ledger. When I calculated that he had exceeded his emotional worth, I was able to make the final decision. Although, it took years and the horse was spared many times, I am still aware of an imbalance between the measurement of Target's and Zambi's worth.

"Which is your favorite horse?"

This question has been asked of me hundreds of times since I have owned multiple horses. Almost before the question mark exits the inquirer's mouth, I exhale the reply quickly.

"I couldn't possibly have a favorite; I love them all the same."

But do I?

Target's life has forced me to examine the conflict between the little girl who loves all horses and the wise woman who measures a horse's worth by how useful he is. Devotion versus practicality. They are sparring foes for sure. This bucolic life is not without heartbreak, difficult decisions and discrimination. What I have learned from these two horses is not to expect perfection and tidy packages. The longer I live with horses the more they mold me into the person I am on my way to becoming. I hope she will be an improvement on who I am now but this journey is not without difficult questions that are painful to answer if I am completely vested in living the mortal truth.

Some of my best rides were on Target. photo D. Allen. Target performed with dancer Eric Bradley for Hoofbeats in the Adirondacks; 2012. photo by M. deCamp

FINAL TARGET
"TARGET"

Rosemary

I glance at the unusual passenger in the seat next to me. Rosemary, my twenty year old green iguana, is with me in route to a book signing. Her job is to beguile would-be readers into taking notice of the book in which she is an important character. Of all the animals who reside at Moose River Farm, Rosemary is the most portable. However, unlike our furry family members, she draws quite different reactions from those who encounter her.

At the start to this drizzly Labor Day weekend, we arrive at the *Adirondack Reader,* a quaint independent bookstore in the town of Inlet, New York. It is owned by retired school teacher Reggie Chambers. Despite rain, the town of Inlet is busy with umbrella toting shoppers squeezing one more vacation out of summer before the Adirondacks transitions into a bouquet of fall foliage. Blazes of red and yellow are already evident in the dense leafy canopy overhead. For me, the school year will begin in exactly seventy-two hours. Where did the summer go?

Once again ten weeks of vacation has flown by. I spent it teaching horseback riding, training and riding horses, visiting with family and waiting anxiously for twenty-five hundred copies of my book to arrive. The latter finally made their way to my house the night before the initial book signing at Moose River Farm one week ago. The event launched the publication of my first book.

It had been an exciting day with so many well-wishers, close friends and family arriving to show their support or to buy a personalized copy. The event was an opportunity for readers to interact with the horses, donkeys, dogs, goats, Fiona the pig and Rosemary. They are the cast of living characters who appear in various stories throughout the first book. Many of MRF's young riders were on hand to guide visitors and answer questions about the animals. Baby donkeys, Bing and Frankie, entertained the crowd with their boyish antics, rolling in the dusty sand and chasing each other around in the driveway. At one point, they discovered the delicious bounty of treats provided by *Ozzie's Coffee Bar* and helped themselves to scones without offering to pay.

Reggie Chambers had brought her granddaughter to visit the animals on the day of the book launch. She had also come to collect copies of the book in anticipation of my book signing at her store the following weekend. Now, with Rosemary under one arm and a box of books under the other, I dash from my car to the cozy interior of Reggie's bookstore. She greets me warmly. Her eyes pop open when she sees the iguana. Within minutes Rosemary and I have our display organized and are ready to greet patrons.

Reggie escorts several customers, especially those with children, over to my table. Youngsters are enamored, while some adults initially are not.

"Is it real?" somebody asks, a mixture of curiosity and squeamishness in her expression. The large lizard lounges leisurely in front of the books on the table.

"This is Rosemary. Would you like to pet her? She is very friendly," I offer a well-rehearsed reply.

"Does she bite?"

"No," I reassure. "She is quite used to people and loves to be scratched right here behind her ears."

"Ears! Where are her ears?"

"On either side of her head," I respond, pointing to the holes behind her eyes that are covered with a tissue paper-like membrane. Next, I scratch the lizard's head so that she stretches her torso upward and closes her eyes. The customer prepares to touch Rosemary with a tentative finger, not quite convinced it's a good idea.

My iguana seems unfazed in unfamiliar surroundings. Her *Mona Lisa* smile reveals little of her opinion about being away from home today, but her easy going temperament lets me know that she isn't stressed at all.

I have brought her as evidence that the characters in my book are real. Although many of the animals have passed away, Rosemary remains one of the oldest and, presently, our longest residing family member. She has survived delivering several large clutches of infertile eggs, extreme temperature fluctuations, and the regeneration of her tail.

"She feels like a beaded belt," the customer reports after bravely touching the lizard. Her hand relaxes as her fingers caress Rosemary's head. The tight expression is replaced with a smile. She begins to identify with the iguana as a fellow living being.

"What does she eat?"

"Leafy vegetables, grapes, zucchini, cucumbers and tofu. This morning she had a scrambled egg."

"How old is she?"

"I have had her 19 years so she is about 20."

"What do you keep her in?"

"She roams around our house freely, but has a heated cabinet she can climb into to get warm."

"Where does she go to the bathroom?"

"On my kitchen floor once a day or every other day."

"She is so interesting."

"Yes, she is, thank you."

Mission accomplished!

Rosemary accompanied me to most of my book signings during the first two years after my book was published. At each venue, she attracted the attention of many, bridging the gap between animal lovers and my book. It was also quality time spent with my lizard in her twilight years. I am grateful to have had the opportunity to share her with so many. But Rosemary's time with me was running out. Two years later she was gone.

The diagnosis was a shock, although I had expected something was wrong for some time. What is difficult with animals is that as long as they are eating and excreting fairly normally, it is easy to deny that anything other than old age afflicts them.

Rosemary had survived a long cold winter in the house that we struggled to keep above seventy degrees. Many mornings I found her stiff and ice cold on the living room floor after she chose to evacuate a cozy heating pad under the footstool. The bitter cold had arrived early in mid-November and had lingered long into May, later than any year I could remember. Rosemary ate well but only if I hand fed her.

On sunny afternoons, she sought warmth from sunbeams that beckoned through the long windows in the deck doors. Occasionally, I placed her out on the back doorstep where she benefited from a dose of unfiltered vitamin D therapy. It also enabled the parietal eye, a transparent scale on top of her head, to determine the time of year. Sensitive to light and dark, this photo sensory organ interacts with the pineal gland at the center of the brain so that appropriate hormones are released during the breeding season or thermoregulation. Although it can't form images, the parietal eye is an amazing adaptation that may explain the evolution of eyes in reptiles.

A lizard's body fat and condition can be observed at the base of her tail. As long as the animal is eating sufficiently, the tail remains plump with taut skin completely concealing the skeletal frame. Rosemary's pelvic bones began to make an appearance at the end of the harsh winter. At first I talked myself into believing her age was at fault. I had been feeding her regularly. But why wasn't her tail fat? By late summer, it was hard to ignore the signs. First, she developed excessive thirst, plunging her snout into any potential water source such as her bath water or puddles on the outside deck. Reluctantly, I began to explore the internet. My heart sank. Renal failure, retained egg follicles, liver disease, and a plethora of other lethal horrors kept me awake at night. I worried incessantly about her. What was I missing? Why couldn't I figure it out, apply the necessary treatment, and move forward into the next twenty-one healthy years of Rosemary's life?

Eventually, my keyword search transitioned from iguana ailments to reptile veterinarians in central New York. Our regular veterinary clinic handled all of our animals except reptiles. My Google search located a clinic in Canastota, home of *The International Boxing Hall of Fame*. Once I made the appointment, there was nothing left to do but wait for the moment of truth to arrive.

"Let me get my book and show you what a normal iguana's body looks like first," said Dr. Barbara Roach as she stepped out the door of the examining room to retrieve a veterinary textbook on reptiles.

"This can't be good if I have to compare Rosemary to a normal iguana," I muttered.

My friend Vicky had accompanied me on the trip and into the examining room. Her silence convinced me she agreed.

The image on Rosemary's x-ray was as clear as the realization that my iguana was probably not going to live much longer. In comparison to the book's image of a normal iguana, Rosemary's lower abdomen was full of a large opaque mass at the dorsal end of the torso. This evidence proved that I could no longer blame Rosemary's symptoms on natural aging. I listened sadly as Dr. Roach professionally continued her diagnosis. The emphasis on tumor, kidney failure, fluid in the abdomen, weight loss, deteriorating condition forced me to see the iguana for the first time as terminally ill.

Rosemary lived in my house longer than any other animal we have ever owned. Only one horse, Windy, who lived in our barn for twenty-four years until his euthanasia at age twenty-seven, had been a part of our family longer. Rosie had belonged to a child who named her baby lizard in honor of a grandmother. When the child needed to find a home for the iguana, she asked me if Rosemary could live in my classroom. I agreed, hopeful that Rosie might provide companionship for our two year old male iguana, Spike. She did. For almost a decade the two iguanas cohabitated.

After the animals were evicted from my classroom, Rosemary and Spike lived a quiet existence in my home until Spike died eight years later. Afterwards, I wondered how much longer Rosemary might last. She did not miss him. I had physically separated them years ago, when it was clear that she was not interested in amorous trysts.

Yet Rosemary continued in good health through cold winters, hot summers and other seasonal fluctuations to which tropical species should find it difficult to adapt. Her reserved personality and faint smile made her a hit among most visitors at Moose River Farm. The iguana continued to entertain so many who *oohed* and *aahed* as she grazed on the lawn or plucked her favorite petunias buds from my planters. Children clamored to deck chairs and sat patiently while Rosie lay on a towel across their laps. The iguana posed for hundreds of pictures, most recently in many *selfies*. Rarely did an encounter with Rosemary result in anything less than amazement and appreciation.

When my book was published, I combed the internet for opportunities to promote it to animal loving readers. The book market is competitive. Attracting attention to one's own title requires careful planning and creativity. At the Moose River Farm book launch, I witnessed the power that my animals had over would-be readers. After all, the book is about animals: the joys and sorrows they bring to my life and the lessons (oh so many lessons) that they teach every day. My experiences with animals are not unique. Perhaps most animal lovers have not had as many interactions with different species as I have; but if they have ever loved a dog, a cat, a hamster, or a deer that frequently visits their backyard, then they will connect with the stories I share.

Rosemary spent that first book signing event sprawled on a table, keeping an eye on activity all around the farm. Her presence gave me confidence to speak to people, engage them in conversation about their own animals and encourage them to scratch behind her ears...once they learned where her ears were. Together, Rosemary and I became a marketing team. Taking her with me on book signings was not only a sure way to attract potential readers, but it also provided us with quality time together away from home. For hours I sat with her in my arms as hand after hand reached out to make her acquaintance.

In the vet's office now, I was forced to accept Rosie's mortality. Emotions boiled over into tears. I turned away from the vet and asked her to give me a moment to compose myself; but I sobbed harder. The vet stepped out of the room again to get tissues for me while Vicky stood silently at my side. With sheer determination I turned off the faucets of my grief. Gulping for air like a stranded trout, I prepared for Dr. Roach to continue the diagnosis.

"Judging from her condition and the size of the mass, we are probably talking about a matter of weeks. She looks comfortable; as long as she is eating and able to relieve herself, she should be ok. As soon as you notice her straining to defecate then it will be time."

My gaze dropped to Rosemary who was lounging untroubled on a towel in my arms. It was the same Rosie, sweet and accepting, only now she was also dying.

"I am so sorry," said Dr. Roach as Vicky and I gathered to leave.

In the reception area, I waited to pay the bill. Rosemary's appointment had consisted of an ultrasound and an x ray to confirm the fatal prognosis; money well spent.

"I just need a minute," I said to Vicky as we approached the parking lot. Once seated inside the car, I allowed myself to weep. Tears gushed in a wave of intense sadness. In its wake was the sobering realization that Rosemary's and my twenty years together were coming to an end. As I calmed, it occurred to me that my prayers had actually been answered. Six months prior to this terminal diagnosis, I had almost lost her in a most dreadful way.

In April, my lack of vigilance almost killed Rosemary. My friends, Missy and Mary Anne, were visiting me during spring break. We had spent an eighty degree day in sunshine that tricked the Adirondacks dwellers into believing the coldest, most extreme winter of the century was behind us. Rosemary lay on the deck most of the day, soaking up much needed unfiltered sunlight. That evening I presented a book talk with Rosemary at the Canastota Public Library. All was well.

The next morning it appeared that winter had returned to humble us once more. Brutal wind and drizzle turned into blowing snow by early afternoon. The last time I had taken notice of Rosemary, she was strutting across the kitchen floor in the late morning. Distracted by my visiting company, I didn't even think about her again until evening. Our dinner was warming in the oven as my guests and I enjoyed a glass of wine. I chopped zucchini and grapes into bite sized pieces, then went to locate the iguana on her heating pad in the living room. She wasn't there. I searched several other locations where she frequently napped. When my search came up empty again, fear shot through me. By now Missy, Mary Anne and Rod were also searching around the house.

My brain whipped lightning fast through the following scenario. Rosemary had just spent a summer day outdoors. She had convinced herself that good weather still existed on the other side of the dog door where she had learned to exit. I dashed out the door, leapt down the steps and sprinted around the deck preparing myself for what I knew I was going to find. Under three inches of snow, I found her lying by the dormant remains of her favorite yarrow plant. I grabbed the still body and scrambled back into the house. My shrieks brought Missy and Mary Anne running into the laundry room as I hastily filled the utility sink with warm water.

Only one word describes how Rosemary looked; dead. She was the color of gray storm clouds. Her mouth slacked open while the rest of her body hung limp. In disbelief I stared at her lying motionless in the water. How had I let it happen?

"This is not the way it is supposed to end," I sobbed.

Mary Anne, Missy and I began rubbing her extremities and her torso under the warm water. She did not appear to be breathing. In my despair, I became aware of Rod pacing back and forth behind us, craning his head every once in a while to observe progress.

"She's gone, Anne. She's gone. There is no use," he admonished quietly.

Those words twisted in me like a dagger. Neither Mary Anne nor Missy turned to console me. Their hands were too busy massaging Rosemary's limbs and keeping her head above water. For an agonizingly long time, we focused on Rosemary. My sniffles were the only sounds in the room. As minutes lurched by, I feared that Rod was right. The iguana's body remained flaccid. Her eyes stared blankly through droopy lids from either side of her head. From time to time Missy stopped massaging to pinch Rosemary's toes. When no response resulted, she dutifully took to massaging again, never once indicating it was time to give up.

"It can't end this way. Why didn't I pay closer attention to her this morning when she was in the kitchen?"

My guests could only soothe me with words. Their hands refused to stop. For another twenty-five minutes, we rubbed Rosemary's body in the warm water. In the back of my mind, I remembered watching a piece on the news years ago. Florida was experiencing severe cold that threatened citrus groves and other temperature sensitive crops in the southern part of the state. Feral iguanas, abandoned in the wilderness by pet owners, were falling out of trees. Although they appeared dead, they began to thaw once tossed into the warm interior of a municipal pickup truck sent out to collect them. Eventually, the truck swarmed with energetic iguanas who returned from the frozen brink none the worse for wear.

The image of the revived iguanas encouraged me as I continued to will Rosie back to life in the sink. Iguanas can survive temperatures in the low forties and upper thirties Fahrenheit. When I found Rosemary, the air temperature was twenty-six degrees. We estimated that she had been outside for over six hours. In the end it may have been the three inches of insulating snow that saved her life by keeping her tissues from dropping below freezing. At that point her organs would have been frozen, destroying the delicate cellular structures.

After forty-five minutes, Missy felt minimal reaction when pinching a toe. Rosemary contracted her leg ever so slightly in response. Slowly but surely, she started to revive. Eventually, her eyes focused and the eyelids widened. We continued our vigil at the sink, for the core of Rosemary's torso was slower to warm up. Finally, when the lizard was able to swim in the water on her own, we deemed it safe to remove her from the sink. I stuffed her under my shirt, securing her between my wool sweater and warm skin while I assembled dinner plates with overcooked leftovers.

At the table we clinked our glasses in a toast to Rosemary's resurrection. With the crisis behind us, we nicknamed her

Frozemary. I kept kissing the nose protruding above my turtleneck and affirmed appreciation over and over for the chance to write a different ending to the iguana's story.

Rosemary's final diagnosis, the one that would ultimately claim her life, was out of my control. The quiet moments after my emotional release in the car allowed me to accept the inevitable. Death on the night of the deep freeze would not have given me a chance to spend quality time with her before saying goodbye.

At home I soaked her every day in the same lifesaving sink that had revived her months ago so that she could relieve herself comfortably. By hand I fed her kale, snap peas, peppers, grapes and scrambled eggs. She spent much of her time on her heating pad by the living room window. When it got too warm there, she was free to move away onto a dog bed or underneath the cabinet that contained our TV. On sunny days, we set her out on the deck. As if a plan greater than we can know was in place, our petunia plants, for the first time ever, survived for several months after they were moved indoors. Pink and purple flowers continued to bloom through late fall, blossoms that Rosemary munched, much to her gastric delight.

The week before Christmas, we knew that Rosemary was ready to die. She refused to eat, spitting out any food that I forced into her mouth. Her wonderful disposition never changed, however, which made the decision to euthanize her difficult. I always look for some profound change in behavior or temperament before I decide to end a life. With Rosemary that change never appeared. Her disinterest in food was the only reason I had. I made the appointment for two days before Christmas, which turned out to be an unseasonably warm, reptile loving day. Vicky agreed to accompany me, yet again, to Canastota for Rosemary's final visit.

On the morning of the last day, I was scheduled for a therapeutic massage. After years of middle age physical discomfort and only temporary relief from prescription medication, I decided to try a holistic approach to self-maintenance. Rod had given me two sessions for Christmas the year before; after finally redeeming them eight months later, I was hooked.

I climbed between the pre-warmed flannel sheets on the massage table and lay on my stomach, face down against the headrest. Breathing deeply, I tried to relax. At low volume, *Enya* performed her mesmerizing new age music. Suzy Stripp entered the room and pulled the sheets up to my neck. She pressed her hands on the right side of my spine and began to push gently into my back. I copied her deliberate heavy breaths in and out. On this particular morning, my head was cluttered. It took some time to chase away the chatter. Eventually, Suzy's hands created a flow of energy that eased the debris from my mind. I allowed thoughts to meander. Anything was possible. Into Rosemary's body I crawled. It was she who was lying on the table under Suzy's hands. I could imagine Suzy carefully massaging the protruding ribs and hip bones. The mental image forced me to see my lizard's deteriorating condition. I crawled in deeper and tried to scrape the killing mass out of her belly.

There was only one heartbreaking truth. In just a few hours, Rosemary would be gone. The loss was going to cut deep and take time to heal. Tears dripped off my nose and splashed onto my hands. Although I knew Suzy would understand, I didn't want her to know. I needed her to continue manipulating my shell, opening spaces for sadness to drain. When Suzy expertly located a sensitive pressure point, the searing pain aligned with my loss and jolted my thoughts. I exited the lizard. Next, I was sitting with Rosemary on my lap. Several children were reaching out to touch her. They bombarded me with questions.

"What does she eat?" "How old is she?" "Where does she sleep?" "How long have you had her?"

The answers poured out like a recording. I had answered them hundreds of times over the last twenty years. I was Rosie's interpreter. All she had to do was sit in my lap and just be.

Switching thoughts again, I was reminded that the next day life at Moose River Farm would go on as usual. Rosemary would be gone; but horses, dogs, donkeys and everybody else who resided there would still require my attention, my care and my affection. I would know when Rod was preparing the burial site. I would know when Rod had removed the body from my car. And I would know when he had placed her into the hole that had been dug to honor her with a resting place.

Later that day, Dr. Roach greeted us compassionately. I held Rosemary. This time my hands would not revive her after she inhaled the anesthetic gas. My eyes stared up at the ceiling for I could not bear to watch the needle puncture her heart. I am grateful to Dr. Roach for providing a painless end to this unique creature's life.

The next day Rod buried Rosemary's body in the corner of our backyard where she had spent many a summer day basking in sunshine. It's comforting to know she is tucked below the earth while we continue with the process of living above ground. In the weeks that followed, Rod searched the internet for an appropriate memorial to commemorate twenty-one years of a special reptilian life. A concrete iguana with the familiar *Mona Lisa* smile watches over Rosemary's grave.

I have no desire to own another iguana now that ours is gone. In twenty-one years, my relationship with Rosemary transitioned from reptilian caregiver to kindred spirit. By the end of her life she was more than an iguana. She was a unique personality packaged within a green scaly caisson.

From Rosemary's longevity I have learned that life is ideally a random beginning, a productive middle and an inevitable end for all living things. It brings a sense of peace to know that of the three phases, my responsibility lies between birth and death. Driven by consciousness of the inevitable end, I want to fill this section of life with breathtaking encounters spent with other living beings. Conveying this goal to young children is difficult because they are not yet able to contemplate their own mortality. It is not appropriate to rush them. However, children benefit from the experience of losing a pet. I reflect on images of the many children who have held Rosemary across their laps, stroking her textured tail. I realize now that I am living the lesson I have taught to children over and over again. Our experiences help fill various tool boxes that we carry along on our path through life. Coping skills are critical tools. We enhance our mental health as we learn to recognize and accept the difference between what we can and cannot control. Finding firm ground on which to stand after tumbling through loss fortifies the strength of our conviction. With each loss my character becomes stronger. With each loss my appreciation for life deepens. With each loss I move forward into the future.

Rosemary used the dog door to exit the house on sunny days.

On TV with host Phil Bayly in Albany, NY. photo by M. deCamp

Rosemary often accompanied me at book signings, taking on the role of teacher. photo by M. deCamp

Eating petunia flowers, her favorite summertime treat. photo by D. Lane

Huxley's Last Breath

In my first book, I wrote about Huxley, a little dachshund puppy who entered our lives at a most significant moment in time. Eight months before his arrival, we had said goodbye to an ancient sixteen-year old dachshund named Luther, marking the third and final loss in our first generation of dogs. That winter we lived dog-less and wondered if we might ever want to be dog owners again after the emotional drain of losing three dogs in three years.

The heart has a way of disregarding emotional reasoning. In late June we brought home a seven week old puppy. Totally unaware of the sadness lifted by his endearing tininess, the puppy we named Huxley proved to be the antidote for Rod's and my grief.

Time passes in the flutter of busy living, and so Huxley also entered the dreaded realm of a canine elder. For almost fourteen years, he snuggled against me at every opportunity when I was enjoying a few minutes on the couch or on the patio hammock. He formed strong bonds with our friends, especially those who spent time housesitting for us. Huxley loved company. Anybody who sat on the couch and wrapped him in a blanket was his best friend. Sometimes it was necessary for him to whimper his desire to have the blanket draped over him. Once it was applied, he rewarded his guest by curling up comfortably against them.

Huxley's life was not without complications. At age two he began to have seizures periodically. They were *petit mal* by nature, not violent, but disturbing nonetheless. During a seizure, his eyes appeared vacant and his body trembled from head to tail. He seemed to be stuck in a neurological spasm, reminding me of the eerie twang that an audio CD makes when the laser gets hung up on a piece of debris and can't read the files. These seizures lasted anywhere from twenty minutes to several hours. At first when Huxley began to have seizures, I panicked, assuming that he needed emergency veterinary care. However, my vet assured me that the seizures were harder on me than they were on the dog. After the episode subsided, Huxley remained quiet for a few hours, but then returned to his exuberant self as if nothing had gone amiss.

Eventually, we began to medicate Huxley daily with Phenobarbital, a powerful barbiturate that keeps the brain quiet. He continued to have seizures from time to time, but perhaps the medication did reduce the number. In hindsight I would never have put him on this drug. It was wearing out his liver and other vital organs. My human need to avoid feeling helpless propelled me to administer the drug.

Like most dachshunds, Huxley also suffered from chronic gingivitis. This condition required deep tooth scalings every other year and resulted in the most toxic smelling breath imaginable. Although his signature *corn chip* body aroma was often overpowered by his rank breath that assaulted our nostrils, it actually endeared him to all who loved him. Huxley frequently yawned, emitting the most noxious odor inches from his human snuggler's face. Rod and I had selectively dulled our sensitivity to the aroma over years of living with dachshunds. We always took pity on friends and family members who held him for the first time. The experience was a hair curling, stomach churning, keeling over experience. There is no odor in the world that can describe it. In her adorable animal memoir, *House of a Million Pets*, author Ann Hodgman describes dachshund breath as smelling like a thousand dead lobsters. This breed characteristic requires a certain degree of olfactory endurance from dachshund lovers. Thankfully, Huxley's owners and admirers were able to pinch their noses and sniff past the putrid bouquet to snuggle the lovable creature.

For the last several months of Huxley's life, his physical health was a paradox. By day he exuded tail wagging energy, participated in a daily walk on mild temperature days, and polished off meals with enthusiasm. His handsome black and tan facial features had faded to gray and gaunt, but his eager interest in life suggested he still felt youthful. Yet, in the middle of the night, his labored breathing woke Rod and me from our own deep slumber. Wheezy inhalations suggested that he could not get enough air into his body. When the raspy gasps subsided, the silence startled me wide awake again, wondering if he had expired between the sheets.

144

Our veterinarian detected a heart murmur. After some discussion, she was not convinced that medication would be in Huxley's best interest quite yet. We agreed. For months we adjusted to the new normal. His energetic days alleviated worry during the oxygen deprived nights. Then one Sunday morning in the middle of January, Huxley did not recover his full respiratory function. Throughout the day, he wheezed and coughed. His ribs heaved visibly with every effort to breathe. All day long we watched him closely and wondered if we should whisk him off to the vet. Aside from labored breathing, he managed quite well. He ate breakfast and tended to business outdoors by way of the dog door. My greatest fear was having to leave him at the vet clinic for observation overnight and full assessment on Monday morning. I couldn't accept the thought of him alone in the clinic.

By the afternoon he had lost his appetite and spent all of his time curled up quietly on his cozy dog bed in the kitchen. I stayed close, petted him and kissed him as much as I could. Several times I interrupted barn chores to return to the house to check on him. Finding him resting comfortably led me to believe I could wait until Monday morning to take Huxley to the vet. In the end it was not meant to be.

In the early evening, I settled at the computer to write. Huxley lay under a blanket in his dog bed at my feet. I kept peeking under the blanket to gaze into his loyal brown eyes. Just before nine o'clock, I was startled by the sound of a sharp *yip* at my feet. With one swift reflex, I pulled the dog bed out from under my desk. Peeling back the blanket revealed Huxley gasping involuntarily. Then silence. His eyes stared lifelessly out from under the blanket. He was gone.

"Rod," I yelped. "Huxley is gone, he just died!"

"What?"

"He is dead!" I sobbed. I picked up the dog bed with Huxley in it and held him close to me. Uncontrollable tears shook me as I whimpered "I love you" under his silky black ears. My words were too late. He was clearly gone.

Years of medication combined with a bacteria overload from chronic gingivitis had probably taken their toll on Huxley's heart. Had we taken him to the vet on Sunday afternoon, the outcome would have been the same. However, euthanasia might have saved him several hours of discomfort. I am not a fan of allowing dogs to die on their own. The responsibility of choosing the time to end their lives is one I take seriously. If I had been encouraged to leave Huxley overnight at the vet's office and he had died alone in the kennel, the guilt would have overwhelmed me. Although I knew he was seriously ill on Sunday afternoon, he did not appear to be in agonizing pain. No doubt his labored breathing was uncomfortable but he seemed content to lie quietly beneath his blanket. He knew I was within inches of him. In the end I try to take comfort in these small details.

Life is precious and, in a way, death is precious too. Inevitably it arrives for each living creature. How we choose to accept it when it calls upon our loved ones can be a deeply moving experience. Living with so many animals has taught me to let them go so that I may continue on a path much longer than the one designated for each of them. Their relatively shorter lives remind me to appreciate each one of my own birthdays. I do not fear getting older. So many humans are denied the privilege. Animals have also taught me to revere quality of life. Longevity is a cruel fate for the critically infirmed. Perhaps a time will come when we can make the same decisions for ourselves that we make for our pets. It is a complicated topic of conversation that makes lawyers and medical ethicists squirm. But are there fates worse than death?

I have found secure footing in conversations with my animal loving cohorts who provide comforting thoughts on this subject. Some may argue that animal lovers who have owned lots of pets and or livestock are indifferent to death. After all, dairy farmers expect to lose a small percentage of their calves because they produce so many. All goatherds can tell endless heartbreaking tales of decimation of their herds from predators, injury and disease. There isn't a horseman alive who hasn't been touched in some way by the devastating decision to euthanize a horse suffering from colic. And dogs just can't live forever. Eventually the time comes when quality of life must be analyzed and difficult decisions made. Thankfully, we can do this for our pets.

What we animal caregivers have in common is that our number of experiences enable us a glimpse into the future beyond our loss. We expect a calm to fall upon the life that still remains all around us after an individual has passed away. The peace encourages us to assimilate our thoughts and process our grief so we can heal. Each experience hard wires our ability to cope and move on. Caring for living and dying animals has taught me this.

Huxley deserved euthanasia, a choice I failed to make for him. In accepting my failure, I must do better for all of the animals who succeed him under my care. Perhaps that lesson is more important than any other he taught me. Like a good student, I want him to know that I have learned it. When *Gilda Radner* exclaimed, *"I think dogs are the most amazing creatures. They give unconditional love. For me they are the role model for being alive,"* I could not agree more. Dogs are the ultimate teachers. They love us no matter what; when their physical time on earth is over, we are left with the choice to honor them and live life by their example. If we live up to being half of the good soul our dogs believe we are, then our time on earth has been well spent.

Below; Huxley with Nina and Niles. 2004. photo by D. Geisdorf

Huxley was a loving little spirit who never failed to lift mine.

Horses Make a Landscape More Beautiful

Donkeys...Who Knew?

"If having a soul means being able to feel love and loyalty and gratitude, then animals are better off than a lot of humans." -James Herriot

The view is spectacular from upstairs in Rod's office. Sitting at his desk on a cushy leather swivel chair, I stare out the window. The sweeping view includes the length of the barn and a one acre fenced in field. Our young donkey Frankie is dutifully leading our over thirty-year old gelding Sandi around in the field. Another donkey, Bing, is watching them from a sunspot where he is resisting the urge to doze. From my birds eye view, I can see Bing's long ears resting at obtuse angles from each side of his bobbing head. Meanwhile, Frankie and Sandi continue to explore the receding snowpack that is quickly evaporating under an early spring blue sky. Despite the fact that the arrival of pesky bugs is months from now, Sandi is wearing a fly mask. The mesh fabric protects his remaining eye, plagued by glaucoma, from irritating sunlight. Sandi depends on the donkey to steer him away from trees that pose undignified hazards for the elderly blind gelding. Sandi appointed Frankie as his seeing eyes by hovering close and following his every move. Frankie accepted his role graciously, allowing the bay gelding to follow at his flank. It is enlightening to watch Sandi adapt by employing Frankie's youthful eyesight to guide him so he can exercise and tend to his horsey needs.

Once again I am privileged to witness the unique characteristics that define my animals' personalities. I am listening and making mental notes that will serve me well in my own times of adversity. For this teachable moment I thank Sandi. When the telephone rings, I startle out of my thoughts. After one more ring my focus is fully detached from the glorious view out the window.

"Hello."

"Is this Anne?" a voice inquires.

"Yes, it is."

"Hi, I am going to put you on hold for a minute. You will be able to hear the radio live when I do. Have you ever been on the radio before?"

"Yes," I affirm. "Thank you."

For the next minute or so I am vaguely aware of the *Car King* bellowing about low prices at its downtown Cleveland, Ohio, location. Next, a sultry female voice beckons, insisting that there is still time to get into shape before bikini season. It's hard to maintain my focus that pulls like a powerful magnet toward Sandi, the donkeys and the receding snow. Bikinis don't even make a blip on my radar.

"Good morning, Anne Phinney!" a booming female voice pipes into the phone.

"Good morning." I reply instinctively.

"My guest, Anne Phinney, is the author of a book called *Finding My Way to Moose River Farm.* She and her husband live in the Adirondacks with eleven horses, four dogs, three goats, two donkeys, a pot belly pig and an iguana. So nice to have you with us this morning."

"Great to be here." I am trying to remember not to use up precious time with unnecessary banter. This opportunity promotes the book, not my good manners. It is the first thing that authors learn about the media. Limit filler words and repeat the name of the book often.

"What is life like on Moose River Farm?"

The interview begins.

Life on Moose River Farm is heavenly. My husband, Rod and I have lived here for thirteen years. The milestone is hard to fathom. In those years we have said hello and goodbye to a menagerie of family members. With the passing of each one, I am left with a sense of awe after all the lessons they taught me. Every day that passes makes it more clear to me what a privilege it is to live this life with animals. It also confirms that I am living the life meant to be mine.

"What has living with animals taught you over the last fifty years?"

"Wow, there is so much; where do I begin? Every day they show me how to live a simple life. In their presence I am content. Their shapes, sizes, vocalities, behaviors, interactions with me and with each other soothe my spirit and my soul. Caring for them is a purpose I appreciate and require, like oxygen, to thrive. Sharing them with others, particularly children who are pleasantly surprised by all of these fringe benefits, brings perhaps the greatest joy. When I am away from home, I wonder about the horses, imagine what the goats are up to and long to have my arms around my donkeys. In the house, there are always dogs at my feet. I also have to watch where I step to avoid mishaps with our iguana. Although there are moments of painful decision making and loss, I am always left with a sense of peace. The animals taught me this acceptance."

"Which one is your favorite?"

"Although they are not children, they are all special members of my family. I would be missing the point of all the lessons learned if I felt favoritism."

When the interview ends, I am given one more opportunity to share the book title and my blog information. A gracious thank you is followed by a hurried click.

For a moment, I sit back in the chair and allow my attention to shift back to the field. Sandi has chosen a dry spot to lie down for a nap. The donks stand close. Bing is nibbling on Sandi's withers. Although he is being gentle, it is enough to prevent the horse from falling asleep. Sandi swings his head in annoyance as if a fly is pestering him in a spot he can't reach above his shoulders. Finally, the donkey stops and chooses to hang his head quietly over Sandi's neck. The bright sun, the faithful long eared companions and the slumber of their elderly charge make me aware that I need not control every situation in the barn. I am responsible for safety, cleanliness and nourishment. The rest is up to forces greater than me. In this case a sequence of events took place that resulted in the arrival of two baby donkeys who placated Sandi's nerves and stole my heart.

"Reba!" I sighed dramatically.

"Aww! Reba!" came the reply followed by a chorus of sympathetic giggles from friends who were with me. They continued to chant, "She was so sweet! We want Reba!"

The little donkey mare had made a lasting impression on me when she pushed her way past two smaller baby donkeys to fill the space provided by my open arms. When she pressed against my chest and dropped her head over my shoulder, I had no choice but to wrap my arms around her. What a love! I have no doubt that she was desperate to show me that, despite being over a year old, she was a better specimen than the two tiny babies competing for my affection. Her gesture won me over.

Unfortunately, the logistics of getting this donkey to the Adirondacks from *Equine Affaire*, a horse expo in West Springfield, Massachusetts, were going to be next to impossible. Therefore, I was forced to peel myself away from our embrace and leave her with her two tiny companions.

What I couldn't leave behind was my piqued interest in acquiring donkeys. Perhaps there was a donkey in need somewhere who could find his or her way to Moose River Farm. Keep in mind I was not alone in this desire. I had accomplices. With me at the horse expo were two children, Haley and Alex, along with two mothers, Vicky and Robyn. All of them were frequent riders and caregivers at my barn. Therefore, I felt pressure.

"Let's get a donkey!"

"It would be so cute in the barn."

"We need a donkey!"

"I want a little baby donkey!"

"Reba! We want Reba," they chorused.

For the next several weeks, we joked and talked about baby donkeys constantly. Frequently I received emails from these friends with pictures of donkeys doing the cutest donkey things, like smiling, pouting, playing with a tire or sleeping with a chicken on top of his back. I also began casually to mention to my horse friends, connected in the industry, that perhaps I might be interested in a donkey if one became available. That is all it took.

"Two donkeys available," read the broken text message from my friend Missy. After an exchange of pictures and information, it turned out that two donkeys, surplus babies from a petting zoo in New Jersey, were in need of a home.

Three weeks later, after making the necessary arrangements, Missy was on her way to visit me with two long eared passengers in her horse trailer. Another friend, Mary Anne, had come along, not wanting to miss out on an adventure that would unite me with two adorable baby donkey stallions called jacks. They arrived in early December. Although snow was late that winter, the days were cold and blustery, followed by nights with temperatures that dropped into the single digits. I worried that the two babies would be in for physical shock to their systems. It was after eleven o'clock when they arrived on a Friday night. Missy backed the trailer up to our indoor ring entrance so we could create a chute to minimize the chance of donkeys escaping and running off in the night.

Once Missy had opened the top doors on the trailer, I could see two sets of long ears swiveling for information in this unfamiliar place. I wondered what the poor babies were thinking. When the ramp was lowered, the rest of their bodies were revealed. Soulful dark eyes, heart stamped muzzles, grey dun colored coats with *cross* markings down the spine, and of course those glorious elongated ears assembled into two whole donkeys, *my* donkeys. Although they were only five and seven months old, they were not tiny by any means. One was taller than the other, and both still had foal characteristics expressed in their fuzzy baby fur. I had already selected their names. As we ushered them off of the trailer and pushed them into their stall, I announced that the smaller one was *Bing* and the other was *Frankie*.

"How did you come up with those names?" Missy asked.

"Bing Crosby and Frank Sinatra, of course. Since it is Christmas time, I wanted names that reflect the season but not too much.

Nothing worse than looking at somebody's Christmas decorations in June. Since I am looking forward to hearing my donkeys sing, I thought they should be named after singers. This time of year we hear a lot of songs by Bing and Frank."

"Oh, I get it, I like that idea," Missy affirmed.

Immediately I felt a connection with the farm's fuzziest new residents. From the moment they stepped off the trailer, Bing and Frankie appeared to have one mission; stand as close to humans as is physically possible. The donkeys must have sensed that this was a good strategy for getting noticed. I obliged by squeezing both arms around their necks and bellies. Although their facial expressions remained reserved, their actions demonstrated a deep trust in human companions. It also proved to me that donkeys are the most affectionate animals in my barn.

The addition of our two baby donkeys, Bing and Frankie, provided a welcome distraction during their first winter. Their long eared presence around the barn was one more reason to smile through chores despite January's bitter cold dips in temperature. The donks provided hysterical entertainment when galloping at full throttle around the paddock with their necks stretched out and their heads comically twisted. They entertained many visitors and their cuddly dispositions endeared them to me. Perhaps the biggest surprise was the contrast they displayed in comparison to my horses.

For over forty years, I have observed horses either deliberately or indirectly while working with them. I can read a horse's intentions fluently and am able to decipher the difference between a lack of confidence and a lack of manners. Of course for each horse I must respond appropriately, without overreacting so that the horse continues to respect me as the leader of our herd.

However, donkey behavior has evolved quite differently despite the fact that, like horses, donkeys are prey animals also. Yet donkeys are more laid back than horses. They will take as long as they need to weigh the pros and cons of complying with my training requests. Their final decisions are based on their need to assess the likelihood of survival if they follow my directions.

Many of the donkeys' behaviors are similar to those of our pig Fiona, who always questions how she will benefit from what I want her to do. With big dewy brown eyes, the donkeys silently weigh the terms of my training. Teaching them to lead with a halter and lead rope was one example. They had never felt pulling pressure around their heads before. Therefore, they couldn't connect this pressure with something they *should* want to do. For a long time they were not convinced that following me was a good idea, even after I emptied my pockets of the apple treats I was using to negotiate the terms of training. Before I knew it, "whoosh," I rushed to the tackroom to retrieve more treats! The tasty morsels of our agreement acted as currency. After several more months of this routine, it was unclear as to who was training whom.

Learning about donkeys has required that I spend hours with them, observing their behavior. It does not surprise me that so much of what they do aligns with the behaviors of children in my classroom. Donkeys strive to please. It is not uncommon for them to abandon a pile of delicious hay to stand as close to me as possible. It reminds me of the child who saves an empty chair next to her in hopes that the teacher will sit there while reading a book out loud. It is a deliberate choice of action that signals the donkey's or child's wish for the human or teacher to be close during activity. (School children have done it since the invention of education.) Donkeys do it when they bond with their caregiver.

All young creatures, human and animal, need to play. In fact when Bing and Frankie are galloping around in the driveway, tagging each other with playful nips and bites, I am reminded of the children on our school playground during their afternoon recess. In both instances, these lively beings play exuberantly, burning off energy while developing strength and coordination. We have also come to realize that students learn through play. Play is not a luxury; it is a necessity.

At the beginning of the donkeys' first summer on the farm, it was necessary to geld or neuter Frankie. Although I hoped to wait until the donkeys were the recommended age of eighteen months, Frankie was already engaging in aggressive behavior with Bing. All day long he harassed the smaller donkey by biting his neck and mounting his back end. Poor Bing tried to run away, but the larger donkey held on tight, resulting in a *piggyback* ride of sorts. The two donkeys provided some detailed sex education for children as they arrived for their riding lessons. For the sake of Bing and impressionable minds, I made the arrangements for Dr. Jen to come and remove the offending glands that were driving Frankie crazy.

The vet performed surgery in a clean grassy patch on the lawn in front of the barn. Dr. Jen sat on the ground between Frankie's hind legs that were tied spread eagle with ropes. An assistant kept tabs on the depth of Frankie's slumber, making certain drugs were easily available so the donkey remained comfortably anesthetized for the entire operation. Donkey castrations require more suturing compared because of increased blood flow. It takes longer to tie off all the severed vessels and prevent leaking. When Dr. Jen was satisfied with her job, Frankie was brought out of anesthesia. Within ten minutes, he was on his feet, completely unfazed by the ordeal. Testes weren't the only thing that Frankie lost that day for it wasn't long after the surgery that Frankie settled down and returned to Bing as an amiable companion, all of his aggressive behavior completely eliminated.

The young donkeys' days were full of all kinds of adventures undertaken between long intervals of browsing. Bing and Frankie initially roamed our property freely, choosing where they wished to be. Their day began before seven o'clock after a breakfast of two small horse treats. The first order of business after exiting their stall was to roll in the dusty sand driveway. Donkeys tend to this task with much more exuberance than horses do. They roll over and over, back and forth, preferring to do so in each other's body print left behind in the dirt. It's not uncommon for them to pee in the same spot as well, much like two male dogs trying to have the last territorial *word* before moving off to begin a different activity.

For two years Bing and Frankie never roamed far from the barn. During the summer they frequently sought shelter within the cool interior of the goat stall. By midafternoon, quite a group had assembled there, including the three goats, all seeking refuge from the sweltering heat and annoying bugs. A whirring box fan provided background noise while the little herd waited for evening to descend, bringing relief from the stifling air. In late afternoon, Frankie and Bing always returned to their own stall for horse treats, a belly filling pile of hay and some much needed rest.

The donks kept themselves well hydrated throughout the day by plunging muzzles into the nearest automatic water troughs. Like kids at a drinking fountain, they took turns slurping deeply. Occasionally, they squeezed both of their mouths into the bowl at the same time, draining all the water before the mechanism had a chance to refill. Although the donkeys still wrestled and bit each other during periods of play, I never thought that their antics were mean spirited as they had been before Frankie was gelded. A year later, Bing was also gelded. Both donks have mellowed into sweet and loving animals who are a joy to spend time with. One of my greatest pleasures is to take them for long walks in the woods. Although Frankie drags behind, ambling at a snail's pace, Bing remains close to me, much like an obedient dog heeling by his master's side. I believe that my company is just as desirable to him as his is to me. There is no greater expression of loyalty than a donkey pressing his body against you while you try to perform chores, such as mucking stalls or filling water buckets. It is their not so subtle attempt to remind me to live in the moment, basking in our mutual devotion to each other and sharing a treat if there happens to be a piece of carrot in my pocket. In these moments, I can't help but abandon my task and join Bing for some quality time together. With my arms around his neck and my nose buried at the base of his lengthy ears, I reflect on *George Eliot's* claim that *"Animals are such agreeable friends—they ask no questions, they pass no criticisms."*

Bing and Frankie arrived at MRF in December, 2012. They were only 5 and 7 months old.

Sandeman's Port

"Horses change lives. They give our young people confidence and self-esteem. They provide peace and tranquility to troubled souls, they give us hope." -Toni Robinson

"That horse was so smart, I swear he had a PhD," proclaimed my friend, Lisa, an assistant professor in the SUNY Morrisville State College Equine Studies program. She was referring to one of the college's school horses who had just been put down due to old age.

Sandeman's Port was also such a school horse. Anybody could ride him. He was trained with push button accuracy to haul novices around the ring. A rider could fall asleep at the reins and Sandi would continue unfazed with the instruction, never putting the rider in jeopardy.

The handsome bay gelding was about twenty years old when he arrived at Moose River Farm. Only fifteen hands, (small for a Trakhener gelding), Sandi was built square with a sound limb and hoof at each corner. Riders experienced a balanced and comfortable ride astride his back because of his solid athletic physique as well as his cooperative personality. His three gears, (walk, trot and canter) maintained a constant speed with the least amount of contact between the reins and the rider's leg.

For many youngsters, the sturdy gelding was the first horse they not only encountered up close but also rode. He was the one with whom they learned to groom, pick feet and tack up for the first time. Sandi graciously sported one of the highly coveted bright neon pink saddle pads without protest. He was cherished by all of us and basked in our devotion to him. Children always wanted to hear the story about the surgical removal of Sandi's right eye that had been ravaged by Uveitis and Glaucoma.

As a riding instructor, I view my school horses as my co-teachers. They take over the instructional gaps that I just can't fill with words or reassurance. Sandi and I taught together like an old married couple who still felt deep respect for each other. I knew exactly what he was thinking; it was as if he had memorized the objectives for each lesson. We both confidently pushed our student to achieve success. Young equestrians are sometimes overwhelmed by so many instructions to follow at once, but Sandi kept their stress at a minimum.

During breaks in the lesson, Sandi often strolled over to me and stopped. I reacted by wrapping my arms around his neck and rubbing his face with my hands. In these intimate moments, I wanted the rider to see that Sandi was not a machine, but a living, breathing being who sought out pleasurable interactions with people. After a minute or so, I "shooed" him back to work under the rider's newly acquired steering skills.

Sandi remained a sturdy fixture in my riding program for nine summers. The removal of his right eye in 2008 did not impair his ability to teach at all. In 2010 the bay gelding fell ill to a kidney infection. Such maladies are rare in horses. The only probable cause may have been his body's adverse immune response to a routine vaccine administered two weeks prior to his symptoms. Thankfully, he fully recovered. After six months of convalescence, he returned to his lesson duties in renewed health. However, age was beginning to catch up with him. Sandi's canter had degraded to that of a *tranter*; hind legs trot while the front legs canter. We limited his lessons and took special care to make certain he rested several days a week. We also made an effort to take him for rides in the woods on long reins where he could enjoy the woods, fields, and river. All of these adjustments enabled Sandi to continue teaching through the summer of 2013.

Sadly, this most amicable horse in the herd became aggressive toward other horses who ventured into his space. Sandi's reactions included lunging full force with ears pinned against his head, mouth agape and teeth bared. The maneuver shocked those of us who knew the gelding as nothing but a gentle soul. However, his reactions were understandable as Sandi clung to the remaining vestiges of his dignity. I was forced to change the turnout routine so Sandi could eat in peace. Thereafter, he was allowed to spend summer days grazing freely around the property by himself without competition from other horses that might cause stress.

Sandi was mostly content with this arrangement except that it isolated him from a herd. His pitiful high-pitched whinnies were proof that horses are happiest when they belong to a group, feeling more secure no matter how low on the pecking order they rank. But Sandi's negative behavior risked injury to other horses as well as to himself.

Meanwhile, our donkeys Bing and Frankie had been forced to accept significant change in their own lives at the farm. For more than a year, they had been allowed to roam freely around the barn, in the same manner as the goats. One crisp evening, shortly before Halloween, the donkeys decided to venture into *Adirondack Woodcraft Camp,* our next door neighbor. On horseback and under falling darkness, I searched for them. Now and then I spotted teasing glimpses of long eared silhouettes galloping through the trees. They had no intention of being captured. Eventually, I located the runaways grazing along a cross country ski trail about a mile from home. Forced by complete darkness to return the horse I was riding to the barn, I accepted my neighbor Mary Gerhardt's offer to join the roundup with her car. While Bing reluctantly allowed me to lead him home, Frankie followed along in Mary's illuminated path. Forced to examine the situation, I made a sad revelation. No longer could Bing and Frankie be permitted to roam freely. With their maturity had come the confidence to explore farther and farther from the barn. Fearing for their safety, (not to mention that of my neighbors'), I felt it necessary to secure them in a paddock during turnout hours. Only on supervised walks were they granted freedom.

Fortunately, Sandi's and the donkeys' situations collided, thus creating an acceptable solution to both dilemmas. Over the next several days, Bing, Frankie and Sandi spent supervised time turned out in a paddock together. Almost immediately, the horse asserted himself as the leader. The donkeys granted him the honor. By the middle of winter, we began to notice that the donkeys seemed to understand Sandi's visual impairment. It appeared that they waited for him to catch up when they decided to move to a different area of the paddock. I truly believe they realized their significance in keeping stress levels low for Sandi. A whole cycle of seasons warmed and cooled the Adirondacks as the herd of three traversed their turnout space together. They looked after each other, shared hay and shared companionship. No matter how perfect the relationship was, however, nothing could protect Sandi from the wrath of advanced age.

Compromised (but not limited) by the surgical removal of his right eye years ago, it was only a matter of time until Sandi's other eye succumbed to Uveitis, (periodic ophthalmia). Although medication slowed the process, by the summer of 2014 it became evident that the battle was being lost. We celebrated Sandi's formal retirement at the Moose River Farm riding recital in July. Many of his former students were present that evening to wish him well. The crowd listened reflectively as we announced the handsome bay's accolades. Sandi entered a carefree phase of life at age thirty with Bing and Frankie at his side.

However, significant change took place over the next year. It had been months since I was able to wrap my arms around Sandi's neck and hold him close to me. His twitching ears against my lips evoked emotions I hadn't felt for him in months, perhaps even a year. In fact lately I had been counting the days until his euthanasia because it was becoming increasingly more difficult to keep him calm. The sedative that Dr. Jennifer Nightingale administered moments ago was working quickly. In my arms I revisited the Sandi who, up until two years ago, had been my long term teaching partner. I was remembering the Sandi who had provided the first giant steps for budding equestrians embarking on a lifetime love of riding. I allowed these images to override more recent depressing memories of an agitated geriatric gelding who lived in a state of fear interrupted by periodic panic. This Sandi from the past was a sharp contrast to the Sandi under my care during this endless winter. For the last few months, he seemed to exist in a state of constant motion fraught with anxiety and an irrational fear of the unknown. Even the constant companionship of his two donkeys, Bing and Frankie, was not always enough to soothe his fears. And once anxiety was ignited, there was no way to calm him down. He circled the ring in a purposeful forward walk, sometimes even daring to trot. His brain tricked his legs into a state of urgency lest the imaginary predator might take him down. Who could blame him for being afraid? He lost weight despite a doubled grain ration. His hooves were worn down to stubby nubs.

Now with his head hanging in my arms, the feelings that I had for him rekindled and burned deep. Galloping in my soul, he was the fuel that kept my heart beating. Horses recharge my emotions and provide daily mental and physical exercise. They are at the center of who I am and who I was destined to become. Through the wisdom of middle age I accept the realization. If only Sandi and I could have remained suspended in the moment of my embrace a little longer, long enough to erase the last several months when caring for him had been difficult. It broke my heart that I could not soothe him. Frequently, I had to correct his lack of manners by snapping the lead rope while leading him; otherwise he would frantically plow into me with the full force of his shoulders. Inevitably while I cleaned his paddock, he careened into the wheelbarrow, fence or wall. It was pitiful.

Worse was the elevated state of fear that consumed him if his donkey companions delayed their arrival to and from the paddock. High-pitched screams of desperation rattled my wits every time. Within minutes the donkeys arrived at Sandi's location, but the gelding was already so worked up that even their presence wasn't able to alleviate the stress. Of course Sandi didn't want anything from me. No treats or soothing words could bring him back down to a level of calm.

As the sedative sank deeper into his neurological tissues, I held Sandi even tighter. Despite our disconnect this winter, I wanted him to know that I was right there. The human who had cared for him on a daily basis since his permanent arrival eight years ago was holding him in an effort to absorb the pain and make it my own while preparing for his final moments. In my mind I thought of all the other humans who had loved him, little girls in particular, who had looked beyond the missing right eye. They had sat confidently on his back, controlled him with ease. In those first moments, many of them had entered the *crazy for horses* stage that afflicts some girls of all ages.

"We're all set," whispered Dr. Nightingale.

The words brought me back to reality, the last minutes of Sandi's last day. She inserted a catheter into his jugular vein, securing it with a suture. Time to walk Sandi outside. My three friends, Irene, Vicky and Missy, followed the procession. Dr. Jen held Sandi's tail to stabilize him while I led him slowly down the centerline of the indoor arena. How many times had he obediently trotted that imaginary line, made a circle, then cantered along the rail? Once through the gate, we traversed into the gray snowy late March afternoon. Sandi's head hung to the ground as he trudged across the frozen terrain.

I like to think that a movie reel of Sandi's life was entertaining him while we ambled onward towards his final resting place. The giggles of all the little girls who groomed and fussed over him before tacking him up for a lesson. Jean's endless devotion to him as he provided safe and educational rides to build her adult confidence. Hopefully, he visited his freedom romps around the property on cool summer mornings before the bugs came out to torment the horses. During one of these liberty romps, Sandi leaped off of a steep hillside down into the sandpit at a full gallop. The only evidence was a collection of hoof prints that abruptly disappeared where Sandi took flight. I hoped that he was remembering his special relationship with our aged mare Makia. For quite some time after her arrival in 2011, Sandi was her paddock mate. She appeared to stir pre-gelding desire in him. It was evident in deep, lusty vocalizations that he sang to her each time she entered his view. I pitied the horse who stepped too close to the fence where Sandi flexed his vocal cords for his lovely Makia. An aggressive charge at the intruder indicated that he would not tolerate competition.

I wondered if he returned in memory to SUNY Morrisville where his teaching career helped transition riders from backyard dabblers to professional technicians in the equine studies program. And then there were the memories I was not privy to. Where Sandi had come from before Morrisville I was not sure, but somewhere he accumulated experience from the first decade of his existence. I hoped those memories were as comforting to him as the ones he had collected at Moose River Farm. Above all I prayed that he felt the love of so many that would be reflected the next day when an announcement of his death hit social media networks.

Along our way, Easau and Zambi trotted to the fence of their paddock when Sandi strolled by. They stood quietly although their necks were erect and their eyes bulged in an effort to collect information. As we approached the next paddock, Spirit and Tango mimicked the first two horses' behavior. Did they all sense Sandi's fate?

Eventually, we arrived at our destination, made obvious by the large hole that Rod had already prepared with the backhoe. Despite a couple of feet of snow that covered frozen earth, Rod was able to dig. Rod's ability to dig this grave was the only reason we did not have to prolong Sandi's euthanasia until late spring thaw. Truth was, I couldn't wait any longer. The anxiety I felt was as acute as Sandi's.

My three friends huddled close, observers to a scene they each have lived through. The knowledge of this embraced me. I wondered if Sandi was aware of similar messages from Zambi, Easau and the other horses standing at the fence. Perhaps the mixture of veterinary chemicals, somber energy, and Sandi's procession toward the idling backhoe infused the air with a smell of impending death that horses recognize.

Dr. Jen issued a few last minute instructions. She did not want the horse to fall directly into the hole, rather alongside where she could monitor his heart rate until it ceased. We adjusted his position for the perfect drop. My hands clung to him while I listened to sniffles among my friends.

"I love you Sandi," I sobbed into his ear then kissed his pumping muzzle.

"Ready?" Dr. Jen asked gently.

"Ready," I choked.

Once his winter blanket was removed, she inserted the syringe of heart stopping sodium pentobarbital into the catheter. I held on a few seconds longer. Then the practical side of my training and experience forced me to release Sandi so that I could step out of the way. For several seconds, he resisted gravitational forces on his bones. Then he buckled to the ground. I knelt on the snow and took up my vigil at his muzzle, kissing and whispering affirmations of love and gratitude for the honor of caring for him in my barn.

"He's gone now, Anne," Jen announced softly, moments later as she removed the stethoscope from her ears. Normal reflexive gasps jolted Sandi's, body but her words sank in. He was gone, he was gone.

The next morning, I spent the day in quiet reflection, caring for the horses, walking with Rod and the dogs and tending to the business of letting Sandi's fans and acquaintances know that he had been put down. On the counter in the tackroom, I found the three locks of Sandi's tail that Vicky and Missy had remembered to clip. My own hair was missing several strands that were now secure in Sandi's left ear.

I was surprised that the donkeys appeared to be feeling low. They remained close together in the indoor arena for most of the day. At dinner time they were not enthusiastic about following me back to their stall where an edible treat always rewarded them. I suppose that they were aware of change in their small herd. Perhaps they wondered where Sandi was and were dutifully waiting for him. Donkeys keep thoughts and feelings to themselves. It's hard to know what they are thinking. Compared to horses, they are genuinely more affectionate; preferring to stand in your way or up close, a request for your attention. In Bing and Frankie's hour of confusion, all I could do was offer extra comfort and affection while we all adjusted to a new normal without Sandi.

At the end of my horses' lives I am left to grieve a close family member. Sandi's loss left me feeling widowed. Our professional partnership had ended years ago when he retired from teaching lessons, but I still honored my vows to care for him until death do us part. In his rapidly declining health I forced myself to examine the inevitability of change. It's coming, like it or not. In death I find peace as long as there are no regrets. Sandi was cared for and provided for until the very end. It is the same honor I will bestow upon all of my human and animal loved ones. My animals have taught me to live a true and appreciative existence, accepting the fact that nothing lasts forever. When loss arrives, it is important to move forward without regret. Vulnerability to predators makes it mandatory that horses must proceed after the death of a herd mate. Although my four geldings stood with ears erect and eyes bulging when Sandi trudged by, they relaxed their posture once Sandi hit the ground. Horses absorb death of a herd mate with no regret. Death is final. Roles shift and new decisions keep the herd safe into the future.

Rod is the grave digger. He is unable to attend the actual moment between life and death. It is just too difficult for him. However, he provides an equally important task that I am unable to witness. With his backhoe he digs a custom sized hole in the ground. To date, I have never watched the process that lowers the carcass, now void of the spirit, into the gaping cavity. I have never watched the vacant shell disappear below the piles of earth that drop from the backhoe bucket. It is just too difficult for me. In our thirty plus years of marriage, Rod and I have grieved the loss of many animals including dogs, goats and horses. His devotion to this last ritual of death is a gift every time.

The hardwiring of human beings enables us to cope through the births and deaths of our loved ones. The arrival and departure of so many animals has tested my coping skills while offering profound moments of realization, reflection and perhaps wisdom. At midlife my own mortal journey is already a legacy of joys and sorrows accumulated, enriched and nourished by horses like Sandi. The lessons learned accentuate the creases at either side of my mouth and deepen those between my eyebrows. It is an honor to live with these special creatures from the moment they arrive at Moose River Farm until their inevitable passage from life. These lines from *Mary Oliver's* poem *In Blackwater Woods* capture the simplicity of what my beloved horses have taught me.

To live in this world

You must be able
To do three things:
To love what is mortal;
To hold it

Against your bones knowing
Your own life depends on it:
And, when the time comes to let it go,
To let it go

From "In Blackwater Woods" by Mary Oliver

Sandi was a steady mount for equestrians of all ages. He and I taught together like an old married couple. Donkeys Bing and Frankie became his companions, providing him with a sense of security during his last few years.

169

Lessons from Tango

Tell me and I forget. Teach me and I remember. Involve me and I learn. -Benjamin Franklin

"Who could possibly take Sandi's place?" The thought percolated in my brain as I surveyed my equine collection. Easau is too spooky. Spirit is too temperamental, Makia is too powerful and Joshua is too sensitive. None of them could possibly tolerate novice riders without assuring them that their first ride was the last.

As dear Sandi, our perfect twenty-eight year old school horse veteran, transitioned into full retirement, it became necessary to move other horses into the "beginner rider" ranks. This is a difficult niche to fill. The perfect beginner horse must be, above all, safe. Next, he must be able to read jaunty, incomplete messages sent from a rider who is struggling to coordinate her body with a horse's movement. The beginner horse must not take these inappropriate cues personally. He must forgive weighty kicks and unintentional yanks on the reins without displaying irritation. It is a lot to ask of our equine partners, but hard to avoid when inexperienced individuals begin the "learning to ride" process. Some horses, like Sandi, patiently accept the challenge while maintaining their dignity. Others make it perfectly clear that they will not. And then there are horses like Tango!

At just under fifteen hands, this compact paint gelding did not intimidate novice riders when they climbed aboard. But once a rider was in the saddle, Tango began to monitor weaknesses in the rider's education. If the reins were not long enough, he refused to go forward. If they were too long, he dropped his head to the ground for a nibble of grass on the perimeter of the ring. If the rider's leg was weak, Tango plodded along with little enthusiasm. If the rider's hands gave the slightest unintentional tug on the reins, the gelding screeched to a halt. He performed none of this disobedience with a sour attitude. In fact, Tango remained patient while waiting for the rider to ask a question that he clearly understood and could answer correctly.

Melinda, a ten year old student, leased Tango so that she could practice her riding more frequently. She enjoyed the challenge of riding the horse in addition to caring for him on the days that she came out to the barn. With great determination, Melinda rode Tango in the ring, working mostly on keeping him next to the rail and moving forward at the trot. Her progress was steady, but Tango frequently resorted to his antics if Melinda got tired or lost focus. Although she had learned to canter on steady Sandi, Melinda had yet to canter the more forward gait that Tango expressed.

The extended beautiful fall weather provided many opportunities to ride on the trail after working out in the ring. A trail ride is a good way for both horse and rider to relax in each other's company after matching wills in the ring. Usually, this phase of the ride occurs uneventfully. However, I always walk along on foot just in case...

"Whoa!" a small voice commanded behind me.

A sickening thought took hold as I turned my head in Melinda's direction. She was navigating Tango across the top of the great hill above our sandpit. Spying the green grass below and without Melinda's permission, Tango decided to abandon the trail and head down the hill for a snack. Of course the sooner he got there the sooner he could eat. Suddenly, he was in full gallop down the grassy slope that would ultimately lead him to the field. In horror I watched Melinda's hot pink T-shirt become smaller and smaller with each thundering stride down the steep hill.

My eyes remained riveted on each of Melinda's pink shoulders. Any second I expected one of them to begin veering left or right, thus precipitating a hard fall to the ground. With all my bipedal might I bolted down the hill after them.

Finally, Tango came to an abrupt halt, dropped his head and began cropping the grass at his feet. From the saddle, Melinda stared back at me.

"Melinda, hop off right now," I ordered through heaving breath.

"What?"

"Get off of him right now!" I ordered, fearful that Tango might begin a victory lap around the field after another mouthful of grass.

172

This time my urgency sank in. Once her feet hit the ground, I knew Melinda was safe.

After what seemed an eternity, I reached horse and rider at the farthest end of the field. "I am in total shock," I exclaimed holding Melinda tight in my arms. "Are you ok?" The words sounded hollow.

"Why did he do that?" she inquired evenly.

I answered the question with a couple of derogatory (nothing too shocking, mind you) expletives about Tango. Convinced that Melinda was fine, the three of us headed back to the barn. On the way we talked about what happened.

"At first I was really scared but then I just knew what to do. So I pushed my heels down and sat up straight. I never felt like I was going to fall off."

"You are one brave cowgirl," I exclaimed. "Nat, I would have been scared galloping down that hill, even with my heels down!"

A few days later, Melinda came back to the barn to ride Tango. Something had changed. She sported a new air of confidence as she prepared him for a workout in the ring.

"Can I canter him?" she asked, casually.

"Well,..I don't...I'm not sure...uh...ok," I responded unable to come up with an excuse not to canter Tango.

And canter they did! Round and round the ring, Tango was under Melinda's complete control. He did exactly what she asked, over and over again. Something had changed in Tango. I watched with a newfound respect for Tango as a teacher...a teacher who doesn't give the answers away, but lets the student discover the answer herself.

The incident down the hill reminded me that sometimes stepping out of our comfort box is just what we need to expand the area of that box. Students who remain at plateaus in their training, math strategies and reading comprehension, often require a dramatic sequence of events to finally break the trance and move forward. In the classroom, however, it is a little safer to promote an exit from one's comfort zone. Assigning brain teasers, interactive math projects and rigorous science experiments to students for extra points can motivate them to work harder. I will go out of my way to search for a novel that might pique the most reluctant reader's interest. If the student is unimpressed at the end of reading five pages, I will help her search for another until she finds one that is so engrossing it's impossible to put down. In the ring and in the classroom, we break learning plateaus by pushing students beyond the limits of what feels comfortable.

Although not consciously, Tango did this for Melinda. His decision to veer down the hill to an oasis of delicious forage forced Melinda to put all of her riding skills into play. Heels down, spine straight, shoulders back prevented her from parting company with Tango's back. In fact it proved to her that correct position was the major reason why she stayed on the horse all the way to the bottom of the hill. It proved to her that her skills were valuable and that she need not doubt her ability to ride, especially when an unexpected challenge arises.

Perhaps in some ways Tango turned out to be a better teacher than Sandi. At first his attitude matched that of the stereotypical schoolmarm from the last century. Without the lemon sucking expression, he taught like a rigid drill sergeant. Only one small patch of flesh on either side of his barrel understood leg commands. The reins only communicated when the rider achieved perfect contact. He offered nothing unless the rider was spot on with her aids. This rigor could be frustrating for novice riders. Communicating with a horse from the saddle requires a synchrony of so many physical nuances. The goal is a light touch here and a gentle squeeze there, but new riders have a hard time with that subtle control. Riders begin with gross motor responses. The timing of their aids or commands lacks polish. Tango, unlike Sandi, had little patience for accidental pinches and imbalances upon his back. He could only withstand so much. Flexibility was not his forte.

Thankfully, the consequences of miscommunication with Tango rarely resulted in a safety issue. Occasionally, he kicked out or threw a half-hearted buck, but only with riders who were requesting a more sophisticated maneuver, the canter for instance. Beginners mostly work at the walk and transitions into the trot. Eventually, Tango began to sort out differences between rank beginners and novices who required a challenge.

Isn't this how my own teaching experience evolved? Although I was certainly more enthusiastic than Tango about my role as a teacher, years passed before my toolbox filled with the confidence necessary to manage my students. Along the way, I collected many errors in judgement. Along the way, I learned flexibility and now know when and how to push my students beyond a comfortable plateau. Experience has paid off, resulting in my ability to address the individual's needs and expectations. At this point in my career I am thankful for the evolution.

As for Tango? *Jane Smiley* summed up his abilities when she said, *"In the end, we don't know what horses can do. We only know that when, over the past thousands of years, we have asked something more of them, at least some of them have readily supplied it."* Although this plucky paint did not choose his role as teacher, Tango eventually owned it and motivated his rider to use the skills that he taught her. Although I held my breath in horror as Melinda and Tango went galloping down the hill, I admit that the event elevated the rider into a higher level of ability from the experience. Like Tango, I became a teacher almost unwittingly; and like Tango, I grew into the role, combining formal training with experiences learned from my equine colleagues. Unlike Tango, I never would have jeopardized the safety of the rider so I could indulge my gastric desires. Yet, by doing so Tango broke a barrier that was inhibiting Melinda's riding progress. He forced her to engage all the skills she had been practicing in her lessons. The unexpected challenge pushed her to apply those skills under challenging circumstances. Perhaps this is what separates mediocre teaching from excellence: knowing when to present a surprising opportunity for a student to prove mastery of skills, to strut her stuff. There is no doubt that Melinda will never forget Tango's contribution to her education in the saddle.

*Tango's owner, Vicky felt confident about his trusty nature.
Tango was a strict teacher and never gave any answers away!
photo by M. deCamp*

Partly Cloudy

"It is the most difficult horses who have the most to give you." -
Lendon Grey

"He is going to kill somebody!"

Studying the black and white gelding, I was certain that the dealer
had not knowingly sold this couple a behavior problem. The dealer's
extensive horse experience and the couple's lack of training were in
conflict, exacerbating the handsome boy's bad behavior.

"Do you want me to work with him while he is at my barn this
winter?" I offered. "The least I can do is evaluate what he knows and
try to ride him consistently for a few months. Perhaps when you
return next spring, he will be more schooled."

After we put the details of the plan in place, the Paint along with
Buddy, his chestnut quarter horse companion, were loaded onto my
trailer and driven to Moose River Farm. They were going to live
under my care for a few months while the male owner spent his
winter in the sunny south. The two horses settled easily into the barn
routine, both perfect gentleman in terms of handling and stall
manners.

A week after their arrival, I began to ride the Paint. It didn't take
me long to assess that his issues resulted from a lack of positive
training. Due to his inexperience, he was what we call in the industry
a *green* horse. As a result of negative experiences, he had developed
defensive coping skills using unpleasant mechanisms to ward off
what he perceived as the *evils* of being ridden. The horse's
recalcitrance was not the fault of the owners or the dealer, but of the
unknown number of people who had handled the horse along the
way. It is a typical scenario that afflicts too many horses in the world
of uneducated trainers and owners. Countless equines are passed
along either for quick profit or to wash one's hands of a problem
horse. Over time, pedigree papers disappear. Unscrupulous trainers
take over; and when egos are bruised by the horse's blatant honesty,
the trainer gives up and passes the animal along to somebody else.
These horses are the juvenile delinquents of the horse industry, akin

to the most unlovable students in the classroom. They are difficult to reach, but actually require more social attention and stroking from the teacher. The difficulty is finding glimmers of goodness to lavish with praise.

I estimated the Paint to be about six years old, perhaps younger, perhaps older; there was no official documentation of his age. The only gauge that I could read was the inside of his mouth. The presence of canine teeth indicated that he had passed his fifth birthday. The presence of a hook or notch on the corner of his last upper incisor indicated that he was not quite eight years old. Therefore, I declared him a six year old. Easy to remember because that would make him the same age as Easau, one of my well documented thoroughbreds.

From the beginning, I felt that the Paint, in his heart of hearts, wanted to do the right thing. Unfortunately, he didn't seem to understand what that was or why it was an important feature in his relationships with humans. In other words, nobody had taught him what the expectations were. The school teacher in me began by setting achievable objectives for the horse. First, he had to understand what my legs were asking him to do when they bumped against his sides. I wasn't trying to be rude. I simply needed him to know that when I bumped him, he should move forward and when my leg was quiet he should maintain the current speed. Clear concise communication is mandatory between horse and human. With this one objective defined and in place, I began to apply it out on the trail.

One of the current owner's complaints was that the horse became terribly upset as he ventured farther away from the barn. The trail that they frequented was a five mile linear trek. Once they reached the end of it, they turned around and headed home. That was when big problems occurred. Unless the Paint was accompanied by his equine companion Buddy, he simply grabbed the bit in his teeth and galloped at full throttle back to the barn. This behavior is not only terrifying to the rider, it is also terribly dangerous. Riding safely requires that the rider maintain total control at all times. Anything less is a disaster waiting for opportunity. No wonder the owner feared the horse was going to kill somebody. He certainly could have.

It is fairly simple to take control of a horse; but unless the rider is skilled and knows how to think like a horse, the method will appear contradictory. With a new respect for the messages from my leg, the Paint was ready to be ridden farther away from the barn. Our trails meander around the property in large loops so that there isn't any place to turn around and head for home. That way the horse never knows when he is on his way back to the barn. He keeps his focus on the rider, the only herd member who can lead him home safely. Of course, eventually the horse recognizes various landmarks and is able to map the terrain himself, but by then he will have developed trust in the rider and will feel confident away from home.

Initially, the Paint screamed for Buddy who remained back at the barn. However, he understood that my consistent leg pressure and the occasional bumps meant keep going forward. He obliged. Occasionally, he made an attempt to bolt back to Buddy, but I was always ready to respond with my legs to thwart his efforts. I valued riding the challenges because each time he failed to get his way, my leadership status was more secure. Occasionally, he came to a complete halt, stretching his neck up to whinny. Then his whole body shuddered from tail to muzzle in an effort to be heard from far away. Instead of punishing him, I circled him around the pressure of my inside leg. It kept him moving forward, in front of my leg, as we say, breaking his focus on getting back to the barn. Progress on the trail continued. It wasn't long before he gave up challenging me and decided to just keep moving onward. Besides, I always led him home, unharmed, to the safety of his herd.

The more I worked with the Paint, the more I liked his energy. When channeled in a forward direction, the horse was enjoyable to ride. In the ring, he learned how to stay balanced so that I could benefit from the physical workout that riding without my stirrups provides. His trot was comfortable, a pleasure to come home to after a long day at school. With rules clearly in place, respect blossomed between the two of us. The Paint accepted riding as a social interaction that didn't involve pain or punishment when he felt confused.

Students in my classroom who suffer like the Paint just need me to be kind and consistent at first. Once they feel confident, they can let down their guard and focus on content and strategy. They can't focus when lack of coping skills have built a barrier that the teacher can't penetrate, no matter what disciplinary consequences she imposes.

To complement our rides, I also engaged the Paint in playful ground work. The cracking sound of a whip raised the energy level that motivated the big horse to cavort. I encouraged bucking, bolting, rolling and any other exuberant behavior. I never tire of watching a horse romp, twist and leap when turned out in a large area. It is a celebration of freedom. The experience is invigorating for both human and horse. My role is to apply pressure by cracking the whip, an action that maintains a therapeutic level of energy that ultimately produces a calm horse. I must mention that the whip never actually touches the horse. How can I expect my fifth grade students to focus on seat work if they don't have a few minutes of physical activity at recess every day? How could I expect anything different from horses?

Once his energy was spent, the Paint chose to abandon his antics and approach me. Seeking his companionship, I mirrored his confident stride and met him half way. We entered each other's personal space where I reached forward to rub his face. In addition, I praised him verbally. He was a good boy, not a monster, not a jerk, just a horse with extra energy who needed to have it channeled properly so that he could concentrate on pleasing his rider.

Next, he followed at my side while I traversed the ring. At this point, his level of energy decreased until his extended body posture from nose to tail signaled total relaxation. At the end of our ground sessions, the paint remained glued to my shoulder when I led him through the gate and out into the driveway. Even the lush green grass on the lawn was not enough of a temptation to break our bond. He remained by my side all the way to his stall.

"Good boy," I praised. He chomped a piece of carrot while my hands stroked his head and neck. Pressed against him, my cheek absorbed the heat from his grinding jowl. The effect was adhesive. I loved this horse. I completely understood who he was.

Winter was one of the mildest on record. We had no snow, unheard of in January. One particular Saturday dawned mildly sunny, reaching sixty degrees by mid-afternoon. It was a perfect day to ride outside. Anticipation motivated me to get the barn chores finished early so that I could spend all afternoon in the saddle. Just as I began tacking up my thoroughbred gelding Easau, the Paint's female owner arrived with the same idea. It had been several weeks since she had ridden him, so I was eager to show her the horse's progress.

I helped the owner get the Paint ready and held him at the mounting block while she climbed aboard. For a few minutes I lingered in the driveway while the owner reacquainted herself with the saddle and the horse underneath her. Satisfied that all was well, I returned to the barn quickly to put a bridle on Easau so that I could join the Paint and his owner.

Leading Easau out to the driveway, I saw that horse and rider were gone. Obviously, the owner planned to enjoy the beautiful day with her horse on her own. Quickly, I squelched my concern, reminding myself that he was her horse, and she had every right to ride him whenever she wished. After mounting Easau, I tried to put the Paint out of my mind so that I could concentrate on my own horse. He deserved my undivided attention while working hard to please me with his efforts. The contrast between the warm January day and Easau's heavy winter coat helped to maintain a low energy ride that was both enjoyable and relaxing.

Suddenly, a faint but piercing whinny penetrated my focus. Adrenaline pumped through Easau and me. I halted to listen. The next screaming whinny was slightly louder, catching the attention of all the other horses around the barn. An even louder scream prompted Buddy to whinny an urgent reply. By now the screaming was accompanied by pounding hooves. Within seconds, chaos was charging up the driveway in the form of a rider-less horse!

Immediately, I dismounted Easau before he could react to the charging steed careening toward the barn. Once the Paint had located other horses to assure him that he had not been abandoned by his herd, he dropped his head to graze on the sparse lawn. According to him, the crisis was over.

Immediately, I escorted Easau back to the barn and hastily removed his tack. Out of the barn I flew on foot in search of the Paint's owner. At the end of the driveway, I caught up with her hobbling stiffly toward the barn.

"Are you alright?" I inquired, relief spreading across my face when it sank in that she was on two feet.

"Yes, I am," she affirmed shakily.

"What happened?"

"Oh, he just seemed so upset out there. He bolted and I lost my balance. I'm alright, really."

"I wanted to go with you to make sure he remained calm. With another horse he would have felt secure," I exclaimed, failing to not sound angry.

I did not want to sound judgmental. After all he was her horse. As a professional, I wanted her to be a successful rider on her own horse. The next day, I stopped in to check on the Paint's owner at her office. Adrenaline is highly effective at masking initial pain after a fall. It can take a day or two before the jarring effects surface as aches and stiffness from neck to ankles. Since I didn't witness the fall, I wasn't sure how hard she had hit the ground.

"I'm fine," she claimed.

"I'm glad to hear that."

She seemed to want the conversation to end. Making light of the incident, she sent me on my way. Perhaps my concern was interpreted as disrespectful. As the proprietor of a riding stable, I am obligated by my conscience and my insurance company to keep everybody safe. It is a huge responsibility. Although this situation occurred between a horse and its owner, I still felt culpable for activity on my property.

Of course the warming trend ended as snow fell. The Paint and I took up our training once more. For the rest of the winter, I pondered the fate of this horse. Unless his owners were willing to join the training effort, the situation was doomed. The couple wanted an uncomplicated trail horse that they could ride all over their beautiful Adirondack property. Who could blame them? Buddy was such a horse, amicable, low energy and safe.

The classy Paint looked impressive under saddle. The only way to cure him of his green status was to ride him consistently and correctly for months on end. I began to wonder if I could find them a suitable replacement and make a trade for the Paint. That way all sides would win, particularly the black and white horse. I also wondered why I was falling in love with this horse.

My first phone call to the male owner of the Paint was met with a mixed reaction. Although he had abandoned the Adirondack winter for the warmth of Florida, it wouldn't be too long before riding weather lured him back to his stunning acreage up north.

"Why do you want him?" he inquired suspiciously. "I paid a lot of money for him; good looking horse but other than that he is a jerk."

"I like the horse a lot. He has potential to be a nice riding horse, but it will take time and consistency to get him there. I like riding him in the ring, challenging him with training and then walking him in the woods. You need another horse like Buddy, who will go forever in the woods at one speed. The Paint is not that kind of horse. He is much younger, with pent up energy that needs to be addressed before you ride him. Unless you are willing to put in the time to spend that energy, he will continue to frustrate you. I have students who train horses. He is a good match for them."

What I didn't say was that I had fallen in love with his horse and did not want to see him go. Since he had bonded with me in our groundwork, the thought of returning him to certain failure was unacceptable to me. This is why I have never been able to buy and sell horses for a living. The emotional cost is too high.

"I have to think about it. I paid a lot of money for him and I would have to consider that in any kind of a deal," he said.

"I understand," I replied trying with all my might not to sound desperate.

For the next several weeks, I waited anxiously for the phone call that would determine the fate of the Paint. These owners were good people, but the thought of the horse returning to disappoint them consumed me with worry. In the meantime, I began to spread the word that I was looking for a safe trail horse. It didn't take long for prospects to fill my email inbox and voicemail. Once again, my dear friend Michele came through with the perfect horse.

"My sister-in-law has a fifteen year old gray quarter horse gelding that she is ready to sell. Scout is safe and sweet and he is always the same whether you ride him every day or once a year. The problem is she thinks he is too good of a horse to hang around in the pasture without a job to do. Her kids used to ride him, but they have all grown up and are living away from home."

Now that I had the perfect prospect, I gathered up my courage to call the Paint's owner and rekindle our conversation about a trade. It had been quite some time since I had made the offer to swap, and I had yet to hear back from the owner. Perhaps he had seriously been considering the idea or perhaps he had not. Reluctantly, I dialed the long distance telephone number. Was I prepared to lose the Paint if the offer was refused?

"Not sure what you have decided about my offer to trade for your horse, but I wanted to let you know that I found a suitable replacement if you are still considering it," I blurted out, trying to keep my end of the line unemotional. After that introduction, I continued to deliver all the information that I knew about the gray gelding. I placed my emphasis on the fact that I knew the owners and knew that they just wanted a good home for their horse. They were not dealers cashing in on a horse they had only known for a short time. If they said the horse was a fantastic trail horse, I believed them. Praying that the Paint's owner believed them too, I held my breath for the definitive reply.

"Well, I don't know," he replied.

I waited for him to continue.

"I paid quite a bit of money for that horse, and I don't want something worth less."

My mind raced desperately to assemble the words that would convince the owner.

"I completely respect your concern. After working with your horse all winter, I have come to the conclusion that he is still rather green. If you were interested in continuing his training consistently, that would be one thing. But you have indicated to me that you want a safe horse to trail ride when time permits in a busy schedule. Between these two horses, the gray gelding is that horse."

In the end, to the owner's delight, Scout proved to be exactly what we were told, a steady mount with unflappable temperament, a perfect gentleman on the trail and an amiable companion for sweet Buddy.

As for the Paint? In the weeks following the owner's decision to trade, I hugged the horse's neck in triumph at every opportunity. I even christened him with two new names that I felt fit his blossoming personality. I named him Partly Cloudy, for his stunning black and white coat pattern with silver dapples under his tail. Since Partly Cloudy is a mouthful, I call him Joshua around the barn.

A decade of learning from Joshua has transpired since his arrival. He is the only horse I own who did not come with a paper pedigree. I have no interest in maintaining well bred horses, but their papers do provide a vague roadmap through their past. At the very least, papers provide a birthdate, breed and location of origin. Joshua's only sign of past ownership is a cross shaped brand on his right flank. I have tried to research the logo on the internet with no luck. His teeth are the only feature that suggests his age and even that is a ballpark figure. I often wonder about his life before he found me. Who trained him and for what purpose? Did he fail in the eyes of this trainer? Did he dash somebody's hopes for competitive glory in the show ring only to be sent away to an uncertain future?

Training Joshua was challenging. He had to train me as well. Traditional rote methods of practice were not enough to produce desired results. Initially, my educated hands and legs spoke to him in a foreign language he did not comprehend. Turning up the volume on my training aids did not help him understand. From behind his ears, I could not read his expression. I had to come down from the saddle and work with him on the ground where I could assess progress by looking at his whole body, particularly his eyes and ears, a horse's most expressive features. As a result, Joshua is at the core of my equine assisted learning program, *Equi-Reflection,* a method of communication with horses that teaches people to speak in body language. The benefits of these *on-foot* sessions with horses goes a long way in connecting horse and rider in a respectful conversation that continues from the saddle. How can two living things form a relationship any other way?

In the classroom it is imperative that I look into my students' eyes whether I am instructing them, inquiring about their weekend, or disciplining a poor choice of behavior. Along with my physical posture, eye contact strengthens our relationship because my expression, words and posture make the situation perfectly clear. The student will know exactly what is expected of him. This alleviates any wishy-washiness, preventing the student from misunderstanding an expected task.

Joshua arrived at Moose River Farm with a chip on his shoulder. His defensive mechanisms had been misinterpreted, giving him a reputation as a wild, untamable temperament like a misunderstood student with a bad reputation. Time and patience enabled the Paint to evolve into a solid equine citizen. Consistent training unlocked his full potential to be a perfect mixture of challenging lesson horse and quiet trail horse. Human perseverance produced an all-around easy going loveable steed. The lessons Joshua taught me are just one more piece of evidence that animals possess strong abilities to guide us toward a better understanding of learning. What *James Baldwin* said about children can also be applied to horses like Joshua. *"A child cannot be taught by somebody who despises him and a child cannot afford to be fooled."*

Joshua required patience and understanding before he could learn the finer points of being ridden. top photo by M. deCamp.

Supreme's Golden Spirit
"Don't judge a book by its cover." -George Eliot

"You have to see this video of a horse I really wanted to buy. Thankfully, he was sold because I really don't need another horse right now. Isn't he pretty?"

"Oh my, he *is* pretty. Why didn't you buy him?"

This was the introduction to a conversation I shared with many friends during the summer of 2009. Every time I played the *Youtube* video recorded by the horse's owner, I was even more disappointed that I had sat on the fence for so long, unable to make up my mind. My hesitation had more to do with announcing to Rod that another horse might be on his way to Moose River Farm. For a period of six years, horses were moving into the barn at an accelerated rate compared to the number who were passing away. And each additional hay-burning, feed-consuming, vet-billing, foot-trimming recipient that came along put additional stress on farm maintenance, not to mention finances. I always carefully consider these components before I fill Rod in on the details of my latest purchase.

Rarely has this announcement been received with a blessing. Rod views every addition to our family as more physical maintenance of our facility. It also gives him more to take care of when I am out of town, a situation that does come up several times a year. In the end, however, after he has spoken his mind and the new horse arrives despite his objections, life settles back into the rhythm that defines peace and tranquility at Moose River Farm. Since Spirit, the golden palomino gelding in the video, had been sold, I was spared this temporary upheaval.

Still, I watched the video repeatedly, becoming more and more enchanted with its subject. His dark golden coat accentuated by the snow white trim of mane, tail and two socks on his hind legs combined in striking contrast. That shade of gold is rare. Most palominos possess a diluted blonde coat that bleaches out under summer sunshine.

Although I was guilty of judging this book by his cover, it was actually his breed that had initially caught my interest. Spirit was an American saddlebred. Typically, saddlebreds are trained for high stepping or gaited competition; but like my first horse, Summer's Promise, Spirit had never been trained or ridden saddleseat. For whatever reason, he had begun his training without the special equipment necessary to make the horse move with high prancing limbs.

Frequently, I perused the bevy of classified websites for saddlebreds who were never trained as such. Perhaps there was a part of me that wanted to recreate the relationship that my sweet mare Promise and I had. Also, there was a part of me that recognized that the saddlebred temperament provides a safe, beginner friendly model and a good choice for teaching riding lessons.

For the rest of the summer and through the fall, I watched the video again and again, always wondering about the golden gelding that got away. Part of my obsession had to do with the resemblances to Promise in the gelding's shape and mannerisms. Whatever the reason, I just could not get over this horse.

By the first of December, the months of good weather fade into the reality of all the cold days to come. It is the price we pay for living in the north country. But what hadn't faded was my intense interest in the saddlebred gelding. How foolish, considering that he had been sold and was already adapting to his new home.

In the long evenings after barn chores are finished and it is too cold to ride, I can be found on the internet conducting either of two searches: horse farms in warmer climate areas or horses. God help me. Shortly before Christmas break, I was conducting an advanced search on *Equine.com* when I heard myself gasp out loud.

"The palomino is for sale....again!"

Updated pictures of the 16.1 hand palomino graced the ad with a caption that read, "A horse to capture your heart." Since Spirit had already captured my heart over and over again in the video, I knew this time he was going to be mine. Since I worried about why the horse was for sale again after only one year in his current home, phone calls to the owner and the trainer ensued. Eventually, I learned all about Spirit's history.

The first time that he came up for sale on the internet, Spirit had belonged to a young college student in Maine. She was a good rider and had been beguiled by the gelding's good looks and potential. Strapped for cash, the college student decided that she should sell her horse who was now moving forward in his training. During the previous winter while I was deciding whether or not I should buy the horse, a young teenager had fallen in love and purchased him. This youngster was enthusiastic about her future with Spirit. She spent a number of months working with her trainer to prepare him for the horse show season ahead. What a thrill campaigning the sun-kissed beauty around the local show circuit was going to be for her! But after a concerted effort, it became apparent that the young girl and Spirit did not make a good match when she was sitting in the saddle.

According to the trainer, Spirit was a great horse and the teen was a good rider. However, together they had no chemistry. He was never going to be the horse she had dreamed about riding and showing, no matter how striking his good looks. The trainer assured me that the horse did not have a behavioral problem. He neither bucked nor reared. He just did not yield to his rider's aids for whatever reason. This situation is common. Some horse and rider combinations just don't mesh.

Now I had a decision to make. Could I transform Spirit into a serviceable lesson horse? Would he and I get along with each other? At least he is pretty. Wasn't I taking a huge risk buying this horse sight unseen and only on the word of a trainer and an owner whom I had never met? Well, yes, but look how pretty he is. The answers to these questions were complicated, but I could justify all of them based on the horse's photogenic presence. There are no guarantees when buying a horse, and certainly there are even fewer when taking so many risks. I seemed to be gearing up for the challenge based solely on what the horse looked like. If he proved to be unsuited to my riding program, I had only myself to blame. For some reason, I allowed the glare from this horse's golden coat to blind my common sense.

While I struggled to make this decision, my teacher voice reminded me of how I try to guide my students toward rational, common sense decision making. In the classroom, shouldn't I be reluctant to allow students to fall victim to poor choices? Isn't it my obligation as their teacher to point out pitfalls of throwing caution to the wind with risky decisions? Choose not to study for a test and a low grade will most likely be the result. Choose to complete assignments later than mandatory due dates and points will be deducted from the overall score. Choose to continue acting inappropriately in class and a trip to the main office will ensue. Purchase a nine year old horse through the internet, sight unseen, after he has lasted less than a year in his current home and any number of consequences might result. But oh, he sure was pretty!

By the end of January, all of the pieces to purchase the gelding had fallen into place. The owner and her mother were excited about his new home and wanted to keep in touch about his progress. Transportation from Maine to the Adirondacks was arranged through a professional shipping company. All that was left to do was wait nine hours while the horse remained in transit on a tractor trailer. At six-thirty in the evening, I received the anticipated phone call that let me know the eighteen wheeler was just about to turn off the main road onto our road. Two and a half miles later, the rig arrived at the end of our driveway.

I decided to unload the horse out there because it was the middle of winter. An unfortunate set of circumstances several years before resulted in a tractor trailer full of hay getting stuck in our driveway for almost five hours. The situation was complicated by the fact that we still needed to unload the six hundred bales of hay stacked inside while trying to figure out how and who was going to tow the truck out of its icy trap. The whole incident has entered family legend. Its dramatic conclusion proved to be both laborious and expensive. It was the reason that I decided to risk walking a horse that I had never handled before, three hundred and fifty feet in darkness to the barn door. Our driveway is tortuous. Therefore, Spirit was unable to see where to this stranger was leading him. The other two horses in the trailer, who had comprised his herd for the last nine hours, were now whinnying shrilly on their way back out to the main road and points west.

In the fading beam of my flashlight, I studied the gelding. Although his ears strained toward the exiting horses, he showed no sign of losing control. With one hand, I directed the dwindling beam of light onto the path, fearing it might expire any moment. With the other hand, I grasped the lead rope and led the newest member of my family toward his waiting herd. He had little choice but to follow me through the dark into the unknown.

"Welcome Spirit," I announced with the same enthusiasm I greet a new student in my classroom. We continued to make our way up toward the barn, his hooves in perfect rhythm with my boots. As we rounded the final curve in the driveway, lights from the barn appeared. Spirit stopped abruptly and raised his long saddlebred neck into the air. His eyes popped open on either side of his head. A small four legged silhouette stood outlined in the warm glow from the barn aisle.

"Bleurr," bleated Lacey the goat who had been pacing in the doorway ever since I vanished into the darkness to await Spirit's arrival at the end of the driveway. Goats are smart and will not venture out after dark when predators are at their most active. Goats prefer to remain close to the safety of the barn. Lacey was scolding me for having broken this life-preserving rule. Normally, I would have answered to assure her that I had made it home in the dark without incident. Instead I remained still in an attempt to keep the energy level low so Spirit's brain could process all of the information attacking his senses in this new place. While he stood his ground, the horses in the barn began reacting to unfamiliar sounds and smells wafting from the driveway. A chorus of shrill and guttural whinnies echoed from the barn.

Horses make a list of pros and cons upon arriving in a new place. They have to weigh their options before advancing further. I could imagine the data piling up as Spirit conducted his survey. He had only a few seconds to decide if he should continue the trek or flee for his life. I waited, knowing that eventually his brain would stumble onto the *Golden Rule* for horses; safety in numbers. The herd mentality dictates that a solo horse is a dead horse. Only a group of two or more can keep each other safe from the predatorily unknowns of life in the wild. Although I live by the adage that horses are unpredictable, there are many circuits in their behavioral wiring that are in fact quite predictable. Sensitive horse people learn how to read and channel these behaviors to keep themselves and their animals safe. Therefore, it did not surprise me when Spirit, still in periscope posture, drew a deep breath in preparation for a whinnying blast to announce his arrival into a new herd. I winced in preparation for a painful assault on my eardrums located just inches below his quivering muzzle.

"Whe uh ohwww ee," choked Spirit. He tried again. "Whe uhhhwww."

The sound was nothing that I had ever heard from a horse before. Although a tremendous puff of breath curled out of the gelding's mouth, the whinny itself was pathetic, lacking any vocabulary the inquisitive barn residents could understand. Even Lacey's scolding bleats ceased. She too wanted to identify the alien approaching the barn with me.

Resigned to his own vocal inadequacies, Spirit lowered his head and allowed me to lead him to safety. Through the barn door he obediently walked down the aisle, seemingly unfazed by low grumbles, pumping nostrils and extended muzzles, all desperate to glean information from the blonde stranger. In that moment I was reminded of the emotions that every new student must experience while seeking an empty seat in my classroom on their first day. Escorted by the fixed stares and whispers of classmates who are not yet sorted into trusting peers, the new student walks a gauntlet into the unknown just as Spirit must have felt until he entered the safety of his new stall. Like the new student, he still has to settle into the community of barn animals and choose those with whom he will feel most comfortable.

Now that Spirit was almost fully revealed under the soft light, I was eager to get a good look at my new horse with the honey colored coat. The signed bank check had been cashed so the gelding was mine no matter what the moment of truth presented. I removed the lightweight blanket and was first taken by his narrow shoulders, a typical trait in saddlebreds. For the last thirty years I have looked at thoroughbreds, quarter horses and Friesians. The "paper doll" thin dimensions of Spirit's front legs might cause one to wonder if these horses lose balance with a rider on their backs. Blessed with knowledge about conditioning and building body mass, I wasn't discouraged one bit by his puny front end. In fact I looked forward to developing the golden chest and rump muscles by riding him up and down hills behind the barn once good weather returned. For the time being, I would spend the rest of the cold weather months just getting to know Spirit and encouraging him to synchronize his rhythm with the rest of the horses on the farm.

It didn't take me long to conclude that Spirit did not have a sunny disposition to match his golden pelt. He was aloof, unemotional, and difficult to connect with, maybe even indifferent. The contrast to Easau, who would sit in my lap if I let him, and Zambi, who would open a door for me if he had thumbs, made me wonder about the palomino's early years, before the two owners of whom I was aware. He acted like an orphan foal who grew up without learning horse rules from an equine parent. I completely understood why a teenager could not connect with him.

On his terms I had to find a way to accentuate his strengths. It was important to forgive him while learning to live with his shortcomings. At first I had to discover what the shortcomings were from my position in the saddle. He was inept at responding to pressure from my leg. Retaliation to the aid included hind leg kicks or refusal to go forward. The more pressure I applied, the more he balked. This behavior surfaced particularly when we were riding out on the trails. It was his way of telling me that he didn't want to go any farther because he wasn't sure what he might encounter out there in the big woods. He was acting like students in my classroom who choose negative behavior as a means to get out of assignments or activities because they either don't understand the directions or they feel that they cannot complete the work. Misbehavior is not an acceptable reaction, but it requires alternative teaching skills rather than punishment from me. Traditional negative consequences for these students do not work. To be successful, they require encouragement from the teacher. I may have the student repeat directions, break the assignment into smaller intervals, or work through the problem with the student filling in answers before I leave them to work independently. Regardless of my strategies, the goal is for the student and the horse to succeed.

Like my misunderstood gelding Joshua, Spirit needed consistency and expectations that he could achieve. Unlike Joshua, Spirit expressed oversensitivity to touch and sound, making it necessary for me to apply the aids softly. My legs slowly squeezed the sides of his torso when I wanted him to move forward. My reins gently pressed the bit against the bars or gums of his mouth. Every move I made in the saddle whispered requests as if I was saying please and thank you. It was important to keep our communication light and airy so that Spirit could relax. The gelding benefitted from ground sessions as well. I believe he was surprised by his desire to approach me after a rollicking good chase in the arena. Instinct drove him to seek my leadership when I stopped shaking a large plastic bag that I use to raise a horse's energy level. With soft eyes and lowered head, he stood while I caressed his head and neck. After following closely at my side for several laps around the arena, Spirit was ready for me to ride.

Riding Spirit after a ground session was a pleasure. Under the spell of our connection, he always appeared to be more receptive to my aids, allowing me to use more pressure without reacting offensively no lurching forward or balking in protest.

By summer Spirit was being ridden by some of my upper level riding students. Courtney, a teenager who had ridden with me since she was in sixth grade, spent a lot of time working Spirit. Riding him was a good test of her own skills, which had developed on well-schooled horses. Serious riders always want to experience new and challenging horses so they can fill their toolboxes with a variety of strategies. Courtney also began to train Spirit over jumps, a skill he performed well and never refused. Over fences he exuded confidence that we hoped to extend into his flat work at the trot and canter.

Consistent training enabled Spirit to improve. Although his attitude did not necessarily soften, he did begin to accept the rider's aids willingly and respond appropriately. This combination is what produces a horse that is safe to ride. Spirit is my first choice for trail rides. Once an anxious scaredy cat, my golden gelding strolls along with a relaxed, enthusiastic demeanor through crunching leaves or blowing snow. He is the best trail companion for other green horses who are skittish away from the barn.

I respect that Spirit doesn't always appreciate my hugs and affection. Not all of my human students are fans of physical contact in the form of a pat on their back or a hand on their shoulder either. As their teacher I must offer praise to inspire motivation. Horses are no different. Gifted horseman, *Frederic Pignon* summarizes the lessons that Spirit taught me to improve as an equestrian. *"May every rider strive for a better connection with his or her horse by observation, closer understanding, and patient groundwork."*

Spirit is proof that not all animal-human bonds result in a perfect balance.

Spirit's sunny exterior hides the challenge he presents under saddle. However, he is a favorite among many riders.

198

Zambezi

"Horses are creatures of habit, all different, like we are. You have to find their formula by being around them." –Rodney Jenkins

"Tragedies come in groups of three so, hopefully, three deaths in four months is the end for a while," I reasoned in my head as I coped with the latest loss on our farm.

By the middle of January, Moose River Farm had suffered the deaths of three animals. Each one forced me through the process of grief even as it overlapped with the next one in line. Emotionally, I did not grieve the losses equally. I began to wonder if I loved some of my animals more than others. Was there a hierarchy in my menagerie that ranked each pet by its distance from my heart? For weeks I pondered this question with great concern, fearful that I might suddenly discover a truth I did not want to know.

Then my twenty-five year old thoroughbred bay gelding Zambezi relapsed with EPM, (Equine Protozoal Myelitis), a parasitic infestation that manifests in the spinal cord of susceptible equids. Although the condition is treatable, there is no guarantee that neurological symptoms will disappear with treatment. Each EPM case is unique depending upon where the protozoa are located along the spinal cord and the degree of permanent damage. Zambi's initial diagnosis in 2000 was proof that timing and extensive research played a large role in a favorable outcome. In the late 1990's many horses with EPM were euthanized because adequate treatment was not available. Among them was the famous *Gifted,* an American Grand Prix dressage star whose euthanasia at the age of seventeen was a devastating loss to his legion of devoted fans. If *Gifted* couldn't be saved, how could Zambi? Yet for more than ten years, Zambi remained symptom free following his first treatment. During that decade, EPM protocol evolved and improved, probably because so many talented, valuable horses had died without an effective remedy.

As Zambi entered his third decade, suspicious incidents began sneaking their way into his conditioning sessions, riding lessons and general milling about. I scratched my head, wondering if something was amiss or if he was feeling the wear and tear of old age. Eventually, long incident free stretches of time helped allay my concern. I was always caught off guard when the next episode occurred, months, sometimes a year or two later. Finally, in the fall of 2012, a series of inexplicable bouts of body lameness prompted our veterinarian, Dr. Nightingale, to treat Zambi with the latest recommended compound for EPM. He appeared to respond favorably, spent the cold winter on vacation from under the saddle and returned to conditioning the following spring looking better than he had in several years. Over the summer, he taught a limited number of riding lessons and lived a life of relative luxury in semi-retirement. The healthy trend continued for another year. The next summer, Zambi suffered several painful hoof abscesses. The soreness laid him up for several weeks of healing once our farrier relieved the pressure with his hoof knife. It was a frustrating few months as abscess after abscess plagued the *Big Z*.

Then in January, Zambi returned to the barn after a brisk galloping play session with his companion Easau in the large field adjacent to his stall. The two horses are free to choose between their stalls and turnout. The gate to the field is open day and night during the snowy winter weather. It is not uncommon to see them frolicking in the field under a full moon in temperatures well below zero. From an upstairs window in our toasty house, I like to watch them celebrate their freedom. Not a fiber in my body, however, wishes to join them in such extreme conditions.

Only slightly winded from the playful jaunt, Zambi greedily sought the hay flake set out for his lunch. Although his front end munched with gusto, the hind end swayed dramatically from side to side. On a twelve-hundred pound animal, this movement is an alarming sight. It left me to wonder what would happen if he fell down. Could he get up on his own? I began to panic.

"What should I do? Should I call the vet? Can it wait until tomorrow? What do you think?" I stammered, conferring with my friend Vicky who was helping me with late afternoon barn chores.

"Well, no, I don't think you should wait," she replied once she had evaluated Zambi's condition with her own eyes.

Immediately, I placed the call that initiates an emergency visit from our veterinarian on a Sunday afternoon. The procedure is the same each time. There is a flurry of phone calls back and forth while the answering service fields the initial call and relays the message to the vet. Then the vet calls me to receive detailed information to help her plan her truck inventory for a visit to my farm.

"What do we want to do for him?" asks Dr. Nightingale or Dr. Jen for short.

It had been more than three years since I met Jennifer on the chaotic August day when she arrived to save Murray. At that time she was only three months out of vet school, a clinically prepared but novice practitioner faced with a complicated case to solve for an emotional client no doubt questioning her ability. Since that hectic day that ended in sadness despite Jen's medical efforts, I have tapped into her outstanding professional abilities on many occasions, including yearly routine vaccinations, donkey geldings, wellness checks and the inevitable euthanasia visits. I hold her in the highest regard because she always acts in my animals' best interests.

Jen gently inquired if she needed to be prepared to put the horse down. Zambi had lived with me for two decades, a startling fact that caught me by surprise. Was this really the end? The big dark horse's arrival was one of my happiest horse memories because it had taken a long time to find him. My mind tumbled back twenty years into the past when I began the tedious task of looking for a new horse to purchase. The story begins when my interest in riding transitioned from jumping fences to the precision of dressage.

My second year of teaching sixth grade began within days of returning from Africa. Barely did I have enough time to put up a thoughtful math concept bulletin board in my classroom before Spike, two baby rats and I welcomed in a whole new group of students with whom we would share our new year. I was quite satisfied in my professional life, having established a routine that made me feel I made a difference in the lives of my students.

Meanwhile, back at our farm, my two quarter horses, Spy and Windy waited patiently for me to return in the afternoons to care for and ride them. Most days my friend Jean joined me to practice her fledgling skills on Windy while I concentrated on Spy's training. Yet, I have to admit riding was becoming blase. I feared my horses were being drilled on the same skills day after day. At that time we didn't have easy access to trail riding where horses get a break from the grind of arena work, I began to investigate other riding disciplines. At this point, my interest in dressage began to pique.

Dressage means training in French. Its roots go back to ancient Greece when some trainers believed that riding practices should encourage the horse to carry his physique athletically and effortlessly with a rider upon his back. In the early days there must have been much discussion among trainers as to how the rider can influence the horse and how the horse should feel when he is responding correctly. I can only imagine the immense range between force and submission that tormented horses as human egos sought to claim master horseman status. Of course the only place these riders could prove their technique's worth was on the battlefield. In the realm of chaos, dressage training resulted in obedience, a factor that probably saved human lives during war.

In the mid 400's B.C., Xenephon, a Greek philosopher, wrote *The Art of Horsemanship.* It appears that Xenephon made emotional connections with his horses. As a result, he realized that humane training methods resulted in harmony when the rider used soft hands and legs to communicate with the horse. When asked correctly, the horse is encouraged to lower his hind end and lift his spine despite weight from a rider sitting on his back. In this position the horse is now at his most efficient in terms of energy conservation. Efficiency results in a *frame,* as it is called, that enables the horse to extend his limbs at both the trot and canter without appearing to careen around the arena as if he is on the race course. Correct frame enables a horse to trot in suspended animation called *passage* and at the highest degree of collection the horse can actually trot in place or *piaffe.* These maneuvers or movements are what make dressage horses appear to dance lightly with athletic agility across a riding arena. The spectacle is even more magical when horse and rider are accompanied by beautiful music. Emotions flow on *Grand Prix Freestyle* night at all world class competitions that I have had the pleasure of watching. What I describe here is a dressage horse at the highest levels. At the lower levels, dressage is simply basic riding and a fundamental understanding of how the rider's body makes the horse move forward, backward and side to side or *laterally*.

These principles work wonders in young horses and novice riders. However, a novice rider cannot learn the intricacies of dressage on a young horse. I would never mount a beginner rider on a green horse. There are too many complicated messages being sent between the horse and his rider. The rider must be intuitive and sensitive in order to correct or reward the horse's efforts. Riders train for years before they are able to apply the techniques needed to train young horses. My interest in dressage developed from an already well educated *seat* or position. I wanted to improve my communication skills so that I could train a horse through the levels that begin at *training* and extend through levels *one to four* before entering competition. Initially, I just wanted to learn the required movements at each level. I knew they would challenge my horses mentally and physically, relieving the boredom we were feeling while training in the ring. I did not aspire to compete at the higher levels.

During training, my body began to make sense of how to solicit a specific response from the horse. As Spy, Windy and I became physically fit from this conditioning, I began to feel more confident about my own abilities. At the same time, I had to recognize that although these two horses tried their hardest, they were limited by their conformation (anatomy), having been bred for other purposes. Quarter horses are bred to sprint for a quarter of a mile. Their breeding selects a short neck and powerful hindquarters. These features also make the horse useful rounding up cattle because he can accelerate and stop quickly in pursuit of stray animals. Although Windy and Spy were athletic jumping over fences and at the lowest levels of dressage, it was going to be a lot to ask of them to perform beyond first level.

Soon it became clear that if I wished to proceed to a higher level of dressage, I needed a different horse. And whenever the *new horse* seed begins to germinate in my brain, it is always initially smothered by the *how- am- I- going -to- convince- Rod -that- a- new- horse -is - a -good -idea* herbicide. In all fairness to Rod, who has been wonderful when it comes to helping me to live my dream, I try to consider his concerns. An additional horse always requires an adjustment to our finances; although I take care of them at home, they still consume a lot of money for hay, grain, farrier, and vet expenses. Rod can't tell the difference between a dressage horse and a non-dressage horse. Therefore, he has a difficult time understanding why an additional horse is necessary when I already have two and can only ride one at a time.

Perhaps this is where the great divide between horsewomen I know and the men who love them commences. To these women, a horse is a dependent like a child, but one who provides therapy, recreation and achievements. To their partners, the horse can be perceived as a competitive opponent who threatens to usurp all of a woman's free time by providing her with a much more pleasurable experience than hanging out with the man. The horse also threatens to unhinge the balance of household finances. I know many women who pay all of their horse's expenses with cash so that their husbands cannot keep track of the amount of money that the horse is burning through. This desperate measure speaks volumes to the importance of the horse in a woman's life; the cost of keeping him is far more economical than the cost of therapy she would require without the horse.

I've been lucky! Rod is neither threatened by the horses nor miserly about keeping track of every penny spent in the barn. Since the horses are in our backyard, I am technically home and easy to find compared to the woman who drives to a distant barn where her horse is boarded. Those women can easily spend multiple hours in the company of their horses while the husband waits like a golf widow at home. Rod has so many projects to keep him busy on the farm that rarely is he waiting for me to leave the barn to entertain him. We do make a point to walk our dogs together, and I do make an effort to finish in the barn between seven o'clock and seven-thirty pm so that we can eat dinner together and talk about the day.

Horses have never come between Rod and me. So once Rod accepted the idea of a new addition to the barn, my enthusiasm drove me to find the perfect equine partner with whom to work through the dressage levels. And what a process it was!

There is no perfect horse. The best candidate needed to be young, safe, sound, a *good mover*, and within my price range, which was under four thousand dollars. I was confident that I could train and condition the right candidate, and I didn't mind working him for a few years before beginning to dabble in low level competition. The only question left to answer at this point was, "Where is he?"

In 1995 the internet had yet to become a useful tool for locating horses available for sale. Instead I had to depend on the laborious task of spreading the word among people in the horse business and perusing the classified sections of both local and equine publications. This made the whole task of searching for my dream horse difficult, with fits of starts and stops as long dry spells were followed by leads on prospective horses.

"So and so is trying to sell his third level dressage horse (I'm listening). It's a Warmblood gelding (Tell me more), beautiful floating trot, (...and?), but he is only 15.2 hands (too small for me)".

"So and so wants to sell her young dressage prospect (I'm all ears). It's a Hanoverian mare (maybe), easy keeper (sounds better), but she has a tendency to buck when she has had enough training for the day (no, thank you)."

"So and so has a large thoroughbred gelding (Oh?). He has huge reaching gaits at trot and canter (yes). He travels easily in the trailer because he has been there and done all that (sounds so easy), but he is eighteen years old (too old, I'm afraid).

"So and so has a horse for sale (really?). It's a tall leggy gelding with four white socks (a beauty no matter what color the rest of him is). He is training at second level with a trainer down around Albany (uh oh). After a finder's fee is added to his asking price, you might need to consider refinancing your house (not happening)".

And so the word of mouth horses drifted in and out of my ears as I crossed each one off my list for various reasons that prevented them from being the *One*.

In early July, I took a trip down to legendary horse trader Phil Quartier's barn in Richfield Springs, NY. I had always found him to be a consummate horseman who made a successful living built on his reputation for buying and selling serviceable horses. What he didn't deal well with were those wannabe horsemen who arrived at his barn looking for a particular colored horse or perhaps a horse guaranteed to go "real fast when he runs." Phil never felt obligated to educate such a patron on qualities to shop for in a safe trail horse. Both Windy and Spy, whom I was delighted to have in my barn, had come from Phil. It was worth a look to see if yet another diamond in the rough might be waiting there for me to find him. Unfortunately, that day none of the four horses I rode touched me as a future prospect for dressage.

Meanwhile, summer sweltered onward into August. I felt an urgency to find this next mount who would take me further in dressage. Where was he? Just like all those years ago when I searched for my first horse Promise, the classified section of a newspaper ultimately led me to Zambezi. X marked the spot on the treasure map classified section of the *Sunday Herald American* from Syracuse.

Within days I was on my way to Cazenovia, just outside of Syracuse, to consider a tall five year old dark bay thoroughbred gelding in need of a job other than lounging around the barn between explosive gallops through the woods. Because the woman who owned him had just had a baby, her life had entered a phase that wasn't going to include horses for a while. Her brother had been riding the horse periodically, galloping the gelding at top speed and jumping every fallen tree and log in sight. The woman feared that an injury was inevitable to either her brother or the horse. Therefore, she felt the best thing was to find the horse a new home.

The tall bay immediately impressed me with his dark good looks and his chiseled cheekbones. His black dappled mahogany colored coat gleamed under summer sun. Soft brown eyes indicated a gentle disposition. A long white blaze extended from between his eyes down to his muzzle. Like a lightning bolt it illuminated the horse's dark exterior. I felt an instant connection.

Under saddle my hopes grew. Perched on his back, I was impressed by the long distance from his withers to his ears. My stocky quarter horses were much shorter in this dimension. On the large bay I had to stretch my torso and arm to reach the *poll* between his ears. He responded positively when I applied my legs to his sides and asked for the trot and canter. After my initial ride, I was confident that this horse could be the one.

A week later the handsome bay was on his way to our farm. I was granted a full seven days to try him before my check was cashed. Seven days transitioned into twenty years of equine and human bliss. Zambezi's large dark, gentle presence is a metaphor for the deep dark African river for which he is named. He has never been anything less than a gentleman with one exception. During my serious years of training, I moved him temporarily to a boarding stable with an indoor arena. During spring vacation when the snow had yet to vacate the Adirondacks, I made these arrangements so I could ride Zambi daily during the long two week break. A young breeding stallion resided at the barn as well. Two mares were being bred on a daily basis during Zambi's stay at the farm. The presence of the stallion and the two ripe females turned Zambi into a horse I did not recognize. He had no focus for ring work. He screamed and bucked during every ride. Finally, I had to take him home for fear that he would injure himself or me. The stallion's scent and mating ritual were overloading Zambi's brain despite being gelded. Once he arrived home Zambi transitioned immediately back to the gentleman I knew him to be.

For five years I trained my bay gelding with one objective to work through the lower levels of dressage. Several horse shows each year provided a gauge for the progress Zambi and I were making. I couldn't afford any more. Besides I found training at home more satisfying than competition. Horses perform their best at home in a relaxed and familiar atmosphere. Away from home horses may feel stressed and not perform as well.

Zambi was a natural athlete with a sweet temperament. He made an ideal candidate for me to work with through the dressage levels. From the beginning, he taught me that less is more. The lightest pressure from my leg produced desired reactions whether or not I was practicing shoulder-in or lead changes. If I practiced one movement too many times, he began to anticipate with big leaps and a heavy pull on the reins or forehand. It was a signal to me that he was ready for something different. I always listened.

Upon Zambi's back I could ride forever without my stirrups. In fact I preferred to ride him without stirrups because I felt it encouraged me to maintain correct posture and weight distribution in the saddle. I complimented my riding by maintaining a high level of fitness through weight lifting. It improved my stamina enabling me to ride several horses a day. The positive feedback I received from riding Zambi carried over to my continued training of Windy and Spy. Zambi taught me how to feel balanced between my hips and the horse's spine. I was pleasantly surprised when this balance transferred to the other horses. I began to feel improved responses when I rode them. With the slightest squeeze of my calf in conjunction with pressure on the rein and from a seatbone, Spy stepped from the walk into a canter immediately instead of trotting a stride or two before the transition. Windy learned to balance his torso on top of his four limbs by distributing equal weight at each leg. That way he didn't have to pull the reins against my hands in an effort to feel balanced. Instead the position of my body showed him how to carry himself.

All learners benefit from specific positive feedback. When teachers' expectations are clear and consistent, students are successful. When students succeed, teachers feel more confident as practitioners of their craft. They fill their toolboxes with positive strategies to inspire current and future students. Thanks to Zambi, my communication skills in the ring and in the classroom improved exponentially. My riding became more respectful of my horses, my teaching more motivational for my students. I believe I heard the great *Monty Roberts* loud and clear when he whispered his famous line *"Horses react appropriately while waiting for the human to get it right."* Perhaps our students respond positively when their teachers get it right as well.

Zambi was also an enthusiastic mount over fences. He loved to jump. Although I did not wish to jump in competition, I did recognize that training over jumps improved Z's athleticism and gave his brain a break from what can become over drill in dressage. Frequently, I attended clinics given by a variety of notable riders and trainers, including Olympians Greg Best and Michael Page. The clinics were exhilarating. Although I always returned home with a greater appreciation for my big dark thoroughbred and his amazing breed, it was his individual easy going personality and eagerness to please me that I loved the most.

Unfortunately, horses age, athleticism fades, and there comes a time when affording them the luxury of retirement is the grandest gesture of appreciation for all the gifts they have given. During that time, I must remain vigilant to the signals that indicate euthanasia is necessary. I had already come close to euthanizing Zambi a year before.

In January, Zambi, along with his companion Easau, found themselves stranded in a field that had frozen into a sheet of ice just outside of their stalls. At some point during my school day, Zambi must have fallen and was unable to establish the necessary traction between hoof and ice to push himself up onto his feet. There was no telling how long he lay there. What was clear, when I discovered him upon my arrival home, was that he was already exhausted from several futile attempts to rise.

After a few frantic phone calls, several people arrived in my driveway eager to assist the prone animal. Unfortunately, efforts to raise Zambi failed over and over again. Each attempt ended when his twelve hundred pound physique collided sickeningly with the ice. Just how much punishment could his body take before he simply broke apart? The thought choked me as my mind scrambled for the solution to end this drama. Meanwhile, a wintry mix of wet snow and rain added to Zambi's misery on the ice.

Despite spreading sand around Zambi and hoisting him with the strength of several men, the gelding was unable to support his own weight once his hind feet made contact with the slippery surface. I began to wonder if, more than the ice itself, an injury to his spine or hips was preventing him from getting up. Immediately, we summoned our veterinarian to the farm. Rex, our school superintendent who is an EMT and an experienced horseman from youth, never left the horse's side, providing me with calm support and advice through the whole ordeal. Shivering in the cold under layers of wet blankets, Zambi appeared to be giving up. We needed to find a solution fast.

Our next plan included dragging the horse on a tarp with the backhoe to an area where the footing was more snow than ice. We sprang into action. In the frenzy of activity, I tried to reassure Zambi by caressing his head, talking softly, and blowing gently into his muzzle. From my location, I became aware of all the individuals who had left other obligations to help my horse. I saw three rowdy young boys from my sixth grade class long ago, now all grown up with children of their own, wanting nothing more than a happy ending to this scene they had stepped into. I saw my neighbors who helped many times when mayhem erupted on the farm. I saw local community members who volunteer as emergency first responders rigging up the apparatus that might free Zambi from his icy trap.

After two and a half hours of crashing failures, Zambi was successfully dragged towards the barn. Several men were then able to slide the exhausted horse off the tarp and onto a pair of rubber mats that had been moved to the horse's new location. Next, I strapped a pair of *Old Mac* sport boots onto his hind feet. The short rest gave Zambi a little strength to try once more. He heaved himself up into the sitting position, then coiled his hocks under his haunches. Mustering all the energy he had left, Zambi launched his full bulk one last time. A roaring cheer from the crowd affirmed that Zambi had indeed found his footing. I believe the big horse was surprised to find himself standing on all fours. Rex triumphantly led Zambi into the barn where, under fluorescent lights, we could assess the damage from his ordeal.

Although Zambi was free from the treacherous ice, his buddy Easau still needed to be coaxed across the frozen surface to reach the safety of the barn. My neighbor, Pam and I returned to him several times during Zambi's crisis, hoping we could persuade him to follow us. But as soon as Easau suspected ice underfoot, he flat-out refused to take another step. Once Zambi disappeared into the barn, Easau became agitated, screaming desperately for his herd-mate to come back. Eventually, fear of being left in the field alone persuaded Easau to follow me along a path that had been generously sanded by one of the local volunteers. Once both horses were safe and secure in the barn, I could breathe a sigh of appreciative relief.

When Dr. Nightingale arrived thirty minutes later, Zambi, now bundled in dry warm blankets, was eating hay in his stall. Miraculously, his injuries were limited to minor bruises, scrapes and stiffness. The vet administered a protocol of IV fluids and pain killers before Zambi was left to rest and recuperate. Over the next few days, he perked up and eventually fully recovered. Dr. Jen's visit had not required euthanasia. However, a year later I was faced with the same decision. If leaning against the wall was necessary to keep him standing, how would he ever get up off the ground after lying down? For many horses this uncertainty is the factor that hastens euthanasia.

I focused on the reality of Dr. Jen's inquiry. Should she be prepared to put Zambi down this time? The vet and I agreed to wait an hour before she headed out to my farm. For the duration I kept a vigil on the horse while he rested. When the hour was up, Zambi's hind end seemed to have gained strength that enabled him to stabilize on all fours. Dr. Jen canceled her visit and the incident was soon behind us. There is no denying that Zambi is in his declining years. I am obliged to stay aware of his condition at all times. When he can no longer get up off the ground on his own, the answer to the question of euthanasia will have to be *yes*.

As I plan for retirement, spending more time with my animals in the barn is what I am looking forward to the most. Retirees like Zambi are being rewarded for the years of selfless service they have provided to my riding lesson students and to me. Observing Zambi now in his twilight years of life, I cannot help but feel empathy. Rest and reflection are gifts we hope for at the end of a long and productive career. My dear horses deserve as much.

At age twenty-eight, Zambi is still with me. His handsome good looks have not faded, but he lacks muscle tone and is slightly underweight despite being offered unlimited hay and large measures of grain. His hind quarters sway weakly behind him, so sometimes he must rest his hip against the wall in his stall. My emotions drift back and forth between sadness and elation when I gaze into his soft brown eyes. They reflect an era when Zambi and I were both much younger; when he and I performed together at a high level of fitness; when I possessed confidence to gallop him around the farm because I trusted him with my life. I revisit the day he surprised me by changing his leading leg at the canter twice after only two strides; a *two tempi change* in dressage lingo. In his eyes I see the devastating *EPM* diagnosis that ended his competitive career but thankfully not his life. This beautiful horse and I have been together for twenty-three years. In that time I too have ended my professional career. So aware of my diminishing levels of energy. I marvel at the woman I used to be; the woman who took care of a barn full of animals at either end of the school day and had stamina left over to ride a horse or two every afternoon. Her boundless energy has faded like that of my big horse's mahogany pelt. I hope I age as gracefully as he has although, I hope, much more slowly. He is a bundle of goodness who has given me nothing but his best. Every day that Zambi can still push his weight off the ground and stand without assistance is one more occasion for us to celebrate.

Zambezi is a once in a lifetime horse; handsome, gentle and always eager to please. Although our horse show career was cut short, he and I have remained together for almost twenty-five years. How much he has taught me is immeasurable.

Dr. Jennifer Nightingale provides health care, wisdom and compassion for all of the animals at MRF.

Equi-Reflection™

"Leadership and learning are indispensable to each other." -John F. Kennedy

For decades the horse industry existed as multiple disciplines that rarely overlapped. For example, those who rode quarter horses remained isolated among their training kin, creating their own interpretation of riding standards. The hunter/jumper community kept to itself and established practices that were rarely questioned because the only people aware of them were riders of that discipline. The Tennessee walking horse fanciers passed down a legacy of artificial aids using ankle weights and chains to accentuate the equine gaits. Nobody seemed to question them. The international dressage community performed and competed against each other within a bubble of acceptable practices. Rarely did anyone question if the use of devices that cranked horses' bodies between a double bridle and a pair of pointy spurs was in the best interests of the horses.

Riders who compete in the sport of combined training jump their horses over extreme obstacles that require a high level of skill to avoid severe injury or death of horse and/or rider. Statistics for the sport of eventing include a staggering fifty human deaths worldwide between 1993 and 2016. That number does not include the dozens of horses killed as well.

The advent of social media resulted in exposure outside of secluded realms so equine disciplines now critique each other. Everybody has an opinion about the methods deemed necessary to inspire a jumper over fences exceeding five feet. The Tennessee walking community received so much negative reaction to its archaic methods of gait accentuation through chains and platform shoes that attendance at their national show dropped significantly. The organization was forced to consider reforming rules and regulations. International dressage is under a litany of abuse accusations due to the method of *rollkur,* a forced stretching of the neck muscles created by pulling hard on the reins, and, therefore, the bit, while jabbing the spurs into the horse's sides. No other training mechanism has received as much controversial criticism as *rollkur*. Social media has created a climate of transparency in the horse industry. Chatty bloggers and tweeters are on constant alert at competitions to report their negative findings. Eventing accidents have been exposed to people within and outside of the horse industry. Anybody can respond as an expert, anybody can respond as a critic. I have mixed feelings about this state of transparency. If the watchdogs reduce horse suffering, then of course I approve. However, if emotional reactions distort the facts, then the horse industry runs the risk of caving to pressure from animal rights extremists.

All the chatter has reawakened my own perceptions about why I own horses. Concern for my horses' wellbeing coupled with the wisdom of age are leading me down a path I am surprised to be traveling. From decades of life as a riding maniac, I have transitioned into a pleasure rider who finds time spent on the ground in the presence of my horses more rewarding than my time in the saddle. From the moment my addiction to horses began at age six, I was driven by my passion to ride them. Caring for them was always a priority I willingly accepted as necessary for a holistic understanding of horses. But riding was the object of owning them. A horse's worth was his potential as a riding mount. In my teens and twenties, that worth included the horse's ability to jump. Injuries incurred by my horses along the way merely interrupted my purpose for owning them. I was sympathetic toward injured horses; but during their convalescence, I wondered whether or not the horse would continue to be useful once he was healed. The summer I hand-walked my quarter horse hunter Windy daily while he healed a suspensory ligament in his lower forelimb, I constantly worried if the injury would prevent me from riding him ever again. It was a discouraging time. These ligaments lack sufficient blood flow so they take months to heal. Meanwhile, I was missing a whole season of good riding weather.

As my interest in jumping transitioned to dressage, the addiction deepened. My body's ability to feel correct responses from my horses encouraged me to drill them day after day until I was convinced the horse had learned how to perform the movements well. I craved getting the *feel* right and worked horses for long stretches so I could enjoy the moments of correctness. Now I often wonder how my horses were feeling. Did they always share my enthusiasm? My wish was always their command. I hope that long walks through the woods at the end of the rides compensated for their gracious efforts.

Makia, my aged thoroughbred mare, gave me many inspiring evenings of training. She was my go-to horse after a long and trying day at school. Under a crisp December sky, with falling snow illuminated by one bright light in the ring, my sagging spirits rose. Mares are notorious for giving everything they have with serious concentration. Makia's goal was to please me. And she always did. But was the mare always up to the task? Were there some evenings when she might have been relieved to remain cozy in her stall? Probably, but I never considered her preferences. We make a deal with our riding horses. In exchange for one productive hour of the day in the riding ring, we feed them and keep them out of harm's way.

As herd animals, horses rely mostly on body language to communicate with other horses. In the company of horses, humans can use their own physical posture and gestures to forge a bond with the horse which uniquely breaks a barrier. The prey instinct of the horse must trust the potentially predacious instinct of the human. That is a lot to ask of an organism that is wired to flee any questionable situation. Only when the horse is convinced he is unthreatened will he join a person. His actions prove that he wants to be convinced because he makes every attempt to read human signals. Powerful emotions are evoked when a bond is forged between horse and human.

Once retired from education, I plan to combine what I have learned from my teaching career and apply it to the assisted learning activities I am currently developing with the animals in my barn. A blossoming philosophy about training horses is guiding me toward the horsewoman I have always wanted to be: respectful, appreciative and kind. Finally, I am using my horses to help people heal by providing them with animal encounters that raise their spirits. Years of observing animal honesty have delivered me to this current philosophical destination.

Equine Assisted Learning

On January first, thoroughbred horses across the globe celebrate their birthdays. In the world of horse racing, this date is used to level the playing field and define qualification credentials for important graded stakes or big money races. Two horses born in January and July of the same year are considered to be the same age and therefore are eligible for any races in their age group. Clearly there is an advantage to being born in January or February. Foals dropped from mares close to the first of the year benefit from more time to grow before their first birthday.

At Moose River Farm, the date is significant because it forces me to acknowledge the age of all my horses for the coming year. On New Year's Day several years ago, half of my ten horses were twenty years old or older. Collectively, their ages ranged from nine years to thirty years. The statistic prompted me to analyze my horseback riding lesson program and the direction that it might take as the animals aged. Although a twenty-year old is not ancient, age is something to consider when comparing older horses to younger equines. Typically, older horses show signs of discomfort from arthritis, sore backs and the ever dreaded navicular syndrome, a condition that causes permanent lameness if hooves are not maintained with proper care and/or medication. Although, many horses enter their third decade with the stamina and fitness of much younger horses, many also lose their enthusiasm for schooling or training in the ring. I must monitor and interpret these factors in each horse, individually.

At the same time, I began to question my own desires as an equestrian. For over forty years, I have lived to ride. Riding was the pivotal focus of my day; I planned all other activities around the number of horses I could ride before going to the house to make dinner. My level of energy was Herculean to say the least. Riding provided me with a pleasing physical fix that I craved every single day, all year round. Occasionally, extremely cold weather forced me to take a break for a few days. As soon as temperatures released their icy grip, I was back in the saddle, riding several horses a day to catch up on the days I had missed.

From time to time, I asked myself what was the urgency to ride so often. My motto has always been: if I want my horse to go well tomorrow, I must ride him today. I also assumed that, after being ridden by many novice riding students, the horses benefited from my experience to correct training. It wasn't necessarily my ego that I fed with this philosophy. I had banished my ego from the barn the year I gave up competing at horse shows. With all due respect to adults who show their horses, I must admit that showing brought out the worst in me.

As soon as I mailed my entry with a check written out for hundreds of dollars, reserved a hotel room for hundreds more, and announced to my poor husband that I would be away with my horse for a few days, I became somebody I never wanted to be. I wasn't abusive. I was driven. During the weeks before a show, I drilled my horses with dressage test movements. I was enthusiastic and eager to receive a judge's feedback, proof that I was training proficiently. Pride in my beautiful animals was the small reward that paid me back after I'd worked so hard to train and manage them day after day. My level of care never wavered. The horses looked fabulous; their toplines from ears to tail developed into physiques that could propel them forward off the strength of conditioned hindquarters. In other words, my horses appeared to be benefiting from the military style precision with which I rode them.

What I failed to notice was that I had left a crucial ingredient out of the training formula. I wasn't connecting emotionally or spiritually with my horses. Rarely did I stand in their stalls and talk to them, pet them and bask in our moment together. Working with them every day was exhausting as I fit the tasks in around an already busy work schedule. Somehow, I made it happen and dropped wearily into bed every night, high on my training progress.

Showing horses is expensive; therefore, I only attended three recognized shows per year. Training continued between show dates. During the winter months, I eased up and allowed the horses to rest, only working them lightly two or three days a week. In those days I rode in all kinds of weather; blowing snow, harsh wind, pelting rain. If the footing in my outdoor ring was sufficient, I rode. This routine continued for years through a succession of horses beginning with my sweet quarter horse, geldings Windy and Spy. Once I accepted that their abilities were limited to dressage basics, I acquired my thoroughbred gelding Zambi in 1995. He was five years old at the time. I began his training immediately, looking forward to working up the levels of dressage to see just how far we could go. Zambi possessed the perfect temperament for my intense training. He worked hard, always wanted to please me and was a pleasure to travel with away from home. The big horse settled into a new stall away from home without concern, ate and drank with gusto and loaded on the trailer without hesitation. His dark bay eye-catching looks made me proud to show him off. I am grateful for these memories and proud of our accomplishments.

When Zambi was diagnosed with the dreaded equine protozoal myelitis or EPM, I gave up competition altogether. The organism that invaded his spinal cord impaired his athletic ability. Treatment helped. Unfortunately, he never regained full strength in his hind end. To be perfectly honest, my decision to stop competing brought with it a sense of relief, rather than a sense of mourning. The fact that Zambi survived EPM, while others, including some of our country's top horses, had not, was all that was important to me.

At the same time Rod was busy building Moose River Farm while the animals and I waited patiently to pack and move in. I began to spend more and more time on the new property. Most weekends, I drove the horses in our horse trailer to the farm so that I could ride and explore the new surroundings. It had been difficult to enjoy trail riding near our home in Inlet because I had to ride across a major road in order to access public trails. The thought of accidentally falling off my horse and having him beeline for home across a busy road was too terrifying to risk. Our new property was miles from the main road. If a horse did accidentally deposit me on the ground out in the woods and run for home, it was extremely unlikely that he would encounter a speeding vehicle in his desperate quest to get back to the barn. I began to enjoy my rides in the woods and anticipated the move that would make riding on the trails an everyday possibility.

Happy in my newly established status as non-competitive rider, I began to consider the horse as a living thing rather than a vehicle for my equestrian success. I began to value my animals as sentient beings, open to feelings as well as to commands. I still loved to ride and to train correctly, but no longer was I driven by a need to compete. Riding could be planned according to how my horses were feeling rather than with a competition deadline in the future. I felt liberated by this change in perspective.

The animals, Rod and I moved to our new farm fourteen years ago. Now when I am conditioning each horse for the next season of riding lessons, I have to consider how the years at the farm have affected him. I am paying more attention these days, listening and watching for signs that suggest I should reduce riding time. If a horse begins to snap his teeth and pin his ears in anticipation of my tightening the girth around his belly, I give him a few days off. I limit riding lessons to once a day for each horse; and all horses are ridden out on the trail to break up the monotony of schooling in the ring. Finally, I am beginning to feel the connection with my horses that I knew had been missing during my competitive days. This shift is a spiritual awakening.

In the fall of 2012, one of my eleven year old riding students lost her mother in a motorcycle accident. The tragedy struck our entire community and left many to wonder about a child's ability to cope with such grief. Her father and I decided to provide her with more extensive barn time in the wake of the accident. It did not surprise me to witness the healing power of horses yet again. In the presence of horses, this child seemed to find control. She gravitated especially toward Makia. The child liked to spend time grooming and riding the gentle mare, building skills to gain confidence. With the world so out of kilter, horses offered the child an opportunity to stand firmly on uneven ground. From the sidelines, I witnessed an intimate exchange between human and horse, the child leaning on the horse for support, the horse holding the child up. In my head I was collecting images of horses as healers. Their noble looks and calm inquisitive natures endear them to most humans. Horses make people feel good. After all, wasn't it my first horse, Promise who soothed me through typically tumultuous teen years? Her quiet presence pushed the anxiety aside. In her company I swelled with pride; I felt both strength and peace.

Often people look for similarities between the human/dog bond and the human/horse bond. While comparing the two relationships, I came to a startling conclusion. Dogs are liars. They love us no matter what. Whether we are in a good or foul mood, dogs want nothing more than to share our time and will wiggle, paw and bark to get our attention. Horses are different. They only trust those whom they are certain are trustworthy. To take a chance might result in failure to survive. Yet herd mentality makes them curious about seeking our companionship. Sometimes the horse hesitates, however, while considering whether or not to trust the person, because horses as prey animals cannot afford the risk. An evolutionary will to survive accepts nothing less than certainty.

Based on my developing philosophy, I began to spend more time on the ground, working my horses at liberty, without tack or restraint. I set new goals as I vowed to handle the horses more, pay attention to ground work and simply be present while my horses were turned out or lounging leisurely in their stalls. It was a difficult commitment considering how limited my time in the barn was. During the winter when the temperature dips well below zero for days on end, it can be challenging enough to clean stalls, fill water buckets and feed grain. Retirement offers a promise of much needed extra time to spend with my horses.

More than anything, I look forward to the incredible bonding that results from working my horses at liberty. When they choose to stand near and interact with me, I know I am communicating on their level. In the reflection of the horse's behavior, I finally see the horsewoman I want to be. As I spent more and more time engaging with my horses on this level, I realized that I was actually developing a program that might benefit people struggling with grief or merely seeking inner calm. I have named this activity Equi-Reflection, to emphasize the horse's ability to respond to human body language. The bond that results between them establishes the human as the leader of their two-creature herd. In addition, many studies show that interacting with horses releases oxytocin, the feel good hormone, into a person's bloodstream. The effect can deliver a temporary sense of peace to an insecure, depressed or grief stricken individual. For the human being, adult or child, this communication with a horse builds confidence and self-awareness that may transfer into her human relationships. She may become more comfortable as a leader among peers or colleagues. At the very least, she will benefit from experiencing her ability to control the horse through simple body cues and signals.

As the concept continued to build in my mind, I wondered if it was a response to the countless comments made to me over the years by fearful adults.

"I have always loved horses, but I am terrified of them."

"I loved horses, but once I was riding and I got thrown; been afraid of them ever since."

"I love horses, but I don't want to ride them."

An Equi-Reflection session is the perfect opportunity for someone to interact with a horse while keeping both feet securely on the ground. A horse's naturally gregarious nature proves to timid humans how trusting equids are. With a few cues from the person's body language and posture, a horse agrees to follow the leader. When the connection is established, it is a deeply moving experience. Horses are prey animals who in the moment of the interaction must *choose* to trust the predator. This is an emotional

222

choice made by the horse. For some reason, the force to trust is stronger than the force to flee. Therefore, it is imperative that humans never betray this trust that I view as a gift from the vulnerable horse.

Horses tune in to human emotions and glean information about the human in their presence. Equi-Reflection sessions teach people how to communicate with horses clearly and assertively. Voice commands are not discouraged, but posture and body movement produce stronger connection. A person who approaches the horse with shoulders back and a forward, purposeful gait will capture the horse's attention and stimulate his curiosity. The horse will inspect this human with a keen eye and assess potential for leadership in their herd of two. In the horse's mind, a good leader means protection and survival. People learn to use their body language to assert themselves when verbal exchange is uncomfortable. Although humans might not be as aware of body language cues, they are always present and read unconsciously during human interactions. The horse's reaction to physical cues teaches people to be aware of body messages and ways to use them. This awareness is one reason why these sessions are so powerful for people who suffer from post-traumatic stress syndrome, depression and grievous loss. The sessions put them back in control of relationships with living beings. Gaining this confidence can be a powerful component in their healing. Although most horses instinctively participate in Equi-Reflection sessions, some are more sensitive than others. Some take little time to connect, while others require more time and proof that the human is worthy of their companionship. Among horses there are extraordinary equines who appear to go beyond the mission to bond with humans. They are the best healers.

Gatsby

"Animals can sometimes take us to a place that we can't reach by ourselves." from the introduction to HBO Sports Documentary: *Barbaro*

Jennifer's grief is so raw she can barely function.

"Robert would have loved this," she sobs. "He loved horses.

Her emotions flow while her hands massage Gatsby's body with a rubber currycomb. The bay gelding sighs and closes his eyes half way. He is not ignoring Jennifer. He is absorbing the pleasure of her touch.

After Gatsby's entire coat is rubbed over, I trade the currycomb for a stiff brush so that Jennifer can whisk the hair and dead skin debris away. Jennifer continues to talk through bouts of tears. Her only son, Robert's sudden death has cheated Jennifer out of a future that every mother looks forward to; marriage, grandchildren after the satisfaction of watching a child blossom into an adult. She feels abandoned. The density of her loss is thick, like the dusty haze enveloping us as she continues to groom Gatsby. Talking about Robert is painful but cathartic. Although I listen, I have no words of wisdom for Jennifer. Sadly, the worst part of grief is that ultimately we are left alone to face it, take control of it and secure it in a manageable place. Time is the most important factor, but time can't be manipulated or hurried. Traditional therapy with a sensitive professional helps. I am confident that Gatsby will also contribute to her healing once he and Jennifer begin to form a relationship. Jennifer is clearly in a state of post-traumatic stress. Out of the blue every aspect of her life has been fractured. It will be a long time before she can fit the pieces back together again, although life will never be the same. Perhaps Gatsby can provide a facet that will complement traditional therapies.

Now that the horse's coat is glistening, Jennifer takes a brush to organize Gatsby's disheveled mane on one side of his neck. He looks almost spiffed up and ready to go to work. Jennifer finishes the grooming session with strong brushing strokes on his long black tail. Gatsby's pleasant expression blinks with appreciation for the lingering effects of Jennifer's body massage.

The black-flies are not too bad this mid-May morning, so Jennifer leads Gatsby by a rope to the outdoor ring. I instruct her on the basics that will make him pay attention to her. I tell her, "He has a tendency to pull to the right if you wish to go left and cross in front of you to the left when you want him to go straight." At the gate I remind her to be assertive with him.

"Make sure you go through the gate first."

"Whoa Gatsby, whoa," she tugs on the lead rope and the horse slows.

"Turn him so he is facing the gate," I continue. "This is the safest place for you to be when you let him go. Before you release him, I want you to stand here in his presence and look at him, really look at him. Unlike your dog, this is a prey animal. Your relationship with him *should* be unnatural because many of your features suggest that you could kill him. Horses don't seem too conflicted by their desire to be with this two legged creature who eats meat. Apparently, humans are worth the risk. Always respect that."

Jennifer is quiet, but her hands never stop stroking Gatsby's face and neck. He closes his eyes as I go on about the two levels of energy that horses have. I try to keep it simple.

"Right now he is calm and low energy, but in order to start our session we have to rev him up a bit. We are going to raise the energy level by chasing him and encouraging him to run."

I show her how to crack the whip by flicking her wrists as she grasps the handle with both hands. The horse is never touched by the whip but the sound gets Gatsby moving out into the open space of the ring. It's hot and humid, but he charges away from us, kicking out a few half-hearted bucks. He races up to the corner of the ring. Jennifer follows in hot pursuit. I chase him back to her when he gallops down to my end of the ring. Gatsby stays close to the fence and trots along, gazing out into the woods. Something out there captures his attention. Jennifer and I turn up the energy by clucking our tongues and cracking the whip. The effect is immediate as Gatsby sprints around the ring exuberantly. Eventually, the horse slows his pace and turns his face toward Jennifer.

"Bring the energy down," I call. "Lower the whip and just stand quietly for a moment."

As she obliges, Gatsby marches with full purpose toward Jennifer. She begins to walk in his direction. When they meet, she reaches out to rub his face and neck. He stands respectfully in her space, appreciating the physical contact. I tell her he is complimenting her body language, grateful that she is easy for him to read. She smiles. I instruct her to be in the moment with Gatsby, feel his warmth, smell his aroma, talk to him.

After a minute or two, I tell Jennifer to stand next to Gatsby on his left side, keeping her shoulder in the vicinity of his eye where the brass buckle of his halter is located. She follows the direction and waits for the next one.

"Now start walking with purpose all over the ring; turning left, turning right, just walk. She grabs his halter to lead him.

"No need to touch him. Just walk."

She resists the temptation to control him.

"Just walk. He wants to follow you. Trust him."

She wills her hands off of his head and begins to walk forward. Gatsby also walks forward, glued to Jennifer's shoulder. They traverse in circles, the predator and the prey clearly united by his desire to feel safe and her desire to lead. I never tire of this moment of revelation.

As instructed, Jennifer walks with purpose, shoulders back and arms gently swinging at her side. It is a signal to Gatsby that she is the leader and he can relax and follow along. When she speeds up, so too does the horse. The bond between them is already strong.

"Now stop," I command from the other side of the fence.

Jennifer halts, but Gatsby walks past her before receiving the message. Jennifer shuffles to catch up to him, but Gatsby has turned to stop in front of her. At this point, I remind her that he has stopped on his own terms because her body language did not speak clearly. He just wasn't prepared or paying attention. Next time she stops, she must define the halt with her body language and wait for him to catch on. She nods her head and they continue to walk together. The next time she stops, she remains still. Gatsby is paying closer attention. He stops too. As they repeat the exercise, I can tell from her smile that Jennifer is enjoying communicating with Gatsby.

"Now we are going to add another command," I say after Gatsby masters the halting activity. "Stand in front of his face and wiggle the whip at him while telling him to back. Be firm and use your whole body to direct him backwards."

Jennifer steps in front of Gatsby's nose. With one command he leans back on his haunches in preparation to step backwards. He takes half a step and waits to see if this is what she wants. Jennifer wiggles the whip as directed. Confirmed that he is doing the right thing, Gatsby takes two steps backward. Instinctively, Jennifer walks to him and strokes his nose.

"Good boy," she fusses. "Such a good boy."

After several repetitions, I can tell they have had enough. She leads him over to the gate where I hand her the lead rope to attach to his halter.

"That was twenty minutes where I didn't think about Robert," she weeps.

Instinctively, I reach out to rub her shoulder. Gatsby stands close and she turns to him for comfort. The power of the horse is never more evident to me than in this moment. He can't bring Robert back, but for a few restful minutes he can interrupt the pain.

Jennifer leads the horse back to the wash stall and secures him on the cross-ties. I show her how to bathe him with Vetrolin so that his muscles cool down. She seems in no hurry. When the horse is soaking wet, I tell her she has one more task.

"Let's take Gatsby outside and let him go so that he can graze on the lawn and dry in the sun," I say.

Jennifer leads him to the grassy knoll by the picnic table, away from all the activity in the barn. Gatsby waits patiently.

"Before you unclip the lead rope, I want you to envision reaching down inside of yourself to break off a small piece of the pain. When you are ready to let it go, you can let Gatsby go. He is going to take that small burden away and carry it for you. He is large and a little bit of your pain won't trouble him. But, it will be less for you to hold onto."

Jennifer turns to Gatsby. From behind I see her shoulders quake. She can take all the time she needs. After a few minutes, she unclips the lead rope. The bay horse lowers his head to the ground and walks off in search of the lush green grass he has been craving through the long winter. The wind is light and the farm is quiet. There is tangible peace that I hope Jennifer can feel. Her gaze remains latched onto Gatsby as he ambles away. In the wake of their Equi-Reflection session, I am convinced that equine assisted activities are my future with horses. Not only does Equi-Reflection feed my passion for working with horses, it also offers a powerful tool for salvaging the mental wellbeing of those who are suffering.

Countless times during an Equi-Reflection session, I have witnessed the moment when the horse chooses to trust the human. Each time, I am as moved as my client is when she realizes the horse has decided to remain close and follow her lead. The behavior is instinctive, not taught. However, it is reinforced by human body language that reveals trust and confidence in the horse. *Allan Hamilton* describes the mission of Equi-Reflection when he admonishes, *"I call horses 'divine mirrors' - they reflect back the emotions you put in. If you put in love and respect and kindness and curiosity, the horse will return that."*

We humans owe a debt of gratitude to the horse for paving our path from early civilization into the industrial age. For thousands of years, we have used the horse to discover new lands, provide protein in our diet, fight wars, plow fields, and win fortunes. By the 1920's we had discarded horsepower almost completely when the automobile evicted equids from their niche in transportation. I am proud to be alive during the era in which we finally recognize the horse's ability to restore faith for those who have lost their way. In the long run, this just might be another favorable contribution from the horse to mankind.

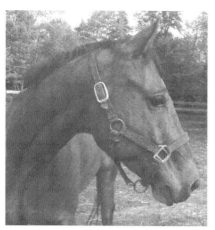

Gatsby made deep connections with participants during Equi-Reflection™ training workshops.

Joshua and Spirit demonstrate a horse's desire to accept leadership from humans.
photos by M. deCamp

Unusual Teacher's Pets
No More Pigs

"By helping you, perhaps I was trying to lift up my life a trifle. Heaven knows anyone's life can stand a little of that." -EB White, (from Charlotte's Web, spoken by *Charlotte*, the spider.)

"No," he said emphatically. "We agreed that Noah was it. No more pigs!"

"Yes, but I have changed my mind and think that a pig would be the perfect addition to the farm," I reasoned.

"No."

Our first Vietnamese potbelly pig, Noah, lived until the age of ten. Sadly, he spent our first winter at MRF in a state of slow decline and passed away in early June of 2005. Although not exactly friendly towards strangers, he was very loyal to his family, allowing me to snuggle close to him until the very end. For more than a year we lived *pig free* while establishing life on our new farm.

The following November, I attended the *Syracuse Invitational Horse Show* with a few of my riding students and friends. Naturally, we found ourselves drawn to a petting zoo among the vendors in the expo hall of the *On Center*. Among the assortment of miniature donkeys, horses and goats was a tiny potbelly piglet. Reaching over the low fence to pet her, I was suddenly overwhelmed with *good* Noah memories; not the ones that included the clothing he had destroyed while incorporating stray socks, shirts and underwear into his 'nest' or the abrasive wear on the fine finish of our furniture after he scratched himself against it. No, I was overcome by thoughts of Noah's sweetness as a tiny pig who "umphed*"* contentedly while snuggling in my arms. The Noah who grazed on our lawn and wallowed in the wet sand of our small beach during hot summer days. The two hundred pound Noah whom Rod hoisted onto the sofa to lie in my arms, (as baby Noah had done one-hundred-eighty pounds earlier), providing comfort for me the evening after our ancient dachshund was euthanized. The Noah who went for boat rides to Rod's family's camp, Sunny Cliff, with us on summer Sunday afternoons, and the Noah who snacked on blueberries in competition with our husky, Mishka, during hikes on the far side of Raquette Lake.

The little piglet that I was stroking was not for sale, but the attendant at the petting zoo just happened to have a litter of potbelly piglets due for weaning in another two weeks. After the horse show, I returned home to break the news to Rod. I wanted another pig!

I can't say that Rod relented; since Fiona's arrival he has, on more than one occasion (particularly when she is scratching herself on the finished woodwork), reminded me that he didn't want another pig. However, just before Thanksgiving, I drove south into Madison County to pick up our six week old piglet with Rod's knowledge but not necessarily his blessing. Like baby Noah, the tiny piglet was adorable! But unlike baby Noah, she had never been handled by a human until this very day. Uniting her with me required the farm owner to chase the piglet around a large stall inhabited by a sow and five siblings. Once the piglet was cornered and grabbed, the breeder stuffed her into my dog crate. During the entire drama, all of the little piglets and their mother screamed in distress as one of their own was plucked from the family and vanished out the stall door.

At the back of the crate the tiny black piglet cowered with legs splayed on the slippery crate surface. Her eyes, wide with terror, broke my heart. She had no idea what was happening to her, who I was or what existed outside of the stall she had lived in since birth.

Originally, I thought I would name her Vanessa, because it was elegant and so lady like. Driving back to Old Forge, I rolled the name back and forth over my tongue while the piglet stood motionless in her crate at the back of my car.

"Vanessa," I sang to her. "Hello Vanessa, my little piggly."

No sound came from the crate. What was she doing back there? My imagination ran wild with the thought that all the stress of leaving her family so abruptly might have killed her. Just when I was about to pull over and check, I heard her feet scrape the bottom of the crate as she changed her position. "Urmp," she grunted quietly.

Meanwhile, the name Vanessa, just wasn't fitting as well as I had hoped. By the time we passed through Utica and began heading north on Route 12, I had tried other names on the tiny piglet. Vera, Winona and Lucy did not fit her either. But when the name Fiona tumbled out of my mouth, I squealed out loud, "That's it, your name is Fiona!"

Acclimating six week old wild Fiona to life in our house was a challenge made more so by the transition from fall to winter. She hated cold weather, standing miserably in the blowing snow and driving rain, refusing to pee or poop. Surprisingly, pigs can go for almost twenty-four hours without eliminating wastes. Frequently, Fiona proves this to me when temperatures plummet below zero for the day. She simply refuses to stay outside and attend to business no matter how much we coax her with food. Thankfully, she is completely housebroken. With very few exceptions when she was younger, she has never had an accident in our house.

Three months after her arrival, I had to resign myself to the fact that my baby pig did not crave the physical contact that Noah enjoyed. I made every effort to soothe her with my voice and beguile her with treats. She always stopped to listen to or sniff my offerings; however, once rewarded, she dashed away, suspicious of my motives if she lingered too long. Perhaps the most heartbreaking realization was that she could never relax when I held her in my arms. When I tried, she retaliated by screaming at top decibel for long exhales that stretched past what I believed was piggly possible. Nothing seemed to appease her. Eventually, I had to respect that Fiona needed my patience as well as space. I gave up trying to hold her.

She reminded me of students I have had in the classroom who just can't seem to muster a smile or offer any significant feedback for my attempts to navigate them on a course of greater good, no matter how hard I try. Unlike self-motivated pupils these students require more patience, kindness and attention from me, no matter how much they resist my efforts. Eventually, we come to some kind of a connection, based only on the student's needs. Over time Fiona and I made a connection, but only on her terms.

Several weeks after I acquired Fiona, I was convinced that I had lost her. Our West Highland terrier, Niles, is the hero of this adventure that happened on our daily animal walk when the piglet was only ten weeks old. By that time, she was following along without a leash in our procession of dogs and goats. At one point Rod and I became distracted when our terriers Nina and Niles took off through the woods in pursuit of a squirrel. By the time we rounded them up again, we realized that Fiona had wandered away. Immediately, we began a frantic search for her with no idea in which direction she was headed. Rod and I separated in search of our tiny swine to no avail. Then we became aware that Niles had disappeared as well. For the next two hours, we searched near and far for both dog and pig, plenty of time for my imagination to envision Fiona drowned in the river and Niles snagged in a trap.

These images haunted me while I retraced the steps of our hike on a six wheeler. Rod combed the trail in the opposite direction on his tractor. Eventually, we met back in the driveway, each hopeful that the other had good news. Disappointed, we headed back out into the woods, refusing to give up the search.

While we were out searching for the final time, my friend Michele and her granddaughter arrived at the farm. They were amused to find Niles and Fiona lying together on the grassy knoll in the middle of the driveway. Perhaps, they thought, we had posed them that way for a picture. Returning home this time, I was convinced that I would never see these two family members ever again. But there they were, lying right next to each other, heaving with exhaustion from their long journey.

I am convinced, from similar events that have taken place in the past, that when Fiona wandered off, Niles took it upon himself to stay close to her and lead the way back home. They must have traversed through the woods, off the trails that we had been scouring. The sight of them safe and sound in our backyard erased the fear that had brewed within me for several hours. The thought of losing the piglet and our Westie was too painful to consider. I escorted Fiona to her bed where she slept without interruption until the next morning.

We lavished Niles with hugs and praise for his heroic efforts that surely resulted in our piglet's safe return. Animals never cease to amaze me. This is one of those events that I have pondered frequently over the years. Niles made the same decision when a visiting friends' beagle got distracted by a wild rabbit and took off in hound dog pursuit. It didn't take us long to realize Niles was gone too. Sure enough, he had stayed with the beagle and was ready to lead her back to the farm once the scent dissipated. After a long empty search, the beagle, escorted by Niles, arrived back to her worried owners' open arms.

Fiona reached maximum size by her second birthday. We estimate that she is easily two hundred pounds. It's unnerving to hear these pigs advertised as micro-minis or teacup pigs. Sanctuaries are full of large potbelly pigs who maxed out at normal weights that owners were not expecting. Compared to breeds of pork producing pigs, Fiona *is* a miniature pig. Some meat pigs top out at over eight hundred pounds.

I love Fiona's presence in the barn. While I perform daily chores, she forages for grain and other tidbits discarded by the horses and goats. Her snout is a force to be reckoned with, capable of detecting the minutest particles of food. She also uses it to gouge my ankles while I measure the horses' feed. Searing pain forces me to drop a handful of grain on the ground. Yes, she has trained me well.

Fiona loves to sunbathe on warm spring days and permits me to douse her with a warm Vetrolin bath when stifling heat sticks around too long in the summer. For the most part, she roams the property freely. When she has had enough of the outdoors, her dexterous snout pushes open the backyard gate so she can make her way back to the house. Unlike Noah, she does not have free run of our home. In a concession to Rod's concern about living with another destructive pig, we have confined her living quarters to a room behind the kitchen. A nest of blankets, that she has torn up and arranged herself, comprises her bed.

Caring for Fiona, is fairly simple most of the time. However, every twenty-eight days, when she comes into heat, managing her becomes quite challenging. On a good day, Fiona goes about her life with one main objective, to find food. Her morning begins with a meager handful of formulated potbelly pig pellets that she scarfs down quickly so she can get on with the task of finding more food. A banquet under the bird feeders provides this reward. Next, she is off to the barn to clean up stray bits of grain that certain horses have flung out of their feeders while eating their own breakfast. Fiona consults her nose like a roadmap that provides her with the exact location of stray grain. With a grunt and a squeal, she pushes her way into stalls where horses are browsing on hay and grain. The horses, for the most part, ignore these greedy intrusions. Once in a while, they lower their heads and pin their ears at her. The gestures are enough to send the pig running out the stall door, grunting in displeasure.

After many hours of foraging, Fiona makes her way back toward the house and the gate that keeps our four small dogs fenced in and safe during the day. With a hefty shove from her snout, the gate pops open, and Fiona enters the dogs' domain quickly, before the spring loaded hinge slams the gate with a clatter behind her. Up the three steps to the back door of our house she drags her full belly. The sound of her snout grinding on the freshly painted dark green door gets our attention. Immediately, we let her into the house. Parched from the hot weather, the pig seeks her water dish and drains more than half a gallon at a time. Finally, Fiona ambles to her bed and cozies up for a long afternoon nap. Tiny pig feet tire easily after one or two hours supporting the bulk of her big body. This nap will last until early evening when an empty stomach rouses her and the process begins once again.

Shortly before Fiona is due to come into heat, her daily routine begins to change. Rod and I have to monitor her constantly for any sign that heat is imminent. Keeping track on the calendar is helpful, but it cannot pinpoint the exact arrival of estrus.

Why all the fuss? Once Fiona comes into her strong heat, she has but one mission in life, a mission so intense that it takes priority over the desire to eat. As a result of urge, Fiona takes it upon herself to leave home. Yup, leave the one place where meals and all the comforts of living a pretty good life exist. Where is she headed? I can only assume to a place where she hopes a boar might be awaiting her fertile arrival! If we are not paying attention, Fiona will simply begin the journey on hoof, down the driveway and out onto the road. Eventually, we catch onto the fact that she has vanished from the property. Then, with the use of our motorized sport vehicle, we are in quick pursuit, tracking shallow cloven hoof prints that suggest she is in a hurry. Frequently, we find her at Adirondack Woodcraft Camp, our neighbor, half a mile or more down the road. Once, she was discovered jogging out to the main road. Luckily, we have always been able to coax her back home where we immediately lock her in the backyard until it is evident that her heat is waning and our homebody pig has returned to her senses, usually within three days.

Fortunately, there is one sign we can count on to warn us that Fiona is coming into heat. That is nesting behavior. I am not sure what the significance of the behavior is. Even if Fiona was to successfully breed, she would still be close to four months from delivering her piglets, so why she is compelled to build a large comfy nest prior to breeding is a mystery. Regardless, the behavior is fascinating to watch because she performs with such determination and purpose. Fiona has successfully built large nests of grass, ferns, and moss. During the winter months, she will nest indoors by gathering dog beds, blankets and any laundry left unattended on the floor. She carefully drags these items into her own bed to create a mass of textiles. To protect our good clothes from destruction, I replace them with old saddle pads that I leave strewn about the floor so she can collect and haul them to the nest herself.

I can't compare living in the house with a female pot belly pig to cohabiting with any other pet. She is unique in all aspects, but she adds a dimension of character that is her very own, endearing her to us for as long as she lives. At times Fiona resembles the most unlovable student in my classroom, grunting defiance at having her feet trimmed or being forced outside to take care of business in sloppy weather conditions. She is prickly, not cuddly. She is leery of guests, so her standoffishness is always a disappointment to them. But Fiona has taught me that her way of life limits stress and keeps her mentally and physically healthy. No doubt these factors are more important than my ego's desire to cuddle with a pig. I respect her needs and make sure that she is safe, comfortable and nutritionally fed.

Call it customized nurturing, the same respect I extend to prickly students in the classroom, for those not jovial and not open to hugs. Like Fiona, each seemingly unapproachable student deserves that I accept his/her unique personality. I need to find ways to make learning available to these students. Perhaps they seek learning the way Fiona seeks food: some from my hands and some from foraging on her own in the safe spaces of the barn. It's my role as teacher to help them find their way to the skills and experiences that will nurture them as they grow. Like Fiona, they require patience and understanding; as I have learned from Fiona, I can't expect to have a their needs; they are not in my classroom to meet mine. I know I can't cuddle Fiona just as I know I cannot coddle all students. Animals like Fiona have much to teach about what educational experts call "individual learning style." After eleven years, Fiona and I have established a warm, respectful connection, on her terms. As *Farmer Hoggett* exclaims in the last scene of the heartwarming motion picture classic, *Babe, "That'll do pig, that'll do!*

Throughout her twelve years of life Fiona has been an interesting character who lives by her own rules and occasionally seeks human companionship. bottom photo by R. Craig

Llamas, Adonis and Bravo

I almost bought a camel. That moment of madness bore into my psyche like a parasitic worm and distracted me for weeks. Shortly before Christmas, it came to my attention that camels resided within an hour's drive of my farm. Furthermore, an eight week old baby dromedary, or one hump camel was up for sale. Curiosity and my love of baby animals guided me to schedule a visit to meet the camels. In the days prior to my appointment, I researched all that I could about camels, using the crash course method that kept me awake late into the night. The genus *Camelus* includes both the dromedary and bactrian (two humps) camel species of modern times. Turns out that the ancestors of these camels were tiny gopher sized mammals that roamed the South Dakota plains some forty million years ago. Five million years later, this tiny creature had evolved to the size of a goat and was beginning to expand its range. Only five million years ago, this early camelid spread into South America where eventually it gave way to the wild camels, both guanaco and vicuna, that roam the plains and Andes mountain region. Meanwhile, the early camelids who migrated north from the plains region made their way across the Bering Strait into Asia to become the large dromedary and bactrian camels we know today. Although I had always associated camels with desert climate, their ability to adapt to both bitter cold and intense heat led me to believe that an Adirondack camel would actually thrive in our harsh winters.

And about that large hump on the camel's back. The fatty cells that comprise the hump tissue are capable of absorbing and retaining a ten day supply of water. More impressive is the fact that camel red blood cells have evolved into an oval shape that facilitates blood flow, especially when the animal is dehydrated. At the end of long intervals, parched camels can drink a staggering forty-five gallons in just a few minutes. This feat alone would kill most animals because the osmotic pressure gradient between the outside and inside of dehydrated cells would cause the cells to rupture!

With heads full of camel facts, my friend Vicky and I navigated our way by GPS to an antique cow barn north of Utica. Several adult

Great Danes barked and bellowed from the barn door where an electric fence prevented them from greeting us up close.

Among the dogs, a petite middle aged woman bundled up in winter barn outerwear waved enthusiastically to attract our attention. Chris, the proprietor of the farm, led Vicky and me away from the boisterous dogs toward her house where the baby camel was currently living in her basement. When Chris turned on the fluorescent lights above his stall, a pair of large brown eyes gazing up from the sides of a fuzzy brown head greeted us. The baby camel stood a full five feet tall. According to him, it was feeding time, a fact he emphasized by bobbing his head like a puppet and gliding back and forth behind his stall door, hoping to attract Chris's attention.

"He was born in mid-October, so he is still on the bottle," Chris shared, paying no attention to the gyrating youngster in our midst. "He will require several more months of bottle feeding, four times a day, before he is old enough to be weaned. That's why I have him over here instead of in the barn with the others. Makes it easier for me to tend to him, especially in bad weather."

I assumed the others included the little fellow's mother. Why he had been removed from her care, I wasn't sure. Camels are not in my area of expertise so I was not entitled to question the woman's motives. Eventually, Chris excused herself to go upstairs to the kitchen and prepare the baby camel's bottle. We were grateful that she had waited for us to experience this most pleasurable chore of animal care.

While waiting, Vicky and I watched the little camel as he careened around in his tiny stall, anticipating the delivery of his meal. By the time Chris arrived back downstairs, the baby had worked himself into a frenzy. I must admit that by this time I was fully intimidated by the camel's frenetic energy. I tried to picture him moving to Moose River Farm and fitting in among my various animals. Due to his price tag, a second camel was out of the question so I would have to work out a plan that didn't leave the camel in total isolation. Not knowing anything about camels, I felt increasingly intimidated.

Chris entered the stall with a gallon bottle of formula. Attached at the opening was a large rubber nipple that disappeared immediately into the camel's mouth. Chris stood with one arm around the baby's neck while holding the bottle upright with her other hand. For the first time, the camel stood fairly still, all of his concentration fixated on sucking.

After the camel had settled, Chris asked me if I'd like to take her place. I did not hesitate. Pleasurable memories of raising my three baby goats earlier that year flooded me with maternal yearning. Mimicking Chris's position enabled me to grasp the bottle with my right hand while my left arm hugged the camel's neck close to me. The little camel bobbed his head up and down, adjusting to the change of human assistance while he pumped the nipple. His fur was soft and warm pressing against me. The sweet smell of formula diffused in the air, mixed with his own camel perfume. I kissed the top of his head and held him tight. The experience alone was worth the visit even if I did not buy the camel.

When the bottle was empty, the little camel continued pacing frantically around in the stall with renewed vigor. I hoped that he would be given the opportunity to spend his juvenile energy. Aside from sustenance, nothing is more important for foals, baby goats and puppies than being given space to run and play. Not only does exercise strengthen growing bones and muscles, but it also provides much needed mental stimulation. Exercise allows juveniles a chance to test their independence by encouraging them to explore further and further from their mother. The baby camel's frenetic energy that intimidated me earlier was no doubt caused by a lack of exercise.

In the weeks that followed the camel visit, I thought about the baby often. If only camels did not grow so big, much bigger than the largest horses. Caring for an animal that I fear is out of the question. How could we ever find a house sitter if we had to go out of town? Eventually, I was able to let go of the idea and move on. While winter staggered through endless months of cold and snow, my waning camel obsession was replaced by a rekindled desire to own llamas.

Llamas are small camel cousins who possess many of the same features, including the large eyed expression, of their mammoth kin. Like camels, goats and cattle, llamas are ruminants; animals who digest stalky cellulose in a large organ called the rumen. The population of bacteria that live in the rumen ferment the starchy structures of edible plants. Like camels, llamas are capable of spitting gobs of stinky green regurgitated vegetation when they are annoyed or threatened. This is usually the only piece of information people glean about llamas. Like camels, llamas *kush* or lie down by buckling their limbs underneath their torso and remaining upright on their chest.

Because of my ruminant knowledge, llamas were among the first animals I had considered adding to our menagerie when Rod and I were married thirty years ago. At the time, they were difficult to locate. Llamas that were available for sale were too expensive for a newlywed couple's budget. Then alpacas, which are similar to llamas but much smaller, invaded the livestock market, promising a fortune to be made from their fiber. Alpacas were also expensive to purchase: twenty-thousand dollars a breeding pair in the mid nineteen-nineties. As a result I abandoned the idea to own small camelids, concentrating instead on abundantly available goats and chickens to complement my horses. Over thirty years later, I could consider buying llamas because the failure of the llama/alpaca market to sustain itself caused a severe drop in prices. Currently, there are more alpaca available than llamas, but both species' prices are more affordable.

Although I needed to refresh my knowledge about llamas, I was fairly confident that I could become proficient in their care once I became acquainted with their special needs. Like goats, llamas are ruminants requiring hay and grass for a substantial diet. The most important concern that I had was the risk of acquiring an aggressive llama. Perusing *Youtube* videos for documented footage of llamas attacking people was enough to justify my concern. In fact some people seek out rogue llamas to protect vulnerable livestock such as sheep and goats. Aggressive llamas will strike, kick and chase anything that invades their territory. Since children frequently attend programs at Moose River Farm, it was imperative that a resident llama be docile and easy to handle. After a lengthy search, I located Dakota Ridge Farm, just south of Saratoga Springs. A couple of exchanged emails fixed an appointment on the calendar and led me to acquire the two most mystical creatures on our farm.

The llama farm's proprietors, Katrina and Gary, could not have been more gracious. They provided Rod and me the opportunity to handle llamas so we could test our comfort level. The farm was home to some fifty-five llamas, fifteen that belonged to people who boarded them there. From the first llama we encountered, a female with a *cria* or baby at her side, we experienced nothing but grace and calm. Several of the other mother llamas put their noses right up to our faces, allowing us to kiss them gently while we rubbed their thick hairy necks. It was quite a soothing experience, not at all intimidating as the baby camel visit had been. Several crias bounced around the paddock, occasionally approaching us curiously. Up close I marveled at their silky soft baby hair. While I petted a gray speckled cria, she stretched her nose right up to mine. At this level I stared into her enormous dark eyes as she stared deep into mine. In that moment I was aware of her sweet perfume and milky breath. The tiny cria did not linger long before dashing away on springy limbs, bobbing and weaving her head in search of mama. I was smitten.

Not once did a llama act aggressively toward us. Katrina was confident that, because her llamas were handled extensively from birth, they had no need to feel threatened by people. We did witness a spitting event when one female, upon whom we were lavishing our attention, protested llama style when other llamas invaded her personal space. All of a sudden, a small wad of green goo shot out of her mouth and up into the air like a silent rocket. It hadn't risen very far before gravity overcame thrust, causing it to descend in a perfect arc and splat on the ground. We laughed at the llama's gooey attempt to shoo other llamas who were crowding her for our attention. They didn't react to the spent ammunition.

We encountered many llamas that afternoon: intact males, gelded males, females, crias, weanlings and yearlings. Every one of them proved to me that this was a camelid that I could handle comfortably. Even Rod was enthusiastic about adding them to our farm. That fact alone made the decision to acquire llamas much more exciting.

One week before Christmas, Gary and Katrina delivered two male llamas to the Adirondacks. Katrina had selected ten year old Adonis, a middle aged, recently gelded male, to teach me how to interact with llamas. Since he had a plethora of experience from breeding to the show ring, he was a natural choice from whom to learn proper llama handling etiquette. Meanwhile, eighteen month old Bravo, a young intact male, was selected for me to train and manage from Adonis' lessons. The addition of any new animal or species to my barn always delivers a welcome distraction, especially when they arrive just before the long winter months. Interacting with the llamas every day and learning their habits provided a new challenge in addition to caring for the established farm members. They changed up the routine of barn chores while incorporating their specific llama needs among the others. They also accompanied me daily on my walks in the woods to exercise the donkeys, Bing and Frankie. The llamas proved to be a perfect fit among all the animals on the farm.

Over the winter months, llamas transformed me from novice handler to educated leader of my small herd. When I wasn't practicing haltering the llamas, earning their trust or leading them on the trails in the woods, I was busy researching their natural history origins and gleaning as much information as I could absorb. It was time well spent during long dark winter evenings after barn chores.

Llamas were domesticated approximately six thousand years ago by South American native people called the Quechua. They captured and bred wild guanacos, small camel cousins, that roam the plains and mountains of the Andes. Guanacos were selectively bred for traits associated with our modern llamas: height and thick coats. *Llama* is a Quechuan term and only a coincidence that it is identical to the Spanish term for *call* or *name*. The animals provided work and fiber during the thriving Inca Empire. In fact llamas were so revered that their remains were often buried with those of prominent leaders to assist them wherever they ended up in the next phase of existence. When the Spanish arrived to conquer this South American region in the mid 1500's, they too employed llamas to carry loads into and out of the mountainous regions they occupied.

In the presence of Adonis and Bravo, I focused on their South American heritage with great interest. Although the alpaca, a smaller cousin of the llama, is bred for softer fiber, my llama's fiber is a unique pleasure to sink cold fingers into. The coarse dry outer layer of hair give way to the velvety undercoat that caresses my calloused hands like polar fleece gloves. In this position I am at eye level with the giant orbs that blink under long dark lashes. They are this prey animal's most prominent feature, enabling him to scan the landscape far and wide for predators. The shape of the llama body takes some getting used to after a lifetime of staring at horse, goat and dog proportions. Llamas have long necks that stretch like church steeples toward the sky and attach to the shoulders at sharp right angles. Horses and goats are curvy with no points. In fact all the training that we do with horses is an effort to accentuate roundness in their posture. Unlike the barrel shape of horses, the llama torso is tent shaped. The spine forms the sharp roof line while the ribs hang at forty-five degree angles like tent flaps.

Most llamas are shorn from shoulder to hip so that heat can dissipate from their bodies during warm weather months. The haircut accentuates their thin waistline that resembles the flanks of racing greyhounds. The llama tail is flat and hairy. It flaps like a ping pong paddle when excitement puts the llama on alert. Llama colors come in an endless variety of brown, black, white, beige and red hues. Small spots, large splotches, and all kinds of regional contrasts like brown hips, white torso, brown head or left side mostly brown and right side speckled brown, create a kaleidoscope of patterns in a grazing herd. Llamas look like a comical assembly of many animals' parts, yet the combination is unique to the species and endearing to llama fanciers. Over time I've come to see the llama as yet another marvel of evolution, perhaps a celebration of another beast worthy to shelter in Noah's Ark.

The first thing Adonis taught me was how to respect his personal space. Unlike goats, donkeys, and horses, llamas do not like to have their faces touched. Reaching forward to stroke the bridge of a llama's nose is disrespectful. Swinging his head left and right or pointing his nose upward was Adonis' clear signal for me to stop. Instead he preferred to lean into my hand, a clear indication that he approved when I reached behind his head to scratch the base of his banana shaped ears. From Adonis' ears I was permitted to stroke his jowls at the sides of his face. When I mastered the technique, he squinted his eyes in pleasure. I could wrap my arms around his neck, scratch his wooly chest and even rub his back without him flinching. He was teaching me the rules; and like all good teachers, he clearly communicated what was allowed and what would not be tolerated. I paid close attention because I wanted to please him. After all, he had been removed from everything familiar to him for the first half of his life. I wanted the second half to be as perfect as I knew he had experienced in the past from his loving owner. After putting up with me through many awkward lessons, I owed him that much.

From the day the llamas arrived, I began to escort them on lead ropes out into the woods for walks. Rod accompanied us daily for the first week until I was confident that I could walk both llamas at the same time. Adonis' large stride and forward strut was easy for me to emulate. He liked to breeze along the trail, his head constantly oscillating like a periscope while his keen eyes and swiveling ears scanned the trees for objects of interest to him. Meanwhile, Bravo, who did not have a long leg span, trotted along at the end of his lead rope behind Adonis and me. The younger llama did not seem as tuned into what was happening in the woods, remaining much more focused on the trail ahead.

I loved interpreting their actions and learning how to read their expressions. Ears back emphasized irritation, not at me, but at an offending llama. If Bravo came too close to Adonis' hind end while we were walking, the older llama would pin his ears to the back of his head and exhale a "puff" sound, indicating that the younger llama had entered his personal space. Bravo replied to the signal by moving away from Adonis. Violent reactions did not occur. Each llama read messages loud and clear, never appearing to challenge the other's wishes. It is a refreshing relationship to witness. After years of observing horses kick and bite each other, goats use their heads to slam rivals in the rib cage, and chickens yank at one another's plumage, all trying to establish the pecking order within their own groups, this comradely give and take was a pleasant relief. In fact the lack of ferocity assured me that I was safe among the llamas even when they were gesturing irritation at each other. I did not fear being kicked, bumped or bitten.

In addition to the puffing sound llamas make when irritated with each other, they also hum. Similar to the bleat of a goat yet softer, the llama hum is grunted in several short continuous measures. Usually, it occurs when the llamas are unsure about what is going on around the barn.

"Umm, umm, umm, umm," they hum when a car drives up to the barn or when they wonder why their dinner is late. Sometimes they hum on our walks, particularly if I veer away from a familiar landmark or turn on the trail. It is their way of inquiring about changes in familiar patterns. I get the sense that they have a need to know what comes next. Llamas don't appreciate surprises. On occasion I have heard Adonis belt out the ultimate llama vocality. It is a combination of a buzzer and a honking horn that penetrates all other sounds that resonate around our farm. The *honk-bzzz* is reserved for occasions that warrant alarm. If he suspects a stranger is approaching the barn from the woods, Adonis will blast and then wait to see if he has effectively sent the offending visitor away before blasting again. Sometimes at dusk he will *honk-buzz* at horses moving about in their paddocks when the descending light conceals them from llama view. He has even sounded the alarm when hawks or wild geese fly low over the barnyard on their way to the river. No matter what provokes Adonis to emit the gravelly vocal tone, it always makes us laugh.

Sitting in their stall to observe the llamas I have become aware of surprising facets of their individual personalities. The younger llama, Bravo, seeks information from Adonis constantly. Every move that the older llama makes causes Bravo to react. If Adonis drinks from the water bucket, Bravo wants to look in the bucket to see if he should do the same. If Adonis cranes his head over the stall door to inquire about a goat, donkey or pig wandering in the aisle, the younger llama squeezes his head through the yoke at the top of the door to see what is going on. From my seated post deep in the hay bedding of their stall, I watch intensely, eager to collect nuances of their behavior so I can become more attuned to their needs. Adonis has a unique way of jutting his lower jaw out to the side while extending his head and neck downward. I am not sure what he is gesturing, but Bravo replies by circling around Adonis to the other side. Adonis then relaxes and both llamas continue eating from the same pile of hay. Although the behavior is a mystery to me, it is evident that, along with many others, it keeps the relationship amicable between these two llamas.

My college education provided me with knowledge and skills to care for my horses, donkeys, goats, pigs and dogs but not llamas. Adding llamas more than thirty years after graduation has forced me to revisit what I learned about ruminants. No need for me to dig out dusty notebooks and textbooks from the last century when internet resources are a click away. In the weeks before the llamas arrived, I was busy refreshing my knowledge of ruminants beyond what I know about goats. By the time Adonis and Bravo arrived, I felt confident that I could care for them adequately and recognize less serious health issues if and when they presented themselves. To prevent *choke*, I made sure the llamas were fed grain in large flat pans. Scattering feed on a large surface assures that a llama cannot fill up its tiny mouth too quickly, causing him to swallow a large wad of grain that plugs up the esophagus. Although choke does not affect the animal's ability to breathe, it does prevent food and gas from passing into and out of the rumen. Therefore, it can have deadly consequences.

I also updated my education about the meningeal worm, a debilitating parasite that invades the brain. Neurological symptoms such as incoordination and dizziness are signals that the animal is infected. The parasite is passed along in deer feces, thus providing exposure to grazing animals. Apparently, llamas are more susceptible than goats and must be dewormed every two or three months with a subcutaneous injection. Although the infestation is treatable, prophylactic measures are far more efficient for preventing damaging symptoms of parasitic invasion.

In my extended research I learned that gestation length is eleven and a half months for an average female llama. This fact was good to know because already I was planning to add more llamas to my newly assembled herd. It occurred to me that perhaps combining llama trekking with the beauty of the Adirondacks could be an activity to offer the public year round. There is such an ethereal quality about llamas that it seemed a natural fit to combine them with hikes through the healing woods. Of course this meant I needed more llamas. By early spring, I had acquired a large female llama with markings similar to Adonis'. Bluff remained at Dakota Ridge Farm in the company of one of their herd sires, Bal Whiskers. Because llamas are induced ovulators, the female will only ovulate or produce an egg when she has been penetrated by a male. Therefore it is difficult to tell when she is in estrus or heat. It is his semen that activates her ovaries. Once an egg has been fertilized, estrus hormones shut down and are replaced by pregnancy hormones such as progesterone. If all goes well, Bluff will arrive at Moose River Farm in the summer with a healthy cria fetus developing in vivo. An ultrasound performed by a veterinarian will confirm pregnancy; and one year later we hope to welcome a tiny cria into the growing llama herd. Thankfully, Dr. Jen Nightingale will be available if Bluff requires assistance, but our vet is very confident that, like most llamas, she will experience an uncomplicated delivery.

The addition of llamas on our farm was an opportunity to become a student once again. This time I took a seat in a virtual classroom that consisted of the internet and devices to access it. My inquisitive nature sent me on a quest to absorb as much as I could about these stunning creatures so that I could offer them the utmost in custom care. Learning about their needs and habits combined with their natural history was a chance to mesh studies in biology with an appreciation of them as art forms. It's as if a cubist has sharpened and exaggerated the conventional horse shape, so familiar to me, and created a jaunty, geometric alternative. Like the fascinating image of the unicorn, the silhouette of the llama charms as it conflicts with conventional geometry of quadrupeds. The unexpected outline surprises; the huge eyes under their luxurious lashes lure me; I want to approach, to stroke, to admire this manifestation of the marvelous variety of the created world. This is learning at its most efficient. While I am giddy with new knowledge, I am reminded that the students in my classroom require the same kind of ignition to fire up their curiosity. I must find topics that jolt their interest or listen closely to what they already find fascinating. Then I can push them to build meaningful reservoirs of information that enable them to work towards their dreams.

Studying llamas has awakened my scholarly interests. I am confident in my research skills after years of studying horses, goats and donkeys. Learning llama has enabled me to revisit my studious young adult self, the girl who would live among a variety of animals when she was educated, when she was competent, when she was grown. I draw upon my own experience when I teach my students how to follow their curiosity into research projects that teach valuable skills. When students really want to learn about a subject, whether it be llamas or gravitational forces, they willingly learn the intricacies of Google and Wikipedia.

It is ironic that this species I once perceived to be vicious is the very same that is guiding me toward gentler animal activities. Why do llamas have such a negative reputation? I have been bitten and kicked by unruly horses, butted by rogue goats, flogged by protective sex crazed ganders and yet never once have I felt threatened by llamas. Their calm nature combined with noble presence beckons me into their space. Katrina from Dakota Ridge Farm says they are mystical beings because they attract attention, lure us to stare and take comfort in their quiet calm. The long neck, springy legs, swiveling banana shaped ears combine into an art form that questions purpose. Yet once we connect with those voluptuous eyes peering from beneath an umbrella of long black fringe, we can't help but succumb to the llama's magical spell. Traversing the woods with Adonis at my shoulder and Bravo in tow relieves lingering stress from the day. They are Buddha and the Dalai-lama rolled into one, my spiritual advisers. Keeping time with my llamas' hushed rhythms, I leave my troubles on the trail behind me.

Bravo and Adonis are the first two llamas that arrived at MRF.
photo by M. deCamp

Top left; Adonis and Bravo.

Top right; Handsome Adonis is appropriately named.

Bottom; Bravo poses with Bluff, Majik and her baby Stormy.

I am Still a Teacher

Opposite Directions

"The meaning of life is to find your gift. The work of life is to develop it. The purpose of life is to give it away." -David Viscott

My educational career has swung like a pendulum back and forth between various learning and teaching trends. When I began teaching sixth grade, professional development opportunities stressed evaluating pupils on a holistic scale. In other words, teachers were encouraged to consider the whole child's strengths and weaknesses when measuring achievement. This trend replaced the idea that student achievement could be based mostly on the numerical value generated by standardized testing. At the end of my career, the trend has swung all the way back to the testing model. Teachers dutifully follow these trends and make the best of them for the sake of the students in their classrooms. After several cycles of pendulum swing, teachers begin to realize that many trends are recycled versions of strategies from past eras. Each time they resurface, they get new labels, suggesting that the education establishment has at last developed the best means of evaluating student achievement.

In my other life, I teach horseback riding to children and adults. I have trained horses for over fifty years. Along the way I have witnessed an evolution of training methods that seek kinder trends. Tight nosebands on bridles, draw reins and other manipulative pieces of tack are still espoused by some to force the horse into a standardized posture. Horses are cranked into a one size fits all *frame*, or position from ears to tail, with little consideration for the horse's individual natural conformation. Like school children all being evaluated by the same tests, not all horses can be squeezed into the same training mold to produce the same performance. Influential "experts" in the education of children and the training of horses seem always to be searching for the quick fix applicable to all.

We have spent too much time in schools and upon horses' backs trying to create the best standards and ways to evaluate mastery of them. I often wonder how many classroom teachers actually believe that the scores from standardized tests help them to be better teachers. Similarly I often wonder how many riders, relying on standard images of what the horse's frame should *look* like, can actually *feel,* with their bodies, when horses are moving in the correct posture. Summaries of test scores and quick glimpses in riding arena mirrors don't always deliver accurate images of students or horses. A teacher learns from her day to day exchanges with her students that each one is an individual, with different ways of learning and of demonstrating mastery of skills. The rider learns with her body how to feel an individual horse's correctness. In addition, the teacher and the rider must learn to communicate precisely and humanely with respective students and mounts. If they are skilled at their work, both teachers and riders add to their tool boxes effective strategies that guide both them and their charges toward success. Both learn to feel almost instinctively when they understand how to elicit the desired response. In the classroom or the riding ring, it's hard and tedious work but necessary when building a foundation for learning and individualized performance based assessment. Students must master multiplication tables before they try to solve complex algebra problems. One can't happen without the other. And yet many instructors continue to pressure riders to learn complex movements despite the rider's lack of basic skills. These situations result in frustrated horses who end up as failed mounts, much the same as students who fail to perform at standardized levels of expectations. Neither are encouraged to reach their full potential. As a teacher of public school students and a trainer of horses, I see parallel perils in over-reliance on universal standards.

Lately, approaching retirement from the public school classroom, I have been reflecting on my students of the past and my horses in the future. It is no longer important that I ride every day, that I train intensely, and maintain a level of fitness from riding several horses. No more testing of students in my future and no more drilling of my horses. Riding the trail casually is all I need to remain connected to my equestrian roots. Working with kids one day a week on my farm is all I need to stay connected to teaching. I know I am where I need to be at this point in my life. I like being at eye level with individual horses and within arms-reach of a few individual kids. I like reading the expressions of animals and children while concentrating on being the best communicator I can be. When all is said and done, it is not my riding or my formal classroom teaching I want to be remembered for. It is my commitment to treat all of my students and all of my animals as individual creatures, each of whom deserves my attention, kindness, knowledge and respect.

Kids Farm Day

"Bless the beasts and the children, for the world can never be the world they see." - Song lyrics by Barry DeVorzon

Over the years, many parents have asked me to consider employing their animal loving children in my barn. Although child labor laws prohibit hiring youngsters, their requests did make me wonder if I could engage young children in an agricultural education program that emphasized animal husbandry. That is how Kids Farm Day was established. Every Monday during the summer months, my farm becomes a place of fun and learning for kids between eight and twelve years old. This is the perfect age range for uninterrupted interest. Once teens discover the social focus of the cell phone, it's harder to engage them, no matter how adorable an animal is.

The children who attend Kids Farm Day arrive in the morning with a bagged lunch and the stamina that they will need for a full day of activities centered around farm life. The schedule begins with animal interactions that include short lessons in care and handling. While digging for worms to feed the chickens, the children and I discuss the importance of protein in their diets. While holding a goose, one can appreciate the density of feathers as a finger plunges into the thick plumage searching for flesh. No wonder geese don't mind cold weather. No wonder a down jacket is toasty warm. Next, each child is assigned to a horse and issued a set of grooming tools. How accomplished a kid feels when she can lift a horse's hoof and scrape out the dirt with a hoof pick. Feeding hay to the horses at noon is a favorite activity that accentuates the importance of routine. Horses become anxious if lunch isn't served on time.

Before they have their own lunch, the kids round up goats, dogs, donkeys and llamas for a hike through the woods. They take turns leading Bing and Frankie. Otherwise the donkeys will gorge themselves on grass and refuse to follow along. The llamas as well must be guided with a lead rope to prevent them from straying into the woods to browse. Meanwhile, the unleashed goats follow a strong herding instinct by bouncing down the trail to keep up with the whole procession of animals and kids. Along the way the children and I squat down to examine yellow trout lilies and delicate white trillium that grow in the woods. Audrey the goat believes we have discovered something for her to eat. She snatches the defenseless flowers before the children and I have finished a thorough examination. We laugh at her greediness while we search for another specimen. Rod identifies trees, pointing out the differences in bark and leaf patterns. The trunk of an aspen is weathered smooth, but birch appears covered with shredded paper.

At the pond, we startle frogs that plunk into the water. Hayden, our longhaired dachshund, does not hesitate to swim after them in hot pursuit. His efforts to catch them are in vain. Under the hot sun, the children, animals and I traverse a green field. Once on the other side, we feel the cool breeze welcome us into the woods. Unfortunately, the deer flies also greet us with chomping mandibles and annoying buzz. A mile later, we arrive back at the farm starved for lunch and a chance to relax before the afternoon session. We secure the llamas, goats and donkeys in various paddocks and stalls so they can enjoy a pile of hay and a long afternoon nap. Although we wash our hands, the memories can never be cleansed away.

During lunch, we casually discuss the events of our morning spent together with the animals.

"Audrey is my favorite goat, even though she likes to butt me," says Tristan.

"I could spend all day with Lowtchee (Friesian mare)," sighs Riley.

"Bing and Frankie are my favorite," claims Molly. "I love their long ears."

"Can I put the tortoises out in their enclosures?" inquires Chase.

After lunch the children participate in homesteading crafts. Pickling cucumbers and making cheese, they witness interesting chemical reactions that they can actually eat! Soap making, knitting and sewing balsam pillows introduce useful skills. We read paper manuals and stained recipe cards, learning to follow directions and to appreciate the history of homely crafts.

Our last activity takes place in the garden. Each week the garden changes as different vegetables ripen and flowers bloom. The children may take a bag full of vegetables home, but the rule is they must pick for themselves. Picking enough beans and peas to serve at dinner is a task that requires focus and patience. If a child is bored after five beans, then that is all they take home. These lessons teach perseverance. Technology, particularly the internet, has certainly enhanced my life as a writer and a teacher. It is a powerful tool that enables information to flow quickly from just a few mouse clicks. However, we should also provide children with pleasurable activities that don't require computers. Kids Farm Day offers those opportunities.

While in the garden, I encourage the children to look for grasshoppers and other bugs that threaten the plants. Any they catch can be tossed to the chickens who patrol the perimeter of the garden in a tube like wire enclosure. Chickens eat insects on their way to plunder the garden. The children also learn how to weed around the carrots and cucumbers without accidentally yanking delicate seedlings. Dirt packs under their fingernails and stains the crevices of their hands. One child tugs at my shirt to show me that the stain on her palm looks like a horse. It does. Another child becomes fascinated with the enormous leaves on a pumpkin plant.

"Why are they so big?" he questions.

"Think about how big a pumpkin is. The leaves have a lot of sugar to produce so it can be stored in the pumpkins that will start to grow in a few weeks," I offer. A few blooms are located at the base of the plant. I show the children where the pumpkin will begin to develop at the base of the flower.

On our way out of the garden, we pluck the few remaining strawberries growing in a raised bed. Hopefully, these experiences will prompt an interest in gardening when the children are grown. I try to draw their attention to the ambiance of the garden, how peaceful it is, how wonderful the dirt feels on our hands; While inhaling the mixture of aromas given off by the plants, I note how satisfying it is to eat food we choose to grow. Teaching gardening to children builds appreciation for our basic needs; food, sun and maybe even human companionship.

The activities on Kids Farm Day stimulate the senses, increasing brain activity. Akin to neuro-exercise, such stimulation is vital for child development. At the end of Kids Farm Day the children leave with new experiences committed to memory. At home they will talk incessantly about llamas, donkeys and horses. They will share anecdotes about naughty goats who jumped into the tractor or horses who massaged their hair in exchange for a back scratch. They will present their family with a bag of vegetables they have handpicked from the garden. The conversations will be peppered with names of other children with whom they interacted at the farm.

Memories are images we take with us, share and eventually look to for comfort in old age. I fear that children will face a deficit of interactive memories if social interactions only take place through a two dimensional screen. The mission of Kids Farm Day is to provide opportunities for children to fill buckets with meaningful memories to take with them as they grow into adults. May they always remember the watchful bold eyes of llamas on our hikes, the soulful bray of a hungry donkey, the sweet taste of fresh peas consumed within seconds of their release from stringy husks, the sweaty aroma of horses, the clack of knitting needles that weave itchy yarn, the earthy fragrance of the woods and the scratchy texture of green hay. May all of these sensations be woven like strands of cloth into each child's memory so that they last a lifetime.

"Tell me and I forget. Teach me and I remember. Involve me and I learn." –Xunzi

Kids Farm Day is an opportunity for children to interact with animals, work in the garden and learn homesteading crafts without the assistance of electronic devices.

Moving Forward

Although the visual image is hazy at times, I can still relate to the heart of myself as a young girl standing in front of a chalkboard in her family's musty basement. The satisfaction she felt in front of her imaginary class is the same that I have felt teaching real students in the classrooms of her future. Her love of horses, dogs and all other animals has led me down a fateful path full of experiences that I could only partially imagine during her childhood. The girl I was then taught me to inspire students with love for and knowledge of animals. Throughout my career, I have seen teaching with and learning from animals unlock the potential in many students. I am indebted to animals for allowing me to tap into their quiet sensibilities and patient interactions as I developed my individual teaching style.

As I come to the end of my formal teaching career, I am transitioning into a future full of exciting possibilities. In a line from *The Four Quartets, T.S. Eliot* simplifies this realization: *"In my end is my beginning."* Physical aspects will change. My classroom will morph into a barn. My wardrobe of trousers and fine wool sweaters can be donated to a thrift store. Instead I will dress according to the season, paying more attention to comfort than to color coordination. My colleagues will possess long ears, swishy tails and an assortment of coat color patterns. Together we will continue our quest to inspire, to challenge, to intrigue. And together we will continue to teach.

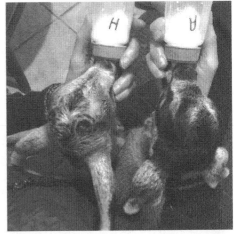

266

The Barn as Sanctuary

Several years ago, my Aunt Anne's memorial service was held at Gwynedd Meeting outside of Philadelphia. It had been more than thirty five years since I had attended meeting for worship. A familiar sense of calm settled upon me as I centered down in the early American decor of the antique meeting house. Although the physical barrier of skin and skull prevented me from reading the thoughts of assembled friends and family, I was reunited with the connection that Quakers experience while waiting patiently for the inner spirit to stir.

During the service, several vocal ministries interrupted the silence. I heard personal anecdotes that reminded me what a special woman and mother Aunt Anne was. Many delivered condolences to my cousins and dear Uncle Morrie. Others provided thoughtful messages of hope and community. Following meeting, we adjourned to the reception area. Nibbling on holiday treats, we received each other with embraces and smiles. After I exited the physical space of the meeting house, I remained enveloped for quite some time in the existential sanctuary of meeting for worship.

Eventually, I returned home to the routine of caring for the animals. My barn is a sanctuary for animals and humans alike, providing shelter for the many horses, goats and donkeys who live with us on Moose River Farm. In the days that followed the memorial service, I came to realize that each morning I attend a different sort of meeting for worship.

I don't sit in quiet contemplation, yet I perform all of my routine chores in a state of meditation. Before centering down, I am greeted by a glorious cacophony as I enter the barn. Shrill whinnies, wheezy brays and ravenous bleats demand sustenance. I oblige by severing twine on hay bales. Once released, pungent grassy flakes pop, making it easy for me to grasp three at a time to toss into each stall. Urgent animal chatter transitions to a chorus of peaceful mastication. The grinding rhythm soothes me in the sanctuary that is my barn.

Here in the pale dawn, I meet with my creature community to prepare for my day. Nothing elevates my spirit more.

Although a formal meeting house is silent, this sanctuary is not. A harmony of grinding molars, pawing hooves and the occasional gusts of breaking wind mingle into white noise. The sounds assure that the animals are well. That reassurance gives me permission to center down to a deeper level of prayer. While my body is busy with chores, my mind meanders, searching for strength that will lift my troubled mood.

Lowtchee, my portly black mare, chews her hay while I sift the piles of manure in her stall and toss them into a wheelbarrow. As if she and I are sitting next to each other on the wooden meeting house bench, I am aware of her satisfaction with life right now as she contemplates the forage in front of her. Once her stall is clean, I push my wheelbarrow to the next stall door. Joshua, a large paint gelding, swings his head to greet me as I enter. The black and white patches of his coat resemble formal evening wear. He too is content with his muzzle deep in hay. I allow my thoughts to surface long enough to greet him, stroking him between the eyes briefly before returning to deep meditation. How will I make a positive difference in a tumultuous world?

My aunt's funeral was held two days after the horrific shooting of children and teaching professionals at *Sandy Hook Elementary School* in Connecticut. The images are raw, the violence, personal. I am an elementary school teacher. This morning I am comforted by the congregation of Moose River Farm's meeting house. In our sanctuary we unite as community. They meditate on a level of gastric bliss. I do so on heartache. It takes the mucking of nine more stalls for my mind to transition from despair to hope. Along the way I desperately seek answers to difficult questions, mostly *why*.

My Quaker education has instilled tolerance and acceptance. I can make a difference today if I make a concerted effort to provide my students with the tools they need to be successful balanced citizens in a world that strives to knock them off balance. My teaching is a small counterbalance to heinous acts, but it *is* within my control. In the end that is all we have, control over our own actions. Although my hoofed society of friends can't articulate meaningful messages, it occurs to me that I have been meditating alongside of them for decades and have borne witness to their peaceful acceptance of what simply is, this moment, now.

I agree with *Gregory Maguire's (*author of *Wicked: The Life and Times of the Wicked Witch of the West)* claim that *"Animals are born who they are, accept it, and that is that. They live with greater peace than people do."*

Eventually, the clock interrupts. My professional day begins in less than one hour. I grasp the long ears of one of my baby donkeys stroking gently. This is the handshake of sorts that will adjourn the meeting. I wish all my animals a good day. Later in the afternoon, the meeting will reconvene. After I serve their supper the animals and I will center down in meaningful meditation, enfolded into the barn sanctuary. *–Amen*

"When I look back over my life it's almost as if there was a plan laid out for me, from the little girl who was so passionate about animals and who longed to go to Africa... Farm animals are far more aware and intelligent than we ever imagined." - Dr. Jane Goodall

Made in the USA
Middletown, DE
18 May 2019